CONFE... SHADOWS

CONFRONTING SHADOWS

An Introduction to the Poetry
of Thomas Kinsella

By David Lynch

NEW ISLAND

Confronting Shadows: An Introduction to the Poetry of Thomas Kinsella

First published in 2015
by New Island Books,
16 Priory Hall Office Park,
Stillorgan,
County Dublin,
Republic of Ireland.

www.newisland.ie

Copyright © David Lynch, 2015.

David Lynch has asserted his moral rights.

Permission has been kindly granted by Carcanet Press Limited to quote from a selection of poems from Kinsella, T. (2001) *Collected Poems* (Manchester: Carcanet).

PRINT ISBN: 978-1-84840-287-4
EPUB ISBN: 978-1-84840-288-1
MOBI ISBN: 978-1-84840-289-8

All rights reserved. The material in this publication is protected by copyright law. Except as may be permitted by law, no part of the material may be reproduced (including by storage in a retrieval system) or transmitted in any form or by any means; adapted; rented or lent without the written permission of the copyright owner.

British Library Cataloguing Data.
A CIP catalogue record for this book is available from the British Library.

Typeset by JVR Creative India
Cover design by Julie Lynch
Printed by SPRINT-print Ltd.

New Island received financial assistance from The Arts Council (*An Chomhairle Ealaíon*), 70 Merrion Square, Dublin 2, Ireland.

10 9 8 7 6 5 4 3 2 1

Contents

1	Entry	1
2	Working-Class Heroes	16
3	Walking Alone	59
4	The Dreams that Died	102
5	The Truth Within?	151
6	Resistance	185
	Works by Thomas Kinsella	267
	Selected Bibliography	271
	Suggested Further Reading	276
	Acknowledgements	278
	Endnotes	279

Also by David Lynch:

Radical Politics in Modern Ireland: A History of the Irish Socialist Republican Party (ISRP) 1896–1904

A Divided Paradise: An Irishman in the Holy Land

*In memory of
the martyrs of the Egyptian Revolution
2011–2012*

1
Entry

Thomas Kinsella's first book of poetry was published the year the Soviet army entered Budapest to crush the Hungarian Revolution, and when the British state, dealing with the Suez Crisis, finally realised that its role in the world was to become somewhat more modest than it had been accustomed to.[1] It was a time that was pre Troubles, pre The Beatles, and (largely) pre TV. The longevity of Kinsella's literary career is thus breathtaking, and made all the more so when we recognise that he still publishes regularly, pushing his life's work into the second decade of the twenty-first century. This long literary life may be a crucial contributing factor to the rather odd and contradictory position Kinsella holds within Irish literature.

He is a writer regarded as central and at the same time marginal, his poetry both canonical and existing on the fringe. It is thus understandable that he has been called 'Ireland's finest unread poet.'[2] As backhanded compliments go, it captures much of the elusiveness of the poet and his influence. His work has been a feature of the Leaving Certificate curriculum for decades, ensuring that recognition of his name remains high. Critics, even those who find his work somewhat obscure, agree on the immensity of Kinsella's achievement, but even so, he is not a regular on Ireland's literary circuit, and poetry sections of bookstores will often carry none of his material. Since the early 1970s, when his readership was arguably at its peak, there has been a steady decline in the numbers of those who read his work.

This incongruity of his recognised importance, coupled with his somewhat perplexing marginality, has created an enigmatic impression around the poetry itself. This is an enigma that some readers and critics have found alluring, others annoying. As early as 1990, Eileen Battersby was writing of the 'mysterious aura which surrounds the poet.'[3]

The waning of his central influence in Irish poetry has been credited to a number of factors.

His 'turn' in style from the structured, ornate early work to poetry of a more modernist, free verse form, dealing with matters of the complicated internal psyche, is often mentioned. The angry and unapologetic anti-imperialist stance of his high-profile 'Butcher's Dozen' poem of 1972, written on the occasion of the Widgery Tribunal, is raised as a reason for his lack of readership in Britain, as well as in a Republic of Ireland that became increasingly politically 'revisionist' during the Troubles. That these are contributors to the narrowing of the audience is undoubtedly true. But there are also more subjective factors, such as the nature of publication undertaken by the poet himself. Since the early 1970s, the majority of his work has been published in short, carefully designed chapbooks called the *Peppercanister* Series. It was a 'small publishing enterprise, with the purpose of issuing occasional special items from our home in Dublin, across the Grand Canal from St Stephen's Church, known locally as "The Peppercanister",' as the poet has written.[4] The series is deliberately produced in short runs, in the hundreds, making each one a special edition. The *Peppercanister* poems have been occasionally collected into book form. One end result of this style of limited publication, however, has been that the writer, widely regarded as Ireland's most significant living poet, is quite difficult to read, not because of the complexity of his verse, but because of the unavailability of his published work. Added to this, the poet has become increasingly distant, to the point of almost non-existence in the mainstream world of Irish literary life, giving few interviews, rare poetry readings, and hardly expected to wander onto our TV screens on a late-night chat show. In an age as wholly extroverted as our own, such behaviour goes against the commercial grain, even while it adds to the sense of mystery and authenticity that are core aspects of the poet's work.

Bono has quipped that he was 'soaked' by Kinsella's poetry in his school days.[5] The U2 frontman meant it as a compliment, but the image is a telling one. There are critics for whom Kinsella's work does more than soak; some have complained of drowning in incomprehension. One critic in the early 1970s commented that the Irish poet had 'brooded himself to pieces.'[6]

The poet's reputation for difficulty and obscurity has become a 'fixed idea' in places, as the poet himself has noted.[7] As with many fixed ideas, however, it occludes a more nuanced reality. Kinsella's work is challenging to be sure, but even the moments of deepest ambiguity, such as in sections of the 1985 collection *Songs of the Psyche*, are not *wilfully* obscure. An appreciation and understanding of the general mindset of the poet and the thematic rhythms of the work makes even the most bizarre of internal journeys into the psyche increasingly comprehensible, and worthy of close reading. One academic has described the early resistance followed by the enjoyable engagement that her class in University College Dublin (UCD) felt when reading Kinsella: 'The initial silently groaning resistance, from the serried ranks – undergraduates' typical mass first reaction to poetry – gives way with remarkable speed to pleasure.'[8] Dr Catriona Clutterbuck sees this change as a product of the 'response-ability' that is required of the reader by Kinsella's poems. She views his type of art as 'radically reciprocal and transferable,' and it makes Kinsella the 'most democratic of major Irish poets today.' This interpretation of Kinsella as an open and engaging poet, his work democratic and accessible to the reader, stands in stark contrast to much critical response.

Kinsella was awarded the freedom of his home city in 2007, and recent years have seen a wave of new critical engagements with the poet's work, after decades of relative silence.[9] The majority of these works belong to the genre of academic, theoretical monographs, providing incredibly rich and new insights into the work. Most have been written by professional literary critics or poet-critics. They have also tended to provide chronological treatments of the work, focusing in particular on the stylistic turn that took place early in Kinsella's career.

This emphasis on the 'turn' in Kinsella's work is arguably misplaced. It is somewhat like zeroing in on the moment that Bob Dylan 'went electric' as the single most crucial event in that singer-songwriter's career. It is important, no doubt, but it may be of more interest to the guitarist or musician than the listener. The formal change in Kinsella's poetry may be of more interest to other poets than it is to readers. The move away from formal verse was signalled in the early 1960s, and certainly by the end of that decade the change was complete. Even in thematic terms, the concerns, topics and interests of the poetry have been relatively consistent since that time. This is not to say that there have not been developments and departures, but if one takes a step back and surveys the complete poetic oeuvre, it is the consistency of theme and the gradual accumulation of insights, rather than rupture, which is the works' most distinctive aspect.

* * *

This study, although building on previous critical engagements, is not in the genre of specialised literary theory. Neither a literary academic nor a professional poet, my primary position of interaction in this study is not even as a journalist. Rather, it is as a close reader, hoping that this contact with the poetry will provide a helpful introduction to other general readers eager to enter the work, but who are searching for a little guidance.

Kinsella, more than many other poets, has emphasised the collaborative relationship between writer and reader. In section 19 of *A Technical Supplement,* he describes a happy evening reading a *'demanding book on your knee,'* underlining sections intently. This active engagement from the reader is the sort of response Kinsella would like from the readers of his own work. In an interview in 1996, the poet was clear regarding the fundamental role a reader plays in the creative aspect of poetry. 'Poetry is a dual effort. The poet initiates an act of communication, while also recording the data, and readers complete the circuit.'[10] But this is no easy collaboration: the poet expects the reader to be up to the task, and the undertaking can be difficult. 'The poems are demanding,' Kinsella has said. 'I am aware of that. And they get more demanding as they succeed each other.'[11] But true to his project, he does not attempt to ease this burden of difficulty for the reader. He intentionally sets the bar high, and he expects the reader to put in the work. The poems 'assume that the act of reading is a dynamic one, the completion of an act of communication, not an inert listening to something sweet or interesting or even informative. They are not meant to increase the supply of significant information, but to embody a construct of significant elements.'[12] Kinsella told *The Irish Times* in 1990 that 'Poetry should be concerned with communication, not entertainment.'[13]

Whilst this highly engaged and reflective mode of reading is sometimes described as 'bridging the gap' or 'closing the circuit', for Kinsella the connection is more creative. This is about more than an understanding between poet and reader – it is about a partnership of sorts. Something new and significant is generated during this reading process, as he writes in section 19 of the 1976 collection, *A Technical Supplement*:

> *Except that it is not a closed circuit,*
> *more a mingling of lives, worlds simmering*
> *in the entranced interval: all that you are*
> *and have come to be*
> *– or as much as can be brought to bear –*
> *'putting on' the fixed outcome of another's*
> *encounter with what what he was*
> *and had come to be*
> *impelled him to stop in flux, living,*
> *and hold that encounter out from*
> *the streaming away of lifeblood, timeblood,*
> *a nexus a nexus*
> *wriggling with life not of our kind.*[14]

This is a dynamic encounter between two lives; it is *'simmering'* with potential and wriggles away alive. The author is not dead here. Certainly not in the way Roland Barthes (1915–1980) read the last rites for the artistic creator by concluding 'the birth of the reader must be at the cost of the death of the author.'[15] The author remains vital in Kinsella's formulation, for he stopped a moment out of flux to render it a work of art. But the author is not the only contributor to this new creation: the active reader produces as well.

It is a seminar, not a lecture; a horizontal rather than vertical relationship; equal rather than imperial. As we will see, the most important intellectual influence on Kinsella's poetry has been the work of the Swiss psychologist and psychiatrist Carl Gustav Jung (1875–1961). Interestingly, Jung's theory on the role of the analyst during therapy has some striking similarities to Kinsella's view on the relationship between reader and poet. While Sigmund Freud (1856–1939) and others had emphasised the role of the therapist as a listener, silently noting the words of the patient, Jung promoted interaction between the two sides, with the therapist actively engaged. For Jung, it is 'a commitment on the part of the analyst that is at least as great as that of the patient. At the unconscious level, both doctor and patient are participating in what the alchemists termed a *coniunctio:* like two chemical substances, they are drawn together in the analytic situation by affinity, and their interaction produces change.'[16] Like the analyst, the reader of Kinsella's poetry is urged to not be quiet, but to speak up and engage.

In section 19 of *A Technical Supplement,* the poet writes warmly of the joys of a nice meal on the patio, picnic on the beach, and reading a page-turner whilst by a tree in the park. But the joy of these pursuits pales against what really matters: '*for real pleasure there is nothing to equal/ sitting down to a serious read.*'[17]

Kinsella's work is a serious read. Humour is not entirely absent, but it is rare. The matters with which it is engaged are generally on the sombre end of the scale. His description in the opening section of the 1973 collection, *New Poems*, of the furious intellectual excitement of his youth *'underlining and underlining'* books and poetry resonates with what it is like to read Kinsella closely. Since his collections are hard to come by, getting your hands on one of the collected works and photocopying an individual poem is one of the most manageable ways of negotiating his work. You will find sections underlined within seconds. By its very nature there is engagement; the rapidly zigzagging pen strokes across the page will etch their own ink marks upon the reader's mind.

The reader's commitment is near physical; as Dennis O'Driscoll (1954–2012) notes, it is as if Kinsella regards the interaction as incomplete unless the reader walks away with some injury or other. 'He expects his readers to wrestle with his poems until they draw the blood of meaning from them.'[18]

But while Kinsella has been quite consistent in the importance he places on close reading by an attentive reader in completing the artistic act of poetry, he has been a little less definitive on the nature of the framework in which such a reading should take place. While in some later critical writing he has emphasised the importance of close reading of individual poems, he had previously stressed the need to see each poem as part of a totality. In a 1989 interview the poet said: 'One of the things that has disappeared, by comparison with the early work, is the notion of a "complete" poem, the idea that a poem can have a beginning, middle and end, and be a satisfactory work of art thereby. The unity is a much bigger one that that. And it isn't a sequence, or a set of connected long poems. It's a totality that is happening with the individual poem a contribution to something accumulating.'[19]

This is how this book approaches the poet's work, actively engaged with the poetry, whilst also seeing the work as an evolving whole rather than hundreds of separate poems. It does not deal with the incredibly important work of translation of old Gaelic literature that the poet has completed, or the prose work he has published through the decades. Neither is it a book focused on the biographical life of the poet. Unlike other writers who live on beyond the verse in the minds of readers, such as Patrick Kavanagh or Dylan Thomas, Kinsella's off-page persona remains remote. Much of the poetry has a strong autobiographical element, although the narrator or poetic 'I' in the work does not always correspond directly with the writer. Biographical and family detail will be touched on when required, but the focus will be primarily on the poetry. It will not be a comprehensive literary theory study, but rather an introduction to the poetry for the general reader that will hopefully prove provocative and engaging, and perhaps encourage more people to read Kinsella's work. The fact that Kinsella has often and comprehensively altered some of his poetry through the decades makes a work like this difficult. Therefore, all work quoted is from the *Collected Poems* (CP) published by Carcanet in 2001, unless otherwise stated.

Literary criticism has become increasingly specialised since the 1960s. Much of its work has been beneficial, in that it has sharpened technique and also undermined the pious pronouncements of old humanist literary certainties. Certainties that led to judgements on works that were meant to be 'objective', however, in fact hid many varied inherent positions – whether sexist, racist, Eurocentric, bourgeois, conservative, or reactionary. As with any specialisation, a helpful shorthand terminology among experts has been developed, but this brings with it the risk of alienating the general reader. Whilst this study will not shy away from some aspects of modern literary theory, it will attempt to keep jargon down to a minimum.

Sometimes there will be close readings of longer poems, but often the book will jump from one poem to another that was published decades later. This is because Kinsella's work echoes within itself across decades of writing, with some poems directly quoting from others. The majority of the work is integrated in terms of recurring themes, built around important personal moments and memories, and favourite intellectual concerns. This repetition, looking again and again at certain personal moments and grand themes, gives the work a sweeping rhythm. Rhythm is still important to a poet, even one like Kinsella, who has for the vast majority of his career not restricted himself to received forms. His work rarely sings with obvious music like much modern Irish lyrical work. But rhythm does not have to be a direct result of poetic tools like alliteration, assonance or end rhyme; it can also result from overall structure and theme. The poet in 1989 said as much: 'The music of poetry, however understood, is of primary importance. Rhythms and rhythmical structures and the rhythm of form – not merely the audible rhythm line by line but the achievement of a totality and the thematic connections amongst one's material – all of that is absolutely primary.'[20]

This work primarily engages with these thematic connections and the rhythms that beat throughout Kinsella's work.

* * *

In 2013, Ireland lost Seamus Heaney, its most famous poet. On the morning that his death was announced, RTÉ Radio ran a special show dedicated to his memory. Along with many other poets and critics, Thomas Kinsella was invited onto the show. Presenter Myles Dungan opened with a long question about Heaney's role as a public poet, but he was interrupted by a Kinsella clearly still shaken by the news of Heaney's death.

'Listen, Miles, I am still in a state of shock.' The deliberate voice was unmistakable. 'I am just feeling how unexpected it is. It really is an extraordinary event, the powerful presence taken from the centre of our scene. My first reaction after the shock, and the shock is still continuing, is the memory of his very earliest poems. I knew straight away that we were dealing with the real thing. But Myles I am leaving you now; it will take a while for me to assess the full extent of that shock. And all I can say is God rest him, and God help us all.'[21] In life, Heaney was vastly complimentary of Kinsella's work. In a close reading of some of Kinsella's poetry from the 1970s, Heaney displayed a real understanding of what his fellow Irish poet was doing. 'Since the late sixties, this deeply responsible poet has been absorbed in a slowly purposeful, heroically undeflected work of personal and national inquisition.'[22]

Heaney's style, persona and ability made him loved by a massive worldwide audience. While Kinsella has never had the same reach in terms of readership and influence, there are literary observers who are happy to position Kinsella's work in the same category as that of Heaney.

Thomas Kinsella was born in the first decade of the new Irish state on 4 May 1928 to working-class parents in Inchicore, Dublin. With grandparents on both sides living in the close locality, the poet spent most of his childhood in different homes in the Kilmainham and Inchicore area. His father, John Paul, worked at the Guinness Brewery, like his father before him, and was influenced by left-wing politics. His mother features rarely in the poetry. He was educated through Irish at Model School, Inchicore. Gaining a scholarship, he was later to go to the Christian Brothers O'Connell School on Richmond Street.

In his youth there was the death of a young sister, Agnes, which features in the poem 'Tear'. There was also a brief period of living in Manchester during the Blitz. This was an important direct experience of what the poet would later call in his notes the 'catastrophe' – a series of horrific events in the twentieth century, including the Second World War, that would irrevocably change the nature of the world, and humanity's perception of itself.

Despite his modest roots, and after applying for a scholarship, he entered UCD in 1946 to study science, soon realising that this was not for him. Sitting an entrance exam for the Civil Service, Kinsella began a successful nineteen-year career that would finish in 1965 at a prominent grade in the Department of Finance, and for a time he was personal secretary to the famous head of the department, T. K. Whitaker. While at university, he had the most important meeting of his life. Eleanor was a 'very striking person, I had no notion whatever of capturing,' according to the poet. 'One day when we were sitting together,' said Eleanor, 'he was eating banana sandwiches. He asked me would I eat one, and I said no thank you. And he said what would you eat? And I said I'd have some lunch, and I thought he was very nice.'[23] Thus began a relationship that would become a marriage in 1955, and would feature prominently in Kinsella's poetry for decades. Eleanor is the poet's great muse.

Other important friendships began in terms of literary publishing when he met Liam Miller in the early 1950s. The founder of the Dolmen Press was of crucial importance in the poet's early career, publishing his early works. He also became close to composer Seán Ó Riada(1931–1971), whose death was marked by Kinsella in verse. His love of poetry had begun early in secondary school, but it wasn't until reading W. H. Auden that Kinsella truly felt that poetry could be important in his life. Serious writing began in the 1950s, and continues to this day.

In 1965, Kinsella left the Civil Service and took an academic posting in the United States; it was also an opportunity to concentrate on poetry full-time. There have been many awards, books and collections since, and he is now regarded by many as Ireland's greatest living poet.

* * *

Despite the critical praise, in lighter moments the poet has himself expressed suspicion at talk that poetry can teach you anything about how to live, or whether it has any point at all. 'I'm really at a loss to explain poetry's function. I mean, it doesn't help to handle the experiences of life. You just record significant encounters. Sometimes I wonder why not just play golf or something else instead.'[24] We must be grateful that the poet committed his life to the artistic act rather than working on his handicap. By 2010, Ireland had more than 350 golf courses. The nation is undoubtedly well served (probably over served) in that department. We have only one Thomas Kinsella, and through a career spanning more than half a century he has served the cultural life of the nation.

His poetic legacy is debated. Gerald Dawe has written that some of Kinsella's work has 'an almost take it or leave it aggressiveness, unique in Irish poetry.'[25] Although I am one of those who have taken it, I do understand why others may leave it. The encounter can be brutal and bruising, but it remains an encounter (I hope this study suggests) worth having.

Poets like Thomas Kinsella often reveal interesting insights into the core nature of life. These insights are the result of dedication, hard work and practice over many decades of craft. Just as in the case of a new band dedicating hundreds of hours to practice in their garage, a soccer player training session after training session perfecting free kicks, or long months of immersing yourself in a new language, we know we can improve our skill set with time and practice. Poets like Kinsella, who see their central work as the 'encounter ... between the individual and the significant ordeal,' by their years of labour in the area of metaphysical and poetic search could indeed have accumulated insights that may be of interest to the rest of us.[26]

Poetry, and art in general, is most powerful when it resonates, and Kinsella's work has resonated with my life with increasing intensity since my late twenties. Living in the Islandbridge and Kilmainham areas of Dublin during the late Celtic Tiger years, I walked the streets and back lanes named in his childhood poetry, a poetic portal into a contrasting era of poverty and struggle in the new Irish state. I have read his walking poems while completing the Camino de Santiago, and investigated his work on nation and place when reporting from Palestine and Israel. While covering the Egyptian revolution as a journalist, his poems celebrating differing aspects of heroism such as 'The Messenger' and 'Dick King' brought context and contemplation to days in Cairo full of tear gas, resistance and deadlines, and his observation in 'Mirror in February' *'for they are not made whole / That reach the age of Christ'* has rung through my mind since I have entered my thirties, questioning the route ahead, contemplating the path behind. In this and many other aspects, the poetry has interested, provoked and infuriated me, but crucially it has always thoroughly engaged.

With poetry that is complex and rewarding, angry and honest, flawed and portentous, it is hoped that this work will encourage others to enter Kinsella's work and read the poems. This offering is made as an attempt at an entrance.

2
Working-Class Heroes

One day while walking through the packed streets of London, a young Cork man working as a messenger for a stockbroker firm was dreaming of home. Michael Collins's (1890–1922) blisteringly brief period as the famous Irish guerrilla and political leader was still in front of him. But through his family Collins had already become immersed in Fenian politics, and had subsequently joined the GAA and the Irish Republican Brotherhood (IRB) in England. London life was very different to the rhythms of the rural country Cork scene in which he had grown up. As he was finding his feet through the massed throng of consumers and commuters, something emerged out of the mess of mechanical modernity all around him that briefly resurrected those rhythms from his memory. There, moving along at a pace more familiar in the Irish farmlands than in the heart of the modern city, an old man on a donkey came forward, making his way down the Shepherd's Bush Road. The image gripped Collins, and he loudly exclaimed, 'I stand for that.'[1]

The old man and his donkey, with its connotations of pastoral labour, contrasted with the urban setting. This rural world was organic and real compared to the alienation of the modern city. Such hostility towards London was not confined to Irish republicans. A decade later, the great modernist poet T. S. Eliot (1888–1965) would deem the British capital an 'unreal city' full of fear, waste and broken fragments in his epic *The Waste Land* (1922).

The old man's appearance did not merely provoke an intense bout of homesickness for the Irish countryside that Collins had left behind. The exclamation in his response has a positive projection in its cry. He is standing *for* something and fighting *for* something, and not merely something that already exists. For the Irish republican, the man and his horse was not a signifier of backwardness or stagnation that compared unfavourably with the innovation and high pace of the city. Rather, he represented the very definition of the positive hope for Irish freedom. Not only would the Ireland he was fighting for be free from British rule, its predominant social structure and mode of production would be rural and agricultural.

Collins was not alone in connecting the rural with his dreams for Ireland. His great rival, Éamon de Valera (1882–1975), made a St Patrick's Day address in 1943 that has been caricatured beyond all that is reasonable. However, even given the somewhat admirable anti-consumerist vision that is at the heart of the speech, de Valera's outline of an idealised Ireland suffers from at least two fatal flaws.[2] Firstly, it bore little resemblance to the reality of Ireland in 1943. Secondly, the vision was so rural-centric that any Irish citizen living in a community where you did not hear cows lowing in the morning could not help but feel excluded. 'The ideal Ireland that we would have, the Ireland that we dreamed of,' de Valera told the Raidió Éireann listeners, 'would be the home of a people who valued material wealth only as a basis for right living, of a people who, satisfied with frugal comfort, devoted their leisure to the things of the spirit – a land whose countryside would be bright with cosy homesteads, whose fields and villages would be joyous with the sounds of industry, with the romping of sturdy children, the contest of athletic youths and the laughter of happy maidens, whose firesides would be forums for the wisdom of serene old age.'[3] For listeners in swathes of rural Ireland whose life was bedevilled by chronic emigration and desperate poverty, the divergence between de Valera's rural dreamscape and their everyday surroundings must have been painfully striking. But at least the broad outlines of their life were included in the Taoiseach's imagination. The urban slum-dweller on Dublin's northside, or Cork's inner city, or the Guinness worker living in his small house in Inchicore, were left in little doubt by the Taoiseach that the type of lives they led were not part of this dream for Ireland. It was almost like they were a national mistake, a residual remnant of the British presence. The urban Irish who had lived for generations in the cities were not quite part of the plan, but de Valera's dream was particularly offensive to those who had recently left rural Ireland to move to Dublin. His vision must have been especially difficult to stomach for the formerly rural Irish who had arrived in the city trying to build a life for themselves and their family. The railway worker in Inchicore who had left his Irish-speaking community in the Claddagh, Galway, not only missed his former life, but was now informed by his Taoiseach that he had abandoned the very place in which the great dream of Ireland was meant to be built.

An acceptance that rural life and the agricultural economy was part of the core DNA of what Ireland should be was also a conviction that proved popular with politicians of the left like James Connolly (1868–1916). The great hero of Irish socialism and republicanism sacrificed his entire adult life to the cause of the urban worker, the labour movement and Irish independence. He would never exclude the working class from his vision of Ireland, unlike some other founding mothers and fathers of the state, and his more hardheaded temperament prevented him from painting visionary pictures of pastoral perfection. He had toured Kerry during a famine in 1898, and became intimately familiar with the drudgery and misery faced by many rural workers.[4] In the long term, he regarded land nationalisation as the answer to the nation's rural economic woes. However, even Connolly believed that the Irish Republic for which he was fighting, even if it were to be a socialist workers' republic, was destined to be predominately agricultural in nature. He called it the 'one important industry of the country,' and that is the way it would remain.[5]

Partition removed the large industrial centre of Belfast from the Irish economy. Following the Civil War and the early decade of the Free State, the focus of mainstream southern political opinion continued to be on rural matters. This orthodoxy remained into the early 1950s, with a protectionist national economic policy and a conviction that agriculture was still the most important industry and rural life the ideal mode of living.

This persisted, despite economic stagnation. The *Irish Independent* editorialised in March 1952 that the rapid rise in emigration meant that there was a 'growing menace to the race.'[6] Thus, some observers felt that the dire economic situation posed an existential threat to the Irish people. Despite this fear, the elite failed to change its set of priorities. 'Any sense of urgency about the issue was weakened by the general orthodoxy or underlying instinctive sense, shared by many in all three major parties, that agriculture was and would remain Ireland's major source of work and wealth, and was the key to the country's economic development,' writes Tom Garvin of the period.[7] Economic debates in the national parliament and newspapers were largely restricted to 'farmer versus ranchers, or the plough versus the cow.'[8] The urban worker and the need to foster industrial development remained a marginal concern. Despite the contention of some historians, the state during this period was not purely a backward, economically inward-looking island of agriculture, adrift from global capitalism. This was because 'Ireland was always part of the modern era. Its role was to provide agricultural produce for the industrial centres of Britain, and this was done mainly in the form of live cattle exports.'[9] A degree of political independence had been achieved, but the Irish economy was still dominated by British economic needs. This was an economic relationship that somewhat bypassed the Irish urban working class.

As in politics and the media, so it is in literature. In the years prior to independence, and the early decades of the Irish state, the focus on the rural as the significant location for Irish identity predominated among writers and intellectuals. The exemplary literary figure for the leading lights of the Irish Literary Revival was heroic, Gaelic, and most often rural. The typical setting was pastoral. When William Butler Yeats (1865–1939), John Millington Synge (1871–1909), Lady Gregory (1852–1932), Douglas Hyde (1860–1949) and others thought and wrote about what the new Ireland should look like and how the new Irish should act, the backdrop was most often one of fields, the characters physically strapping, simple and Gaelic.

The generally positive connotations surrounding rural life was contrasted with the morals of the growing urban middle class that Yeats disliked so much, and also with the urban working class, who seemed a little too British to fit into any uncomplicated reconstruction of Irish identity. It also reflected wider trends in the literary modernist movement at the time, which sometimes exalted the peasantry as heroic and organic compared to the corruption and lack of authenticity of city life. The peasantry were often the object rather than real subjects of this work. Yeats compared the Sligo countryside of his youth to an innocent, childlike idyll, uncorrupted by modernity.[10] The peasantry, for him, were often mere vessels to carry images rather than real and complex humans.

Of course a swift pen-picture of such a dynamic literary movement does it an injustice. The themes of the Irish Literary Renaissance were rarely homogenous, its perceptions of Irish identity nuanced. Whether it was the complicated, questioning Mayo peasantry of J. M. Synge's *The Playboy of the Western World*, or the life of Dubliners in Sean O'Casey's great trilogy of plays, there were countercurrents and critiques coming from within the revival. But it is not reductive to conclude that the movement's general thematic fixation was with the pastoral setting and the rural character. Even when we skip a generation and address what is regarded as the first great poetic counterblast to the Yeatsian dream of what Irishness is, the urban experience is still largely absent.

Patrick Kavanagh's (1904–1967) 'The Great Hunger', published in 1942, was a rejection of the idealised vision of Yeats. Published a year before de Valera's St Patrick's Day speech, this is a long poem full of real, broken humans repetitively working the Irish fields rather than the muscular heroes of the Taoiseach's dreams or the idyllic Celtic twilight countryside of Yeats's imagination. By facing the deprivations of rural labour in 1940s Ireland and the aridity of its social and sexual life, Kavanagh's poem was a sharp and necessary readjustment to the unbalanced Yeatsian legacy from the Irish Literary Revival. But if it was a needed riposte, it is again a largely rural one. The battle over Ireland's national identity, over what it meant to be truly Irish, would take place, figuratively, in a field. But what of the battles on the cobblestones, back lanes, inner-city tenement housing and the growing suburbs? Why this comparative lack of focus on the urban?

Suspicion of the nationalist loyalty of the working class, particularly the Dublin proletariat, may have been a factor. A legacy of the history of the Pale (a region of Ireland around Dublin under English control in the Middle Ages) perhaps; the lingering use of the pejorative 'jackeen' to describe a Dubliner speaks to this. Dublin was regarded as the most 'English' of the cities, a place where the Union Jack could fly unperturbed. The stories of Dublin slum-dwellers turning on the rebels of 1916 fitted into this narrative. The politics of organised labour and socialism were denounced by leading nationalist figures like Arthur Griffith (1872–1922).

That the Dublin working class in reality never fitted into this stereotype need not delay us here, but as Declan Kiberd has shown, in the conscious modern recreation and invention of Irishness that took place between the death of Charles Stewart Parnell in 1871 and the Irish revolution, the most significant factor in the invention was the relationship with the English.[11] With England rejected as an imperial and occupying force, the colonial masters had been associated with the industrial and urban in many nationalists' eyes.

Thus, the industrial and urban were damned by association. The Dublin working class proved problematic to the more narrow conceptions of what Irish identity would be. As is often the case with difficult things, they were regularly ignored. English-speaking, soccer-playing, urban slum living with an eye towards international trends in popular culture, they may have been Irish, but not as Yeats or de Valera (in their different ways) wanted to know it.

The 1960s and 1970s brought a shift in economic policy towards a greater focus on industry, and there was an increased urbanisation of Irish people's lives. However, the perception that 'rural Ireland was real Ireland' continued.[12] The country remained politically conservative, the power of the Catholic Church still strong.

This was the backdrop from which Thomas Kinsella's long poem 'The Messenger' emerged. It was not a moment of national concern that sparked its creation, but rather personal loss. In May 1976, the poet's father, John Paul Kinsella, died, and the poem was published two years later. The cover was designed to replicate the front page of *The Sacred Heart Messenger*, a popular religious magazine in Ireland at the time. The symbols on the front cover are proletarian rather than pious, the starry plough rather than the cross. That one bookshop in Dublin was said to be offended by *The Messenger* because of its sacrilegious design gives a sense of the type of capital city into which it was published in the late 1970s.[13]

'The Messenger' is an extraordinary elegy for a father, critically commemorating the life of worker, trade unionist and family man John Paul Kinsella. It is an artistic act of love that retrieves a life full of hope and courage, disappointment and bitterness. But by tracing this life, the poet also salvages a marginalised radical, political and social tradition, resuscitating the memory of a Dublin urban experience that may have been lost in the back lanes and shadows of the capital city.

They might not have fitted into the bucolic dreams and official visions of the founding fathers and mothers of the Irish state and writers of the Celtic Twilight, but in reality these urban Irish were there, working, loving, striking, losing and striving. In 'The Messenger', the lives lived on these poor Dublin streets get their moment on the poetic stage.

* * *

As an introduction to Thomas Kinsella's work, 'The Messenger' is an excellent place for a reader to commence their engagement.

Coming towards the end of what is the most important and fruitful ten-year period in his writing career, this sprawling, muscular elegy is arguably one of the most impressive poetic creations by any Irish writer since independence. For those readers trying to grab a hold of the most significant themes and consistent forms in the Kinsella canon, all of it, or at least most of it, can be found here. In terms of form it is episodic and often fragmented, yet tight in subject and development. Thematically there is the delicate dance between the historical and personal, the careful rendering of specific national and familial moments and the strange delving into the internal psyche of poet and father. There are the favoured words like 'half', 'turned away', 'deeper', 'egg' and 'pearl', which appear and reappear across his six-decade-long output. There is the sense of family tradition, the restrictions of organised religion, an imaginary explanation of the central themes of Jungian philosophy, a cast of figures of public proletarian heroism like James Connolly and James Larkin, and private working-class valour like Kinsella's father and grandfather. And there is a dragon. Yes, a dragon who raises its reptilian head during an argument between father and son. The mythical reptile slides in during a dispute, and is the symbol of the unmanaged ego, the half-spoken tension and half-ignored friction that looms large between the men.

> *A dragon slashes its lizard wings*
> *as it looks out, with halved head,*
> *and bellows with incompleteness.*[14]

Early in the poem, the reminiscences of John Paul's life begin following an incident at his funeral. An inappropriate comment by a man in a managerial position at the Guinness Brewery enrages the poet. The unthinking words about his father, that *'He lived in his two sons,'* angers the narrator, who counters that his father's existence had its own legitimate independence beyond the lives of his children. Although he was a supporter of great communal causes, he also possessed an inner fire of his own. He lived in his *'own half fierce force,'* and this force propels the narrator into a series of recollections about his father's political, working and personal life. It is telling that it is an unwelcomed comment from an individual from the capitalist class that sparks the fury, for 'The Messenger' is a proletarian poem written from the perspective of the labouring class.

John Paul was originally from the Liberties area of Dublin, but after marriage moved to different houses in Kilmainham and Inchicore and worked in the Guinness Brewery. During his time at the brewery he was involved in attempts to found its first trade union. Brewery workers had not traditionally been known for militancy, and in a 'paternalistic' firm like the Guinness Brewery, the drive to unionisation came later than many other sectors. As early as 1911, trade union leader James Larkin was chiding the brewery workers for their lack of action. 'Is it not time you took your place by your class and organised yourself?' he asked a crowd of workers in Beresford Place in July 1911.[15]

Through 'The Messenger', Kinsella charts his father's life in reverse, beginning with the image of his dying father in his dressing gown at home, and then slowly tracing backward to the Dublin urchin all excited in his new job as a postal messenger boy. By inverting time's arrow, Kinsella allows the inherent disappointment of the later life to be uplifted by the end of the poem, with the hopefulness of his father's early idealism (aside from the very brief final scene from the funeral). It is a case of technical form triumphing over living inevitability.

In a series of scenes, John Paul's life is depicted in carefully evocative vignettes. In one, John Paul is reading Marx as a young worker. His politicised mind lingers upon the vision of tragic inspiration forever burnt into the collective consciousness of the Irish socialist left.

> *Connolly strapped in a chair*
> *regarding the guns*
> *that shall pronounce his name for ever.*[16]

Later a faithful follower of James Larkin and his proletarian proselytising, John Paul became active in the fight to form the first trade union in the Guinness Brewery. Kinsella recalls his father at a Labour election rally outside the Black Lion pub in Inchicore, fiery and heroic.

> *It is outside the Black Lion, in Inchicore.*
> *A young man. He is not much more than thirty.*
> *He is on an election lorry, trying to shout.*
>
> *He is goodlooking and dark.*
> *He has a raincoat belted tight*
> *and his hair is brushed back, like what actor.*
>
> *He is shouting about the Blueshirts*
> *but his voice is hoarse.*
> *His arm keeps pointing upward.*[17]

He is a man of dashing action, of progress, passionately shouting as he points to the sky's limit. The Black Lion is a well-known pub in the area, and its deployment is a familiar technique of analogy by Kinsella. His father is depicted as a young lionhearted activist in a series of set pieces that have a cinematic quality to them. Later, John Paul and his own father will be recalled working together on the Guinness barge, where *'The old lion-shoulders expand in the Guinness jersey.'* This is *'his father's den'*. The big cat is of course a symbol of courage, but in working-class socialist history there is also Percy Bysshe Shelley's (1792–1822) famous rallying call to the oppressed in 1819 in 'The Mask of Anarchy', to:

> *Rise, like lions after slumber*
> *In unvanquishable number,*
> *Shake your chains to earth like dew*
> *Which in sleep had fallen on you:*
> *Ye are many – they are few.*

Kinsella's father was a reader of Shelley in his youth, and late in the poem the contents of the young John Paul's *'Gentlemen's*

Sixpenny Library' are outlined. It is said to include *'Shelley, unbound.'* Earlier in the poem, Kinsella, a semi-aware child, is led by his father's hand out of Mass as the parish priest roars in anger from the altar. His father is a man of conviction, rejecting the propaganda from the powerful pulpit. Under his father's protection, the young Kinsella sees the priest:

> *— thick white hair, a red face,*
> *a black mouth shouting*
> *Godless Russia after us.*[18]

But he is not only a father, worker or socialist; he is a lover as well. The moment of the poet's conception is envisioned, with young lovers lying by a riverbank in Wicklow. It is the one scene in the poem where the urban setting is replaced by the rural. Love is made surrounded by the busyness and growth of nature. It may be easier to imagine sex enclosed by the warm glow of nature rather than in the dark, narrow houses in the back lanes of Kilmainham and Inchicore.

> *A gossamer ghost arrows and hesitates*
>
> *out of the reeds, and stands in the air above them*
> *insect-shimmering, and settles on a bright*
> *inner upturn of her dress. The wings*
>
> *close up like palms. The body, a glass worm,*
> *is pulsing. The tail-tip winces and quivers:*
>
> I think *this is where I come in.*[19]

Before the poet comes into the scene, his father's early years are sheltered by his own father, a Guinness barge captain and cobbler. The class-conscious political beliefs of father and grandfather have a progressive, positive energy to them. The image of them reaching out, like Larkin's famous outstretched arms, reoccurs. It is the straining of their class for better conditions and a general refusal to accept that their modest background will hold them back in life. They are on the move. John Paul points 'upward' on the election lorry. Earlier, as a young adult, he sits alongside his own father in his cobbler's workshop. Both men stretch and point their bodies, the son attempting to emulate his father's skill, but also to emulate the leading figures of labour history and the great class battle of the Dublin 1913 Lockout.

He reaches for a hammer,
his jaw jutting as best it can
with Marx, Engels, Larkin

howling with upstreched arms into the teeth
of Martin Murphy and the Church
and a flourish of police batons,[20]

And later in the same section, the symbols of skilled labour, socialist politics and intergenerational respect combine:

Son and father, upright, right arms raised.
Stretching a thread.
Trying to strike right.[21]

All this reaching is evocative of a wider sense of a working class on the collective march, stretching for something better than the disappointing present. It is pulsating with heroism, with the strong belief in the socialist movement of the early twentieth century: that the working class was progressively, maybe inevitably, moving towards power. This doctrine of the historical inevitability of working-class victory was strong among many of the most class-conscious workers in Europe, and ran parallel with a desire to develop their own intellectual horizons. Betterment of the class would mirror personal betterment. John Paul was a member of the Left Book Club, he read widely and was interested in music. Thomas's younger brother, John, would become a composer in adult life. The poet would in a later interview call him a 'very concerned' person.[22]

The poem delves deeper into the past, where the young John Paul emerges *'bursting with pleasure'* from a dark home on a narrow street in Dublin's Liberties. The hopeful socialistic enthusiasm in John Paul the trade unionist is replicated in the youthful, innocent dreams he had on entering his first job as a messenger boy. The excitement of the new post mirrors the intellectual excitement of the bookish and inquisitive boy outside his working hours. He is at the start of his adventure, and economic restrictions were not going to stop him.

> *He is all excitement: arms akimbo,*
> *a thumb crooked by the telegram pouch,*
> *shoes polished, and a way to make in the world.*
>
> *His eyes are bright,*
> *his schoolmaster's tags fresh in mind.*
> *He has a few of the Gentlemen's Sixpenny Library*
>
> *under the bed* – A Midsummer Night's Dream,
> Sartor Resartus, The Divine Comedy, *with a notebook,*
> Moore's Melodies, *a trifle shaken ... Shelley, unbound...*[23]

By placing the instances of political action so close to that of this adolescent hyperactivity, the poem may call for a reading that would judge John Paul's political and labour activity as childish. But such a reading would need to ignore the genuine appreciation that permeates the verse. When recalling his father making a speech on a Labour platform, Kinsella is sceptical, yet believes that it is in such moments where something precious is found.

> *Goodness is where you find it.*
> *Abnormal.*
>   *A pearl.*[24]

A world shaped predominantly by people like his father would see disappointment continue to darken lives and death destroy everything, but where temporal society would be decent.

> *The eggseed Goodness*
> *that is also called*
> *Decency.*[25]

The dilution of the political programme of trade union activity and socialism to 'Decency' would trouble many active adherents to the cause. The socialism espoused by Karl Marx (1818–1883) and Friedrich Engels (1820–1895) declared itself scientific, based on laws in the social and economic sphere that had as much validity as laws in the natural sciences. This insistence on the scientific basis of socialism may have strengthened the intellectual backbone of some followers, but in truth the vast majority of socialists did not think that socialism would improve their lot because it was *true*, but rather because they believed it to be *righteous*. Thus, 'Decency' is not the most negative of qualities to celebrate. Indeed, the poet is also praising the lived experience of such politics through the individual characteristics of his father. He practised what he preached. He wanted society to be fairer, more equal and more decent, and in turn he was a decent man himself.

Most of the poem's energy is weighted towards its end, with all the vigour of youth, in contrast to the onset of illness and looming death that shapes the early sections of the poem. John Paul, ill and feeble, is now:

> *Corded into a thick dressing gown*
> *he glared from his rocker*
> *at people whispering on television.*
>
> *He knocked the last drops of Baby Power*
> *into his glass and carried the lifewater*
> *to his lips. He recollected himself*[26]

But the early sections are not entirely devoid of passion; although perhaps weak in body, the fighting spirit still marches on. The poet's father remains angry over an obscure pension dispute still unresolved from his time in the Guinness Brewery. Even at this moment, late in life, the beating heart of the trade unionist is still there. Not content to ruminate on his own, he organises his fellow pensioners and continues the class struggle.

> *His last battle – the impulse*
> *at its tottering extreme:*
>
> *muster your fellow pensioners, and advance*
> *pitched with them*
>   *('Power to the Spent!')*
>
> *against the far off boardroom door.*
> *All about him, open mouthed,*
> *they expired in ones and twos.*[27]

This last march evokes paradoxical feelings of respect and futility. The boardroom is far off because of the vast distance between the working-class pensioners and the rich of Dublin. But this distance also means that it cannot be reached before the marchers die. There will always be a battle that cannot be won, a victory unattainable before you breathe your last. The call for the transfer of power mockingly echoes the historic demand of Russian workers. This is not the great battle cry of the October Revolution, 'Power to the Soviets', which was still reverberating through the minds of activists of the European left like John Paul Kinsella in the decades after 1917. This is a far more feeble clarion call, but it is a call to action nonetheless. The pensioners in one final battle win our admiration for their last march of resistance towards their former employers. Whatever the result of this struggle, they cannot resist their mortality.

This demonstration against injustice becomes grimmer with each step, as it slowly but inevitably morphs into a death march with John Paul's comrades dropping down dead by his side. The Guinness boardroom may be resisted and fought against, but our collective mortality cannot. Time is our ultimate master, and no slave revolt, however well organised, can topple it.

This is classic Thomas Kinsella. He prevents any reader from becoming so utterly consumed by admiration for the active resistance of his father that they forget the dark, shadowy side of the story. This is not a one-sided rebel poem to be recited at a protest or meeting to rally the activists. It is the signature of this poet that the reader is never allowed to forget that the shadow of death hangs over all of this. We are blocked from losing ourselves in the seductive rhetoric of solidarity or the heroic actions of collective struggle. We may admire, but such admiration is hard-won and ultimately marginal. It cannot truly be felt without a constant awareness that futility stalks every step taken by John Paul and his ageing comrades.

Kinsella's refusal to consecrate these actions unquestionably, or to glorify class struggle or political resistance, means that the poem stands as a creation of profound reflection rather than simple elegiac celebration. The actions of his father, his grandfather and their fellow workers and trade unionists are not called into question politically, but rather existentially. Righteous resistance may bring a heroic valour to life, but resistance, no matter how righteous, cannot prevent the end of everything. The poem at its core says that the person who confronts this, internalises it and continues to fight, is the most admirable of all.

This existence of ultimate futility must be confronted honestly; although Kinsella's father's political struggles are recalled within a tone of respect and admiration, the tone is substantially qualified. The socialist hope for equality and democracy, as personified by his father, is ultimately flawed.

> *For there is really nothing to be done.*
> *There is an urge, and it is valuable,*
> *but it is of no avail.*[28]

It is of no avail, not so much because of some inherent political or economic faults, but rather because such a progressive project is rendered almost meaningless when set beside life's constants: disappointment and death. To the action-ready Leninist who yearns to know what is to be done, the poetic voice replies with the sobering *'really nothing'*. This is gloomy to be sure, but to recognise this truth, and from its wreckage somehow to rescue shards of hope and continue the fight, is perhaps the most heroic, and certainly the most honest, struggle of all. The poem suggests that his father with his *'half fierce force'* has not reached a totality of understanding of this truth; his rage against the economic machine is somewhat unbalanced.

The narrator's voice is subtle. It does not call his father out for idiotic innocence in his activism, but rather it questions what the point of it all is. The contradictory conclusion is both stark and equivocal: it is pointless, but still worthwhile. This conclusion is not the sort of rallying call that Larkin would have roared out to his followers during the 1913 Lockout, nor the type of lines that John Paul would have shouted on the election lorry outside the Black Lion until he was hoarse. Why raise the passions of an audience to concentrate their minds on some injustice, and to forge their intentions to some collective action, only to then say: this is all well and good, but really in the long run it means nothing? That is not good politics.

Kinsella is a poet, not a politician. If he were a politician, a left-wing critic could perhaps damn these lines as the product of the poet's weary bourgeois adulthood. But reflexive critical scorn at Kinsella's reflections would be misplaced. For even though he believes his father's struggle to be *'of no avail,'* there is an urge to do good, *'and it is valuable.'* The tension between this desire to do good and the nagging, whispering awareness, if we are truthful, of the presence of meaninglessness, is starkly faced by Kinsella. It is a more total and truthful response to reality.

The old men on the death march *'against the far off boardroom door'* must have some intimation that this is true for them also as they watch their comrades fall by their side, one by one, but they march on regardless. It is this staring at the apparent futility of life, not turning away from it, and still believing that the fight is worthwhile, that forms the honest core of the exacting, marginal victory of the progressive cause. Kinsella brilliantly juxtaposes the protest march against economic injustice with a lifelong march in protest against the ultimate injustice: the inevitability of death itself.

John Paul Kinsella and his comrades are not broken old men; they are working-class heroes, bravely marching against the tyrannies of Capital and Time.

* * *

'The Messenger' is noteworthy, both for the historical moments from modern Irish history to which it alludes, and also for those that are absent. The focus is heavily biased towards the events that directly impacted the labour movement in the period during the birth of the Irish state and the few decades that followed. The 1913 Lockout, the most defining set-piece battle in the modern history of the Irish working class, is prominent. The clash between James Larkin and his union members with William Martin Murphy (1844–1919) and his employer-supporters lasted for months, and ended in defeat for Larkin. But despite the loss, its impact, especially on the consciousness of Dublin workers, remained strong. Its most recent historian has called it 'the nearest thing Ireland has ever had to a socialist revolution.'[29] Those who lived through it, such as Kinsella's father and grandfather, were deeply shaped by the intense period of class consciousness it created.

The poem also mentions the stand against the fascist 'Blueshirts' in the 1930s taken by the small Irish left (among others), and evokes the drive to unionise workers in the Guinness Brewery. Absent, though, is the War of Independence (1919–1921) and subsequent Civil War (1922–23). The 1916 Rising makes a graphic and memorable appearance, but only in the very specific image of the most prominent socialist in Irish history meeting his fate. James Connolly's killing by the British forces for his role as one of the Rising's leaders was a massive blow to the labour movement in Ireland, just as the fight for independence was entering a critical stage. As mentioned in 'The Messenger', Connolly was tied to a chair to face the firing squad, but his entrapment also reflects the political power of the Irish working class, tied up and restrained following the foundation of the southern Irish state. The older John Paul, corded into his dressing gown, mirrors the image of Connolly, with proletarian power strapped and constrained.

While 'The Messenger' beats with moments of powerful energy, the hopes of the Irish socialist and labour movements after the defeat of 1913 were continually to be disappointed. John Paul may be dashing on the election lorry, but the fact that his voice is hoarse as he strains to be heard means that many people may not have been listening to his radical message. And generally, in Dublin, they were not. While the working class in many other European countries built powerful political and union blocks, the Irish political left was puny in comparison. The concerns and hopes of the urban poor were increasingly ignored by the political and economic elite. Ireland became a conservative capitalist state, under the strong influence of the Catholic Church, where the interest of the agricultural sector predominated over that of urban citizens. Compared to their economic equivalents in Britain, the 'Republic's working class, by contrast, withered in political, social and cultural terms' following the establishment of the Free State.[30]

Despite this, James Liddy claims that Thomas Kinsella has remained loyal, to an extent, to his father's political tradition. He has 'stayed in the tradition of his father; the labour voice mostly, though not totally, represented in the

Labour Party, the dark horse of the republic which has never quite seen electoral legitimacy.'[31] This is true, to a point, but must be qualified. The politics espoused by his father in 'The Messenger' were very much to the left of the Labour Party. When remembered in 'The Messenger' as an activist in the 1930s and 1940s, this was a period of strong radical socialist influence in the party. The Communist Party of Ireland (CPI) attempted a policy of infiltration of the Labour Party, and party branches in Inchicore and Kilmainham were among those in which the CPI's influence was strongest.[32] The father, like most left-wingers at the time, had a certain respect for the Soviet Union. When Germany attacked the Soviet Union during the Second World War, Kinsella's father turned to his son and foretold that Hitler was 'finished'.[33] Radical opinions were to be expected in the 1920s, 1930s and 1940s as this was the period of the continental crisis in bourgeois democracy, during which a battle between fascism and communism continued throughout Europe.

These great ideological and military struggles on the continent had a fainter echo on the island of Ireland. The Irish working class often preferred its heroes to be closer to home. James Larkin, with his broad body, arms aloft and mouth wide, makes an appearance in a later Kinsella poem, 'The Pen Shop' (1997). Larkin as roaring superhero, arms pointing up, almost ready to take off, is contrasted to the actual marginality and powerlessness of the urban worker during the early decades of the Irish state. It is almost because of this defeat and marginalisation that the Irish labour tradition projected onto Larkin the sense of heroic power that it lacked.

While there are these moments of entrapment and powerlessness within 'The Messenger', they are rare. In fact, members of the working class, through the personae of father and grandfather, are portrayed as creative, complex and active agents in the story of their lives. As Michael Pierse has written, this sense of agency is often missing from depictions of working-class characters in general Irish literature. Workers do not often do it for themselves; they are being done to, and are more often than not the helpless victims of history rather than generators of it. But 'being working class is not the same as being a passive victim of powerful social forces; it is part of a collective, active, organic and historical process of identity formation.'[34] The men in 'The Messenger' are certainly not passive victims. They live life with a zest that is often thwarted and disappointed, but continues despite this. Kinsella's writings are repeatedly, if not overwhelmingly, inflected with class concerns. Although his later life as a successful civil servant, academic and poet may have separated him from traditional working-class life, his early years in such a politically conscious environment and in the small communities around Inchicore left a lasting impression.

In 'St Catherine's Clock' (1987), there is a distant memory of childhood when the young poet was brought out to the Naas Road to visit *'our best cousins.'* There exists an unformed youthful perception of class difference within the greater family, which combines with a knowledge that, though the poet's immediate family may be poor, it does not mean they do not present the best face possible.

> *I know I was not bold*
> *even if I did terrible things.*
>
> *I was always dressed properly,*
> *and minded my brother.*[35]

He was taught by his family to take pride in his appearance, and to acknowledge that poverty in practice did not mean poverty in spirit. As a result, there is little sense of embarrassment about class origins, or a major inferiority complex. On the contrary, there is something approaching class pride.

And I always remembered
who and what I am.[36]

John Brannigan has claimed a general 'absence of class-based critique in Irish Studies,' and it is true that literary critics seldom view the work of Thomas Kinsella through a class lens.[37]

The absence of class interest in the literary criticism of Irish literature could merely be a reflection of the marginalisation of class-based politics and social movements in the Irish state, which has witnessed since its foundation 'the diminution of labour issues in subsequent decades, and the disappearance of such unbridled and unconcealed working-class solidarity with the foundation of the Free State.'[38]

But despite this marginalisation, there has remained a tradition of Dublin writing focused on the working class, which contains its own repeated themes. Pierse has identified hostility to the power of the Catholic Church and concern over how the state's education system fails the urban poor as key elements in this Dublin genre.[39] Both figure in Kinsella's work over the decades.

'The Messenger' finds its place in that tradition of neglected literary treatments of Irish working-class life. Not one-dimensional, never clichéd, the men (the absence of women is noteworthy) of the poem live as workers, lovers, craftsmen and fathers, disappointed, infused with the hope of social change, as striker and as excited adolescent. They are actors in both their own and their country's history. History is not done to them (as is arguably the case of O'Casey's great trilogy, for example); they are agents of it. Disappointed agents maybe, but still making attempts to shape their future. 'The proletarian appears in Dublin's writing as a conflicted figure of commitment to community and dissent from orthodoxy, as a conduit for radical ideas and a disempowered, disenchanted pariah in its own state,' writes Pierse when describing literature from the capital since the death of O'Casey in 1964.[40] The men of 'The Messenger' fit this description to a large extent, in all their contradictory impulses. The poem is a dynamic and non-idealised portrayal of the Dublin working class, rendered by one of its most talented scions.

* * *

This life of political engagement and action was not the one taken by most Irish workers in the early part of the twentieth century. Even at high points of the labour struggle, like the 1913 Lockout or the mass strikes during the War of Independence, many remained disengaged, or involved only slightly. Is there a sense of meaning or even heroism that can be salvaged from such lives?

In contrast to the activist, politically engaged example of working-class life featured in 'The Messenger', Kinsella's poem 'Dick King' serves as a suggestive counterpart. Published in his 1962 collection, *Downstream*, the poem honours a differing aspect of potential proletarian heroism. it originally emerged in early draft form as two separate poems.[41] In its published edition, 'Dick King' has two distinct sections stuck together, which remain clearly separate in form and tone. Despite the jolt to the reader that the formal and thematic shift brings, the poem does not creak on its hinge, as it is held together by an evolving portrait of a family friend and neighbour from the poet's childhood.

The second section of the poem has a pleasant, simple rhyming sequence over six four-line stanzas. But in the soothing, recurring rhythm, the repetition of King's daily grind of work, the greyness of his personal life and the uprooted nature of his existence in Dublin are grimly painted. Like many thousands of internal migrants in Ireland, King has moved from west to east, leaving rural Ireland in search of work in the growing capital. Originally from the Claddagh area near Galway city centre, King was a neighbour of the Kinsella family in Inchicore. The poet recalls him being 'always around' his family home.[42]

An initial reading of King's life, or at least the part of his life based in Dublin, generates feelings of pity. The dull routine of work is relentless and uninspiring. Unlike Kinsella's romantic poetry-reading father, who knew from Shelley, *'If Winter comes can Spring be far behind?'*, 'Dick King' has no seasonal respite; everything is constantly bleak.

> *And season in, season out,*
> *He made his wintry bed.*
> *He took the path to the turnstile*
> *Morning and night till he was dead.*[43]

The seasons may change around him, but his experience never gets to move beyond the bleakest period of winter. It is a life of dull proletarian grind, controlled by the set time of the working day.

The rhythm of organised industrial time was very different to the more organic time management of rural Ireland, and a shock to internal migrants like King. Time is very structured in capitalist production, an experience that has often stunned those who previously worked in the countryside. A modern anthropological study into the process of 'proletarisation' of rural workers in the plantations and mines of South America demonstrated that the peasants had not previously regarded time as something they had abstractly to follow or keep. Looking at this example and other 'traditional' societies, Michael T. Taussig found that 'time for these people is not abstracted from the tissue of life activities, but is embedded in them. It is not "clock time" but what we could call "human time" time is social relations.'[44] But as the South American peasants began life as mine workers living to established hours set by their boss in the pursuit of profit, time took on a life of its own. It was something that loomed over them, scared and controlled them; they begun to associate it with the devil, for it had morphed into 'an abstraction, but also a substance, it passes, it can be wasted, it can be saved and so forth. Moreover, it is animated: so we speak of fighting against it.'[45]

There is a similar feeling of shock towards time in King's case. His move to Dublin does not merely mean a new development in his naturally evolving life; it is more like being born again, with time starting anew.

> *By the Southern Railway he increased*
> *His second soul was born*
> *In the clangour of the iron sheds,*
> *The hush of the late horn.*[46]

This 'second soul' is not only born in the noise and fuss of industrial, urban Dublin, but also in a different language.

His former life in Gaelic-speaking Galway is not merely an old life from which he has evolved; it is a totally different one. There has been a rupture rather than a development. In all the anxiety brought on by this new and alien birth, the domestic home provides little respite. In the face of radical change, his partner hangs on doggedly and dogmatically to old certainties, her repetitive prayers mimicking the daily drudgery of his working day.

> *An invalid he took to wife.*
> *She prayed her life away;*
> *Her whisper filled the whitewashed yard*
> *Until her dying day.*[47]

But our feelings of pity towards Dick King are greatly tempered by the narrator's empathic judgement in the opening of the second section of the poem: '*Dick King was an upright man.*'

'Upright' is a pose that brings backbone and rugged respectability, if not to a life, then certainly to an individual. And there is little doubt that the poet respects this man, a forerunner to 'Vertical Man', a 1973 elegy he would later pen for his great friend and composer Seán Ó Riada. But what is the nature of this respect that King garners? What is the value of this upright stance, when we are given in rhythmical detail an insight into his monotonous, pitiful existence? Surely Dick King's quiet, unquestioning reaction to the reality of working-class life contrasts unfavourably to the more activist, heroic actions of John Paul Kinsella in 'The Messenger'?

If we engage with modern theories of heroism, we can find some provocative perspectives as to how Dick King may be regarded as an upright and even heroic individual. King's daily routine could arguably be celebrated as an authentic 'life of revolt,' a personal story of heroism in the eyes of existentialist writers like Albert Camus (1913–1960).[48]

For Camus, all humans were destined to search for a meaning in their lives, but there is no meaning 'out there.' The absurdity of life comes from the incongruity of man's passionate search for this meaning, and what Camus calls the 'unreasonable silence of the world.'[49] Camus rejects two options that man seems to have in the face of this absurd incongruity. One is suicide, which he regards as the ultimate defeat. The other is a 'leap' into faith (it does not necessarily have to be religious), where man ignores the meaningless nature of life and finds solace in elaborate theological, philosophical or political systems of belief. Camus rejects this as another form of suicide, this time calling it 'philosophical' suicide.

In the face of the absurd universe, Camus proposes a number of possible lives that man may lead that could provide some level of satisfaction. Some, such as a life led to excess with the feeding of a gargantuan appetite, personified by Don Juan and his sexual excess, or the life of an actor or conqueror, do not concern us here. It is Camus's controversial celebration of the life experienced by what he called the 'absurd hero' that allows a possible reading of King's life as heroic.

In Camus's most significant philosophical writing, *The Myth of Sisyphus* (1942), a life of routine, such as Dick King's, is celebrated as 'virile' and honourable. In Greek mythology, Sisyphus is punished by the Gods for wrongdoing. His punishment is to roll a massive rock up a hill, and then, having reached the top, he is forever doomed to watch the rock roll back down the hill. He must repeat this action forever – a very long shift indeed. Camus uses

Sisyphus's predicament as a metaphor for the daily routine of the worker under industrial capitalism. But Camus does not recommend that Sisyphus should organise with his fellow working slaves to form a trade union and strike a blow against the Gods. Rather, the Algerian-born writer celebrates Sisyphus because he lives a life 'without appeal.'[50] The knowledge that his regular labour is meaningless does not lead him to despair, resignation or suicide. Instead, this hero displays toughness and awe-inspiring fortitude (in the eyes of Camus, at least) by his indefatigability. He smiles when he is returning down the hill every time. King's similar resoluteness in continuing his working routine echoes that of Sisyphus. Camus believed that man 'is defeated in advance,' but despite that, 'everything considered, a determined soul will always manage.'[51] Dick King's second soul, born in the railway works, may not sing with hope, but it manages and it is determined to keep going every day.

It is precisely the absence of hope that Camus admires in Sisyphus. Unlike John Paul Kinsella, whose life fluctuated between hope in progress and disappointment in actuality, King does not experience these changes of emotional seasons. King takes the same path to the turnstile each day. His scheduled route is a set, predetermined hike that is predictable and plodding, '*Sixty years he trod / The dull stations underfoot / Fifteen he lies with God.*' There are no flashes of adventure in these walks. In contrast, Kinsella's father often stepped off the well-trodden path, whether it was with his leftist politics, the marches against the Blueshirts or turning his back on the powerful altar and leading his child out of Mass. He could also take steps that approached the wantonly dangerous rather than classically heroic, as he did when some dispute in work led him, in a combination of anger and foolhardiness, to swagger in front of his work colleagues.

He brandished his solid body
thirty feet high above their heads therefore
and with a shout of laughter

traversed a steel beam in the Racking Shed
and dared with outstretched arms
what might befall.[52]

Behind such ostentatious and childish displays of physical bravery, there lay layers of accumulated disappointment and thwarted hopes for betterment. But although these dangerous steps are questionable, they are brave, and it is impossible to imagine Dick King taking such risks. Camus would be attracted to the more mundane steps taken by King rather than John Paul's more dramatic strides, for 'continuing to toil without purpose, continuing to live in a world that provides no reason for living, itself provides a reason for living.'[53]

Sisyphus is thus for Camus a heroic, working-class everyman because he lives without hope. The absurd hero understands the set-up that is his life, but continues nonetheless. 'It happens that the stage-set collapses,' wrote Camus on the ordinary worker who understands what Sisyphus did. 'Rising, tram, four hours in the office or factory, meal, tram, four hours of work, meal, sleep and Monday, Tuesday, Wednesday, Thursday, Friday and Saturday, according to the same rhythm – this path is easily followed most of the time. But one day the "why" arises and everything begins in that weariness tinged with amazement.'[54]

Although a reading of King as an absurdist hero is attractive, in the end it fails to convince. For the heroism in Camus's theory requires the hero to recognise the futility and absurdity of his plight, and to continue on regardless. There is nothing in the poem to sustain a reading whereby King was aware of the folly of his daily routine. Thus, he cannot be 'upright' or heroic in the sense that Camus understood. So from where does King acquire such an upstanding gait and the admiration of the poet?

We must briefly consider a conservative reading that would recognise honour in the actions of Dick King in the sense that he sticks to his daily routine without causing trouble. In contrast to 'The Messenger', which crackles with the energy of class struggle, there is no politicised labour strife here. This is not the class-conscious worker, angry at the unjustified gap between rich and poor. This is the atomised man, with his head down, putting one foot in front of the other, getting through his day of alienated labour, pushing the rock to the top of the hill and watching it roll down again. Such acceptance is consoling to the capitalist, or any defenders of the status quo, for such workers are not likely to demand major change. But again, given the overall thrust of Kinsella's work, and the political sensibility it displays (however faintly sometimes), it is not convincing to regard Dick King as an exemplar of stoic, working-class obedience to the daily dictates of capital.

The poem does reflect an appreciation for the stoical strides forward that a person takes, despite life's difficulty. Such stoic admiration remains in a poem published almost three decades later. 'The Stable' (1990) is about an elderly neighbour in the Percy Place area of south Dublin, a Mr O'Keefe, who every day brings his horse and trap along the same route, '*Unbothered for forty years / he took the path from the stable door / to the garden tap, and ran the water / into the bucket under his thumb.*'[55] O'Keefe is in the lineage of Dick King, unheroic, it seems, in all but his daily doggedness. A level of respect is won for sticking to the routine, for not becoming resigned. There is also a regard for King, which is also seen with O'Keefe, which comes from his loyalty to a profession, doing the job, and doing it well and consistently. 'It is also the staggering evidence of man's sole dignity: the dogged revolt against his conditions, perseverance in an effort considered sterile.... It calls for a daily effort.... All that "for nothing", in order to repeat and mark time,' wrote Camus.[56] Indeed, Kinsella's own description of his working literary life often echoes the routine and hard labour of this type of man. Although the creative act is dissimilar to wage labour, the work that goes into the poetry is described as painful, full of long hours of preparation and sweat. Kinsella is not the poet of instant inspiration; it is not the same as William Wordsworth's (1770–1850) 'spontaneous overflow of powerful feelings.' His poetry is created by a combination of the doggedness of Dick King, the passion of his father and the craft of his grandfather.

But Dick King is not 'an upright man' purely because of his ability to stick to the daily grind. In the poet's memory, King is not a man of honourable backbone because of anything he did during his working hours. The real source of King's dignity and admirable qualities can be found in the less structured, more dreamlike opening sequence of the poem. Here, King is shown holding the hand of the young Kinsella as they both stand on the west end of James's Street, not far from the Kinsella family home. The tonal atmosphere is one of intergenerational awe from the child's perspective, and the offering of loving safety from the elder. The young narrator feels protected by the older King:

> *When I sheltered my nine years against your buttons*
> *And your own dread years were to come.*[57]

King is the archetypal 'old man' figure, a person of wisdom who gently takes the young poet by his hand and delicately introduces him to some of the more difficult aspects of the world, such as death.

> *And your voice, in a pause of softness, named the dead,*
> *Hushed as though the city had died by fire,*
> *Bemused, discovering ... discovering*
> *A gate to enter temperate ghosthood by;*
> *And I squeezed your fingers till you found again*
> *My hand hidden in yours.*
>
> *I squeeze your fingers.*[58]

It is in his role of guide, as the gatekeeper to knowledge, that King's life is given a structured meaning and significance. He leads this initiation process for the child. It is the unfussy continuation of an important historical ritual of guidance. In the eyes of the child, King is a heroic source of wisdom. He is an elderly Old Testament prophet standing on James's Street watching the horses drink water from the fountain. A millennium-old process of passing on knowledge is taking place. It is an important ritual, which finds its validation beyond the Southern Railway yard or the four walls of King's home. Its validation is in the memory of the poet.

Unlike the strikes, revolts and resistance of working-class politics, there will be few popular ballads written about this. Separately, in autobiographical prose, Kinsella has written of King as a 'protector of my unformed feelings.' His memory of this older man, who always seemed to be around the Kinsella home, is a warm and respectful one. His emotional memory of him is 'of selfless kindness.'[59] This is the reason he remains in the poet's memory long after his death.

In your ghost, Dick King, in your phantom vowels I read
That death roves our memories igniting
Love. Kind plague, low voice in a stubbled throat,
You haunt with the taint of age and of vanished good,
Fouling my thought with losses.[60]

King is a type of hero as the imparter of wisdom and an early guide in Kinsella's life journey. His fist is not stretched upwards like James Larkin's or John Paul Kinsella's, but is lovingly cupped around the young poet's hand, protecting and guiding him through the early questioning of life's mysteries.

In 'The Messenger' and 'Dick King', Kinsella explores two differing aspects of working-class heroism: the fighter and the mentor. 'Dick King' is a celebration of 'ordinary' wisdom from 'ordinary' people. It remembers how, even in the midst of banal routine, people can quietly live out heroic roles in the minds of those who love them most.

* * *

It is not only the repetitive, unrewarding aspect of his work that is the source of disappointment in Dick King's life. There is also a cultural and geographical unsettledness that permeates the poem. This unsettledness may echo the wider anxiety or nausea that existential twentieth-century writers like Camus, Jean-Paul Sartre (1905–1980) and Martin Heidegger (1889–1976) have characterised as bedevilling modern man. After centuries of certainty that the purpose of life was the will of God, sceptical modern man is concerned about what, if anything, can be positively asserted about the meaning of life. What Sartre described as the 'foundationless foundation' on which modern man precariously stands is because the rock of certainty has been replaced by a swamp of subjectivity and hearsay.[61] For Camus, the loss of meaning can make man feel like an exile; he is exiled from the former sense of meaning that the world held. He lives 'in a universe suddenly divested of illusions and lights, man feels an alien, a stranger. His exile is without remedy since he is deprived of the memory of a lost home or the hope of a promised land.'[62]

This exile leaves a sense of unsettledness, or what Kinsella would call in a later poem 'unfitness' in 'Tao and Unfitness at Inistiogue on the River Nore'. This was a 1978 poem written under the influence of eastern Taoism. While the unsettledness in 'Dick King' and other Kinsella poems may have an element of a general existentialist, zeitgeist anxiety, it is in the narrowly national context that its essence is more clearly apparent.

A sense of unease can occur at different levels. On the one hand, there is the existential sense of unease with humanity's role in a universe that is devoid of objective meaning or structure. On the other, there is a sense of unease arising from emigration, or 'not fitting in' with a new location you have moved to. Kinsella is interested in both, and in several of his works juxtaposes these conditions.

This latter sense of unease is a product of the migration patterns that took place in Ireland in the late nineteenth and early half of the twentieth century, from struggling rural communities to urban areas like Dublin in Ireland, and abroad to the cities of the US and Britain. While the emerging political and literary elite valorised agriculture and country living, in reality many people were leaving a rural Ireland that was mired in perpetual economic crisis. An imbalance in population distribution is a feature of many colonised and post-colonial states, and Ireland was no different. Dublin expanded rapidly, and Irish communities grew in the great cities of the US and Britain, while rural Ireland stagnated because of emigration.

King, a native Irish speaker, had left Galway to travel to Dublin in search of work. It was never going to be an easy process of fitting in.

> *By the salt seaboard he grew up*
> *But left its rock and rain*
> *To bring a dying language east*
> *And dwell in Basin Lane.*[63]

Although the narrator already concludes that the language is dying, there is a feeling that its fate was sealed with the relocation to the capital. The gradual loss of Gaelic, and the accompanying culture, may have been a process set in train by centuries of cultural and economic imperialism, but this urbanisation of the Irish-speaking minority in the independent state helped to accelerate the process. King's migration to the capital was a journey replicated by tens of thousands of rural Irish, a trip of necessity made against the backdrop of official paeans to the importance and benefits of rural living. The official narrative from the political elite was that 'real' Ireland was in the countryside. While the elite of political and literary Ireland were promoting a journey into the west, in reality much of Ireland was heading east. For King and his ilk, the change in circumstances was profound, as significant as any emigration to London and New York. It was as if a completely new second life had begun. The orthodox ideology persisted that farmers were 'the moral and economic backbone of the country,' as Declan Kiberd has written.[64] That this was so made the internal migrants yearn for their former lives even more. 'The myth was given a further lease of life in each generation,' continues Kiberd, 'by the urbanised descendents of landless labourers or by failed small farmers keen to create a compensatory tale of rare old times. Marooned in an unplanned city of tenements and housing estates, many people experienced real guilt-feelings for the "crime" of being Dubliners at all.'[65]

The engagement between rural and urban experience was not always smooth. As Tom Garvin has noted about Dublin in the decades following independence, 'rural ways of familial and social organisation succeeded in transferring themselves to the city, and Dublin remained for a time an uneasy mixture of rural and urban styles of life.'[66] If this was true generally of Dublin in the first half of the twentieth century, it was especially true of the Inchicore, Kilmainham area of west Dublin in which the Kinsella family and King lived. Already regarded as existing on the very edge of Dublin's urban core, the area in Kinsella's youth was a place where rural Ireland's influence was never too far away. The popular perception at the time was 'that one mile west of Inchicore, the bog begins,' according to some Dubliners.[67]

In early poems, Kinsella voiced this unsettling geographical sense in reverse, this time for a working-class Dubliner in a rural environment. In his ornate early poem 'Another September', the setting is reminiscent of the final bedroom scene in 'The Dead', the short story by James Joyce (1882–1941) The poet narrator experiences a feeling of distance from his sleeping partner, which makes him question how much he really knows his wife. Like Gabriel Conroy in Joyce's story, who discovers a previously unknown tale of lost love in his wife's past, the narrator in 'Another September' sees his lover in a disconcerting new light. But what sparks this new feeling of estrangement, for Kinsella, is location. The couple has woken up together in his wife's family home in Wexford. Surrounded by the unfamiliar and rural, his wife is cast anew against what is, for the poet, an unaccustomed backdrop. She is welcomed by the natural world around her.

> *Domestic Autumn, like an animal*
> *Long used to handling by those countrymen,*
> *Rubs her kind hide against the bedroom wall*
> *Sensing a fragrant child come back again.*[68]

But while the rural world may celebrate the return of a beloved daughter, its attitude towards the male, urban poet is rejection.

> *– Not this half-tolerated consciousness*
> *That plants its grammar in her yielding weather*
> *But that unspeaking daughter, growing less*
> *Familiar where we fell asleep together.*[69]

Echoing 'The Dead', the poem resonates with a deep-seated feeling that we can never truly know the other, even if it is our lover. There is also significant patriarchal panic present, with the man no longer able completely to know and control the female. He cannot dominate her past, her interior memories and her relationship with the countryside. No matter what advantages patriarchy bestows on man, he cannot totally dominate his wife. Towards the end of the poem, his separation from his partner becomes even more pronounced when he imagines her in the company of numerous symbolic figures of womanhood: '*Moving like women: Justice, Truth, such figures.*' This is a world of symbolic history in which she can mix, but from which he is excluded.

But it is the uncomfortable experience in the natural, rural setting that looms large. The poet narrator is *'half-tolerated'* – he does not fit in, any more than the experience and aspirations of the Irish working class were tolerated within the new Irish state.

Leading Irish poet Eavan Boland has recalled how important her first reading of 'Another September' was as part of her own poetic development. She read it 'when I was scarcely out of my teens, my ears and eyes still dazed by Yeatsian rhetoric. This hardly seemed from the same tradition. In a way it wasn't.'[70] What attracted the young poet was this very unsettledness of the urban poet in the rural, domestic setting. Boland found the context most refreshing. Rather than a heroic poem situated in the outdoors of a wild Irish pastoral setting, this poem was domestic, populated by ordinary people. It was in 'a bedroom, moreover, located in the new Ireland, where downright working lives were lived.'[71] It was difficult to imagine Yeats or Kavanagh doing it in quite the same way. 'In the Irish poem, as I understood it, this was new. The locale of the pastoral had been suddenly and unceremoniously shifted.... A domestic scene where everything is human and from which the demigods of the pastoral are banished.'[72]

The unsettledness that the narrator experiences in 'Another September' was read by the young Boland as familiar and comfortable. Twenty years younger than Kinsella, Boland represented a new era, less burdened by the expectations felt by the first generation born after independence. That first generation, Kinsella's generation, were well aware of what their parents had sacrificed in creating the new state; they were schooled in the dreams of what the new Ireland was meant to be. But they became adults in the disappointing reality of their parents' dream. By the time we reach the late 1960s, when Boland was entering her late twenties, that sharp distinction between hope and disappointment is not so stark, and the original dreams of the revolution are more distant, possibly weighing less heavily on Boland and her peers.

In Kinsella's long poem 'Nightwalker' (1968), his peers are becoming middle-aged. They are portrayed as being uneasy as they wait for the suburban train before work every morning. Uncomfortably *'scratching in our waistcoats'* and *'(twitching our thin umbrellas)'*, the uniforms of middle-class suburban life are ill-fitting, maybe a bit too British, too resonant of imperial, bourgeois garments.

In 'I wonder whether one expects', which opens the 1962 collection, *Downstream*, the life of the middle-class senior civil servant living in the suburbs differs greatly from the popular perception of what a poet's life should be. After listing the attributes that are commonly expected from a poet ('absent-mindedness', 'expert sex', 'a ready rage', etc.), the more prosaic content of the poet's daily routine seems ridiculous.

> *But surely not the morning train,*
> *The office lunch, the look of pain*
> *Down the blotched suburban grass,*
> *Not the weekly trance at Mass...*
> *Drawing on my sober dress*
> *These, alas, I must confess.*[73]

Something that is 'blotched' has connotations of an existence that is not correct, a life that is marked by error. This can be read in the narrow sense of the poem, meaning that the poet is hardly expected to live such a boring suburban life. But there is a wider understanding of the incorrectness of this residential living on the outskirts of the city. It is neither the rural-based rugged life that the dreamers of the Literary Revival and political elite had hoped for, nor the working-class urban experience in which the poet was brought up. It is faintly foreign, with suburbia more a British or American phenomenon than authentically Gaelic. It was certainly not the stuff of heroic dreams.

* * *

By resuscitating Dublin working-class experience in 'The Messenger' and 'Dick King', Kinsella has helped to force it back into the canon of Irish literature and cultural imagination. Such resuscitation contributes to undermining the sense of unsettledness that surrounds conceptions of how the urban Irish are to fit into national identity. Kinsella expands the narrative of Irish history and identity to the back lanes, whitewashed houses, walled gardens, factory gates and picket lines of Dublin's working class. By bringing to life its heroes, with their hopes and disappointments, Kinsella has helped broaden the scope of Irish identity to include the city and its labourers.

3
Walking Alone

Trying to follow in the literary footsteps of Thomas Kinsella will keep you fit. Few writers have taken their readers on as many long-distance strolls as this Irish poet has. A number of his most important long poems are structured around wandering journeys where the poet narrator interacts with the environment around him, provoking images and recurrent themes. Walking as a form of archetypal journey is a popular ordering device in literature. In the Irish canon, James Joyce's *Ulysses* is assembled around a series of walks across Dublin. But while Joyce's characters, particularly Leopold Bloom, have their heads up to greet people, Kinsella's wandering persona is not so social. He normally has his head down, *'reading the ground.'*

As James Liddy observed, 'Kinsella's peregrinations are frequently, though not always, peopleless.'[1] The walk is an occasion to contemplate both the natural and man-made world around him. The walker interacts with what this world represents rather than the people he passes on his path. The sympathetic passer-by would regard the poet as having the gait of a man deep in thought. A less sympathetic stroller may see haughty arrogance or the introverted loner. Whatever the exterior may look like, internally, the poetic imagination is on the move. Through a series of walking poems over the decades, this narrator confronts everything from the persistent implications of history and politics on the modern Irish state, to encounters with the first ancient settlers in Ireland, to journeys into the deepest layers of the personal unconscious.

In 'A Country Walk' from the 1962 collection, *Downstream*, Kinsella describes the easing effect a solitary stroll has on a tensed mind, and how it nourishes imaginative growth. His head sunk by draining domesticity, he leaves his in-laws in Wexford with a burst. '*I swung the gate shut with a furious sigh / Rammed trembling hands in pockets and drew in / A breath of river air.*'[2] So begins a physical and mental journey. Externally he walks along the riverbank, and internally through imagined Irish history, stretching from the earliest mythological sagas, through the Norman Conquest, towards a cynical contemplation of the modern, independent state.

In his early strides, his continuing tension remains clear, but after drinking the soothing waters from a nearby well, things begin to improve.

> *And soon proceeded with a lighter step*
> *Down the river valley, wide and quiet.*[3]

Walking is creative and medicinal, '*Each slow footfall a drop of peace returning.*' The stationary, icy mindset that had frozen his senses is beginning to thaw as he strides onwards. Walking is healing, a practical way of dealing with everyday stress. But its benefits do not cease at this level; it also has a creative aspect, and an enabling impact on the poet's imagination.

* * *

Kinsella's most significant poem from his early career, the 1968 'Nightwalker', is a jagged modernist hike. The poet's opening footsteps in this long poem are made into a moonlit, suburban Dublin landscape.

> *My shadow twists about my feet in the light*
> *Of every passing street lamp. Window after window*
> *Pale entities, motionless in their cells like grubs,*
> *Stare in a blue trance.*[4]

The poet stomps across the capital, undertaking a metaphysical journey that sees him traverse issues such as the loss of the Gaelic language, corruption in the political elite, the legacy of the Irish Civil War and the debates surrounding the economic policy of the Seán Lemass-led government. His imaginative walk finally comes to a halt at an ominous body of water. 'I have heard of this place, I think / This is the Sea of Disappointment.'

As the sun sets on his middle age, Kinsella does not slow down. He is out again, flexing his leg and brain muscles, in 'St Catherine's Clock' (1987). This time the poet takes a long ramble through personal and political history, beginning at his home on the Grand Canal in Percy Place, Dublin 4, and ending in his childhood haunts of Inchicore and Kilmainham. After he leaves his front door and begins to stride forward, he marks the beginning of the journey with a moment of personal ritual.

> *The whole terrace*
> *slammed shut.*
> *I inhaled the granite lamplight,*
> *divining the energies of the prowler.*[5]

In his poetry in the 1990s, the poet is again prowling at night around the back lanes and streets near his Percy Place home, spotting an unwelcome shadowy figure on his travels – an omen of destructive development in his neighbourhood.

But it is in the walking itself, the constant moving, where the ideas are dislodged from the unconscious and allowed to swirl inside the conscious mind. The very act of walking leads to the cracking of the poet's frozen anxiety, created by icy inertia. With each footfall, the stodgy solidity of a tensed mind becomes increasingly liquefied, allowing the artistic imagination to flow. In short, walking helps you to relax and think big, facilitating what German critical theorist Theodor Adorno (1903–1969) would praise as uninterrupted thinking. 'As long as thinking is not interrupted it has a firm grasp upon possibility,' wrote Adorno, and it seems that in the case of Kinsella, uninterrupted thinking is often facilitated by getting out there and walking alone.[6]

Walking also helps narrative, and narrative is one significant way whereby structure can produce meaning in literature and life. As Maurice Harmon has noted, many of Kinsella's meanderings are 'archetypal journeys into the underworld of death and suffering leading to ultimate clarification.'[7] While this poet prefers to walk alone, he does so in the understanding that he follows in the footsteps of many millions before him who have made similar archetypal journeys in life and art.

* * *

What propels people along? What makes them put one foot in front of the other?

In 'Survivor', from the 1973 *From the Land of the Dead* collection, the male protagonist is lying in a cave. This ancient man is reluctant to take his first steps out into the open, to heed the call of adventure and to leave the safety of his home. '*The cavern is a perfect shell of force*', and he feels protected and comfortable there. The paucity of movement and action in his life means that he lacks a strong sense of self-worth, but this is compensated by the absence of ordeal that striving and adventure will undoubtedly bring. His stationary existence is contradictory, but seductive.

> *Curled in self hate. Delicious.*
>   *Head heavy. Arm too heavy.*
> *What is it, to suffer:*
>   *the dismal rock nourishes.*
> *Draughts creep: shelter in them.*
>   *Deep misery: it is a pleasure.*
> *Soil the self, lie still.*[8]

But this situation cannot last: '*Something crept in once.*' What crept into the cave enters the body and '*under the head*' of the man. This wriggling thing, like the serpent in man's first garden, is a disruptive influence on the passivity of the cave. This cave, unlike Eden, is not paradise, but its qualities are clear: the absence of striving lessens the ordeal of life. Even so, this thing, slithering into the cave, begins to work on his dreams. This writhing thing is the 'herald' of myth, and it calls man forth to begin his journey. The call is to leave the cave, walk out and to launch the adventure and ordeal of life. Of course one could turn away from this call, but in Kinsella's work this is a negative response. 'The herald's summons may be to live, as in the present instance, or, at a later moment of the biography, to die,' according to Joseph Campbell.[9] Whichever it is, it is a call to action, and 'all moments of separation and new birth produce anxiety' says Campbell.

    Once awakened by the herald, this new awareness of the journey ahead makes man dream and hope for betterment. This hope begins a process of movement as he strives for some new goal. The dark nourishment of the cave is no longer enough: man has his eyes on a bigger prize.

> *A new beginning. An entire new world*
> *floating on the ocean like a cloud,*
> *distilled from sunlight and the crests of foam.*[10]

Once the new goal has been imagined, man must leave the cave and begin the adventure to reach it. It takes the former cave-dweller on a classic sea voyage, this time in search of new lands. Taking to the seas, the adventurer and his crew reach an island that has many obvious positives: '*Paradise. No serpents. No noxious beasts.*' This Erin is mysterious, but the land is initially generous to the new arrivals. The call that began the adventure was heeded, and the payoff seems evident.

> *No lions. No toads. No injurious rats*
> *or dragons or scorpions. Only the she-wolf.*
>
> *Perpetual twilight. A last outpost in the gloom.*
> *A land of the dead. Sometimes*
> *an otherworldly music sounded on the wind.*[11]

But this new island, just like other mythical visions of lands of milk and honey and shining cities on the hill, can never fulfil the totality of hope that man has projected onto it. If hope is the propulsion for striving, then disappointment is more often its result. The island no longer just gives, but begins to take, mercilessly:

> *Everyone falling sick, after a time.*
> *Thin voices, thin threads of some kind of sweetness*
> *dissolving one by one in the blood.*[12]

As Maurice Harmon has observed, these ancient people are looking for paradise, but they merely find a new beginning, as they are 'undergoing the fundamental process of searching, absorption, suffering, death and renewal.'[13] There is no paradise, because if paradise existed there would be no ordeal, no movement, no opposites, no progression, no waste, and therefore no learning.

In 'The Dispossessed', from the same collection, a garden before the Fall is shown to be peaceful, where the inhabitants have learned *'that we must be virtuous without hope.'* But such a situation is inherently unstable. The denial of hope is to deny a core aspect of human consciousness, for the man in the cave at the beginning of 'Survivor', and the occupants of the first garden in 'The Dispossessed', are actually hopeless. Without the conscious capacity to create new goals for themselves, they are more like drugged-up prisoners, safe and happy, but in chains. When the satanic creature arrives in the garden, *'and lifted His unmangled hand'*, it does not take much mischief-making for it to have the inhabitants questioning their position.

Walking forwards and facing life's ordeals can sometimes bring unbearable costs. The journey may consist of experiences of such horrific terror that when the person returns they are struck dumb by what they have experienced. In '38 Phoenix Street', from the 1974 collection, *One*, Mr Cummins is an old neighbour from Kinsella's childhood who is *'always hunched down'*, looking sad, facing the stove in the kitchen. *'A black rubbery scar stuck on his white forehead'* tells the tale of his nightmare during the Great War.

> *Sealed in his sad cave. Hisshorror erecting*
> *slowly out of its rock nests, nosing the air.*
> *He was buried for three days under a hill of dead,*
> *the faces congested down all round him*
> *grinning* Dardanelles! *in the dark.*[14]

In this moment of overwhelming horror, the body continued to fight on although the mind had blanked out with pain. The biological life drive is to survive, to continue the journey, even when consciousness has lapsed. He was found when another soldier noticed a *'thread of blood / glistening among the black crusts on his forehead.'* But the shock and trauma of war has returned Mr Cummins to his point of origin. The knowledge he has gained on his journey was so powerfully evil that he is left hunched and sad. He no longer faces the journey in front of him, but is *'turned away towards the bars.'* The bars are of the kitchen stove, but they also recall the bars of the prison in which he now resides. His journey is over; he is *'Sealed in his sad cave.'*

The small flat in Baggot Street in which the poet lived before his marriage during the early 1950s is evoked constantly through his decades of poetry. It is a dark, cavernous place, where the young poet finds intellectual sustenance in his reading and early poetic work. It is also a lonely and arid location. Friends like Seán Ó Riada drop by, but even then their presence is more intense than relaxed. In the preface to 'Her Vertical Smile' (1985), the poet recalls listening to Gustav Mahler for the first time with Ó Riada, the music 'filling the mean little space: the unmade single bed, the dusty electric fire glowing in the grate, spattered with butts.'[15] It is a time of sombre solitariness and bedsit poetry.

This is the poet's cave. Outside there was the security of the civil service job in the Department of Finance; inside was the safety and sustenance of the flat where he experienced intense intellectual growth. In 'Memory of W. H. Auden', the variety of thoughtful investigations are hinted at: *'Jesus in History. Man and his Symbols / Civilisation Surprised in her*

Underwear,'[16] but it is Auden's work that first brings a feeling that poetry can be the medium through which to best digest these intellectual investigations.

But the journey out of the cave, the strides into real adulthood and full-time poetry, will only come when the call is accepted and the cave is departed. This coincides with the arrival of Eleanor into his life, the enabling figure that allows for growth and departure from the dark but nutrient flat. In the 1999 collection, *The Familiar*, the poet recalls the flat prior to Eleanor's arrival. '*I was on my own, fumbling at the neglect / in my cell, up under the roof / over Baggot Street.*'[17] But the process begins with the building of a loving relationship, the stepping out into the world and facing his journey more fully – a journey devoted to poetry. This meant leaving the bleak safety of the flat.

Long after the flat was departed, it reoccurs as a dominant motif in Kinsella's poetry. In 'Survivor', the cave is described by its important function in world mythology. The Baggot Street flat plays a similar role in the poet's personal life story.

> *It is spoken of, always,*
> *in terms of mystery – our first home...*
> *that there is a power holding this part of the mountain*
> *subtly separate from the world, in firm hands;*[18]

The cave for the ancient survivor and the flat for the poet have functioned as second wombs where the traveller can find time to build up the necessary skills and fortitude before beginning the second part of the journey into adulthood.

Leaving the flat is just one of a number of important points of departure that repeat in the poet's work. The original move to Baggot Street represented the significant departure from his childhood neighbourhood in Kilmainham and Inchicore. In the important poem 'Phoenix Park', published in 1968, departure from Ireland to the United States, the final abandonment of his civil service life and the beginning of his work in academia and full-time poetry, is the overarching narrative of the poem. That this moment brings more a sense of apprehension than hope is because of the poet's temperament, but also because of concerns over his partner's ill health. In the 1990 poem 'Rituals of Departure', moving house in the US, this time with young children, is recalled. Their tears in the back of the car are a reminder of the break that any move from a family home can represent. The *'high red oaks'* outside the home are symbols of the roots the family had sunk in the area, but are also reminiscent of the Tree of Life, of which we are all branches.

In the intricate, bruising lines of this long love poem, the poet narrator in 'Phoenix Park' celebrates the female muse as an enabling persona. It is 1960s Dublin; the poet has left his flat and is now married. The poet and his wife take a trip to the hospital in the Phoenix Park, where Eleanor had received treatment for TB. The couple is also deciding whether to move full time to the United States and begin a new life for themselves. The poem, set on a typically damp Dublin day, is saturated with hesitation and decision: should they stay or should they go? Do they move forward into the next part of their journey, or do they remain? It is a time of decision and indecision, of trying to find a structure for their shared journey out of the confusing mess of options and factors that need to be weighed.

In the chaos that the poet finds around him, he discovers some semblance of structure in the feminine. But this structure of movement is not one of constant progress;

it is not an easy celebration of victory over adversity. No, there is an appreciation that movement in life means loss as well as gain.

> *Laws of order I find I have discovered*
> *Mainly at your hands. Of failure and increase.*
> *The stagger and recovery of spirit:*[19]

There is uneasiness to the human condition, an inability to be satisfied because of a consistent feeling that something is missing inside each of us. The need to fill this constant void pushes us forwards towards some new content. But forward, it seems, to no set end point, no complete life satisfaction, no shining city on the hill, no end of history.

> *That life is hunger, hunger is for order,*
> *And hunger satisfied brings on new hunger*
>
> *Till there's nothing to come,*[20]

In 'Phoenix Park', the poet narrator regards the '*positive dream*' that is '*undying love*' as something that strengthens the impulse to keep going. But while this enables progress, there is also an image of frightening nothingness into which we stride, pressing our bodies out into empty meaninglessness.

> *That, while the dream lasts, there's a total hunger*
> *That gropes out disappearing just past touch,*
> *A blind human face burrowing in the void,*[21]

A world '*disappearing just past touch*' is reminiscent of 'that roar which lies on the other side of silence' that George Eliot writes of in *Middlemarch*. It is also an example of a mysterious eloquence that is not often associated with Kinsella. Literary critic Denis Donoghue writes that 'Eloquence, as distinct from rhetoric, has no aim: it is a play of words or other expressive means ... its place in the world is to be without place or function, its mode is to be intrinsic.'[22] The blind human face forcing itself into a void of meaninglessness around us is an image resistant to easy dissection, but it is one that intrinsically reflects a 'post-God' apprehension, on the one hand of the apparent senselessness of life, and on the other of man's inherent impulse to forge ahead in search of ultimate meaning.

This journey is thankless, and never reaches a destination, but it seems that we accumulate something worthwhile along this process. This positive accumulation is symbolised by crystals:

> *Till there's nothing to come; – let the crystal crack*
> *On some insoluble matter, then its heart*
> *Shudders and accepts the flaw, adjusts on it*
> *Taking new strength*[23]

The vision of humans reaching out in hunger for something beyond their fingertips is common in Kinsella. In the poem 'Finistère', a band of ancient seafaring emigrants stand on the northern Spanish shore, contemplating a difficult journey ahead, and deciding whether to stay or go.

> *We hesitated before that wider sea*
> *but our heads sang with purpose*
> *and predatory peace*[24]

In 'Finistère', the sailors decide to set sail, heeding the call to adventure with hope in their hearts. During the journey they encounter the inevitable cycle of hope and disappointment along the way. But if hope and the call to adventure is part of what gets humans going, the most basic of drives — hunger, shelter and sexual — are certainly also part of the propulsion. In the 'Prologue' of the 1974 collection, *One*, ancient man stands upright and begins.

> *Up and awake. Up straight*
> *in absolute hunger*
> *out of this black lair, and eat!*
>
> *Driven rustling blind over*
> *fragments of old frights and furies,*
> *then with a sudden hiss into*
> *a grey sheen of light. A pale space*
> *everywhere alive with bits and pieces,*
> *little hearts beating in their*
> *furryfeathery bundles, transfixed.*
>
> *That. There.*
> *Hurling toward it, whimswift.*
> *Snapdelicius. So necessary.*
> *Another. Throbflutter. Swallowed.*
> *And another.*
> *The ache ... The ease!*
> *And another.*[25]

The factors pushing human movement here are clear. They have existed since primordial times, and continue to drive our steps forward. There is a desire to appease our needs, and once we have filled this void we experience a momentary satisfaction.

> *But with the satisfaction*
> *comes a falling off*
> *in the drive, the desire.*
> *The two energies approach and come to terms,*
> *balance somehow, grow still.*[26]

The initial needs such as food and shelter are fulfilled, and then the construction of more complex civilisation can begin.

In *A Technical Supplement* (1976), humankind's conception of itself as fundamentally different and better than the rest of nature is mocked. A description of man's anatomy is quickly followed by a gruesome blow-by-blow account of a day spent in a slaughterhouse, where the '*Huge horned fruit*' of cow and sheep are methodically torn asunder on an industrial scale.

In section 8 of the collection, a lizard eats another (unidentified) living thing, with deliberate violent jerks. Just as humans munch on the '*horned fruit*', the lizard's devouring of another life leaves the reader uneasy with the absence of morality. There is an ethical nothingness here; it is something monstrous.

> *Stone still*
> *holding it sideways in its jaws.*
> *With a jerk, adjusting it*
> *with the head facing nearer.*
>
> *The two staring in separate directions.*
>
> *Again. The head inside the mouth*
> *and the little hands and feet and the tail*
> *and the suddenly soft round belly*
> *hanging down outside.*

>   *Again.*
> *Splayed hind legs and a tail.*
>
> *A tail.*
>   *Then*
> *a leather-granite face*
> *unfulfillable.*[27]

Man's countenance may at times show expressions of hope and at others disappointment, but at all times, like the lizard, it is unquenchable. We are restless, moving forward, striding ahead. Lucy Collins regards desire rather than suffering as the propellant within Kinsella's poetry, for desire posits a relationship with something beyond the present state, as it must 'be aware of what we lack in order to desire it,' and thus leads to a 'refusal to accept things as they are.' Suffering, on the other hand, leads us merely to be 'sensitive to our own pain.'[28]

    This suggests that the lesson, if it can be called that, is that there is no turning away from this inevitable movement between hope and disappointment; to strive and to grow is to fulfil this destiny. Waste is also a fundamental part of the process, often bemoaned, but impossible to ignore. Kinsella has been rather ruthless in his own life and work when it comes to accepting waste, dropping previous positions and discarding poetic practices. Waste is a natural by-product of growth. As a student he walked out of a science degree when he knew it was not for him, and his departure from a top civil service job in the mid 1960s would have been perceived by many as 'wasting' a career. He ruthlessly discarded strict, metrical poetic writing and the numerological system he used in some of his work, and turned his back on concerns of critical and public acclaim, focusing instead on his own marginal poetic structure. Waste is thus to be endured as inevitable, its process absorbed with the recognition that any propulsion in life will leave elements of natural debris in its wake.

In 'Mirror in February' (1962), the narrator contemplates himself in his bathroom shaving mirror. His concern that he is no longer young may seem excessively melodramatic (he is only 33), however, the wider theme of ageing holds relevance. Outside, the natural seasonal changes can be seen in the garden's annual developments, and are accompanied by destruction and waste.

> *Below my window the awakening trees,*
> *Hacked clean for better bearing, stand defaced*
> *Suffering their brute necessities,*[29]

The slow death inherent in nature mirrors his slow demise; as each season passes, the inevitable comes closer. Like the trees, however, such destruction and waste is not always bad. In humans, the ageing process can help you to learn more.

> *It seems again that it is time to learn,*
> *In this untiring, crumbling place of growth*[30]

The apparent oxymoronic clasping together of *'crumbling'* and *'growth'* is of course not so strange in the Kinsellian view of walking forward in life. In the 1973 'Hen Woman', the young poet is standing in the back yard of his grandparents' home. He spots a beetle carrying a piece of excrement on its back, moving slowly across the back yard. Waste is absorbed into a part of the life process by the beetle. The insect looks seasonal, *'like a bronze leaf'* and is only *'inching across the cement.'* The slow crawl of the beetle, full of waste, was noted in ancient Egyptian society, where the scarab was an important symbol of the heavenly cycle of growth and waste. Here, the scarab in Dublin gets on with its working life, with a grim routine reminiscent of Dick King's daily walk to work.

> *The serrated brow pressed the ground humbly,*
> *lifted in a short stare, bowed again;*
> *the dung-ball advanced minutely,*
> *losing a few fragments,*
> *specks of staleness and freshness.*[31]

This is also the work process of the poet, where waste is inevitable. Waste can also provide sustenance to other beings, like the beetle or the flies on the cow dung in 'Tao and Unfitness at Inistiogue on the River Nore'. Waste is to be expected, not celebrated or feared, but faced and endured, hopefully a source of learning and knowledge for the next engagement in the journey.

Thus, despite all the ordeals inherent in beginning the journey, there is nothing for it but to leave the cave and walk on.

* * *

The walking in Kinsella's work is always solitary, and the critical perception of this poet as a loner and an outsider is a persistent one. Kinsella has mentioned the 'scattering of incoherent lives' that made up his poetic contemporaries who were first published in the 1950s.[32] It is true to say that his generation of Irish poets did lack the obvious connections that the writers of the Irish Literary Revival shared, or the English 'Movement' poets, or later the Irish poets of the 'Northern Renaissance'. But with Kinsella, this isolation is not merely a product of generational poetic culture; there is also an obvious personal inclination towards walking alone.

When questioned about the perception of him being a 'loner' in a 2002 interview, the poet did not reject the characterisation. 'I have never belonged to a group of poets,' he answered. 'Poetry was always a solitary matter, having nothing to do, for example, with a time in a university.'[33] His poetic generation is one from which he feels disconnected, but it nonetheless figures irregularly in his work. 'In Memory' (1990) is a poem written on the occasion of a funeral of one of the poets who had established themselves in the 1950s. The sombre gathering of his now elderly contemporaries leads Kinsella to survey their lives:

> *Some left the country, or disappeared*
> *as though they had never been.*
> *Others stayed in irregular contact*
> *our conversations growing more general.*[34]

Although time has made conversations more general, it becomes evident that many of the relationships were never that close to begin with. They were individuals who just happened to share a time and space when their published poetic careers began; connection did not develop far beyond this happenchance. Some of this tension and lingering spite between the ageing writers leads the narrator to an explosion of incredible misanthropy, the ferocity of which leaves the reader needing to catch their breath.

> *The narrow face of envy.*
> *Hardness of heart. Self.*

> *False witness. The irreducible*
> *malice and greed of the species.*[35]

You would have to conclude that these squabbles must have been on a fairly epic scale to produce lines of such forceful anger. In a later poem, 'Open Court' (1991), a literary bar scene from sometime during the late 1950s is brought to life in jaunty couplets. The poet departs on another journey by foot: *'From Stephen's Green I set my feet / contented into Grafton Street.'*[36] He enters a *'sty'* of a bar, which is playing host to literary Dublin. Patrick Kavanagh is apparently depicted as the *'ruined Anonymous'*, raging in the corner. This character somewhat entertainingly raves against Dublin, cursing the day he ever left the Monaghan countryside, to which he was famously adverse: *'Accursed pity / I ever came to Dublin city.'*[37] The characters spitting misanthropy and anger at literary Dublin and its hangers on is not something lacking in Kinsella's own poetry. Some of the pen-pictures in 'Open Court' are memorable, such as the older male author who accompanies a young female student to the bar. *'He halts a moment, losing track / His palm slips lower down her back.'*[38] There could also be some rather nerdish enjoyment to be found in guessing which unflattering pen-picture depicts which writer from the era, but the fun in that is minimal and unrewarding. Peter Denman is right to fault the poem for its humourlessness and 'bile',[39] and it is clear that the writer has little warmth for his generation. This is a perfectly reasonable response, but the poem's observations are often overly cruel, like *'Three poets sprawl / silent, minor, by the wall.'*[40] Even if it does make the reader wince at its animosity, 'Open Court' also exhibits that core Kinsella trait: it is unremittingly honest. There is no attempt on the poet's behalf to ingratiate himself with his fellow writers; the poet is steadfast against any misty-eyed, nostalgic turn towards a past literary era. The Dublin literary scene of the 1950s is not glorified, but darkly and cruelly depicted.

It seems that Kinsella was never very clubbable in the artistic sense. For example, he refused membership of *Aosdána*. Established by Taoiseach Charlie Haughey in 1981, the organisation is filled by peer nomination and election, and is limited to 250 living artists, who receive a stipend. Kinsella's stated reasons for his refusal to join have ranged from the self-regarding to the socially critical, all of which may have rankled with some of his fellow writers. In 2001 he told *The Irish Times* that it was a 'matter of standards.'[41] He believed that he would be standing for higher standards by standing outside the organisation, although he did add that there were members whom he held in high regard. In an interview a year later he developed a wider criticism of *Aosdána*, including a broader critique of the intentions of the ruling political elite, and former Taoiseach Charles Haughey in particular. 'The atmosphere of its establishment – as a clever but marginal embellishment, at minimal cost, in the years of aggrandisement under Haughey – contributed to the same feeling,' he said. 'The very title, taken from a meaningful social and artistic function in Ireland's integrated past and applied meaninglessly, embodies this emptiness.'[42] In a 1989 interview he amusingly described the Irish poetry scene as a 'blood sport'.[43] Whatever the situation, he was more comfortable, it seems, walking on the margins of literary Ireland.

When describing his essential poetic theory, it is always as an individual, never as part of a movement, or even within a broader tradition of Irish writing. In 'At the Head

Table', the poet narrator describes his work in terms that chime with Kinsella's reputation and self-image.

> *I have devoted*
> *my life, my entire career,*
> *to the avoidance of affectation,*
> *the way of entertainment*
>
> *or the specialist response.*[44]

But the reaction, the poet maintains, to such endeavour had been *'Dislike. Misunderstanding'*. In 'Worker in Mirror, at his Bench', a craftsman fields questions about his practice from members of the public who are baffled by the strangeness of some of his work. The craftsman answers the public as best he can, telling them that *'Yes, everything is deliberate,'* and *'No, it has no practical application.'* The routine and hard labour in the work is emphasised; this is not the explosion of inspiration from the romantic artist, *'Here the passion is in the putting together.'* It is technical, demanding, a pulling together of various materials from the exterior and interior worlds. The narrator describes his work as trying to create ' — *states of peace nursed out of wreckage.'* This line evokes the famous line in T. S. Eliot's *The Waste Land*: *'These fragments I have shored against my ruins,'* which acts almost as a credo for modernist poetic structure. Out of the wreckage of technological society, an era of total war and administrated genocide, the modernist poet is to rescue all that can be salvaged from what can still be regarded as worthwhile, and to forge it together to prevent total disintegration into a popular culture swamp of subjective rubbish.

The association of work practises and public response between the glassworker and poet are clear. The worker says, '*It is tedious, yes. The process is elaborate / and wasteful.*'[45] He admits to being in awe at the '*massiveness*' of other artists' achievements, but this does not lead him to despair: '*I have leaned my shed/ against a solid wall.*'[46] In the face of the understanding smiles of his audience, the worker outlines how the artistic act is about listening to the forces that move him, and letting the materials interact with each other. What he is describing is a deeply solitary affair:

> *I tinker with the things that dominate me*
> *as they describe their random persistent coherences.*
> *Clean surfaces shift and glitter among themselves.*[47]

When the artist begins to articulate his dark view of humanity ('*We all are vile ...* '), his audience's reaction changes rapidly from polite smiles to turning around and leaving his craft shop. In a more mocking and complex tone, in 'Self Release' from the difficult 1985 *Songs of the Psyche* collection, the narrator addresses his readers. He wonders aloud if they would rather he did not deal with the vague matters of his obscure unconscious, which constitute the collection's main preoccupation. In a violent image, he visualises stabbing the part of his brain that creates the internal psychological interests that grip the attention of the poet. After numbing that part, he could become less morose and intense, and maybe get back to writing the sort of accessible poetry that his many early readers and critics loved:

> *Then you would see how charming*
> *it is possible to be,*
> *how fluent and fascinating,*
> *a startlement to all,*
> *internationally, and beyond.*[48]

The '*and beyond*' brings self-mocking humour to the address, but the narrator is hinting that to be true to his art has meant that he must be true to what he regards as important. And if that means losing readership because he must bring literary life to the complexity of the personal unconscious, rather than writing perfectly crafted poetry about beautiful landscapes or young love, then this is a sacrifice of popular acclaim that he has been willing to make. There is a feeling that the poet almost equates marginality and isolation with authenticity and quality, or at least regards popularity and critical success in literature as a far from foolproof guide to its brilliance. In a November 1996 interview the poet said: 'You can't deny that public response is very pleasing, but public response can be off-key too.'[49]

In section 12 of '*A Technical Supplement*', there is a statement defending the marginal position as the point from which art can be its most challenging, non-conformist and important. '*There, at the unrewarding outer reaches, / the integrity of the whole thing is tested.*'[50] The placing of '*unrewarding*' and '*integrity*' so close together speaks to the poet's understanding that work that may seem unrewarding in the sense of not generating huge public or critical reaction can still have integrity and quality.

* * *

After his early walking away from strict form, Kinsella's work has most often featured a 'modernist' tone and structure. Modernism in terms of literary form and content is more associated with the early period of the twentieth century and linked to exemplars such as T. S. Eliot and Ezra Pound (1885–1972) in poetry, and James Joyce and Virginia Woolf

(1882–1941) in prose. In terms of poetry, its output was associated with free form, fragmentation, a poetic narrative voice that was not always steady, multiple perspectives and free verse.

Instead of a strict set of criteria, modernism is better understood as a literary rejection of classic nineteenth-century forms and a reaction to the onset of the machine age, massive cities, the rise of popular culture and the horror of the First World War. 'Modernism can therefore be thought of as an impulse to reshape literature and expand the borders of the possible in written language ... It is also a term that has hardened around certain writers and texts who aspired to this agenda of remaking,' writes Peter Childs.[51] For Tim Armstrong it is modernism's 'declaration of non-complicity; the preservation of a space which future generations might recognise as freedom' that was its most important aspect.[52] But to capture the connection between societal change and literary reaction, it remains Marshall Berman in *All that is Solid Melts into Air: The Experience of Modernity* who described it best, writing that the experience of the energy and flux of modern life cuts across class, geographical, ethnic and religious divides. It was an experience that seemed to unify everyone in its general impact. 'But it is a paradoxical unity, a unity of disunity: it pours us all into a maelstrom of perpetual disintegration and renewal, of struggle and contradiction, of ambiguity and anguish. To be modern is to be part of a universe in which, as Marx said, "all that is solid melts into air." '[53]

Many modernists felt that one way of resisting this disintegration was to create difficult art that would not be vulnerable to easy dissolution. It could survive the maelstrom. The concept of accessibility and the rejection of mass appeal was always a point of tension within modernism.

As Joe Cleary notes, 'The modernists ... were for the most part determined to maintain a Chinese wall between a demandingly intellectual and non-commercial high art and commercial mass culture.'[54] For many modernists, the key sign of authenticity in art was in the ferocity of its rejection of mass society. The genuine perplexity of much of the population at the work, such as Joyce's *Ulysses* or Eliot's *The Waste Land*, was a sign to many modernists that they were on the right path. The route of artistic authenticity was through a dense difficulty of theme and experimental forms of creation.

For some critics, modernism was an elitist rejection of popular culture.[55] For others, like Adorno, it was an attempt to preserve great art from the homogenising effects of the 'culture industry'.[56] Kinsella's work was never much affected by the 1960s' explosion in popular culture. This stood him in contrast to a fellow Irish poet such as Paul Durkan. As Theo Dorgan has written of Durkan, he was a poet who was 'interested in what is potentially positive within the new mass culture.'[57] This could not be said of Kinsella. Although *Nightwalker* was published in the late 1960s Kinsella is not a 1960s poet. Approaching 40 in the late 1960s, the 'revolution' in popular culture that exploded in the western world had little impact on his work. While Philip Larkin moaned that sex happened only around the time of the first Beatles LP, which was too late for him, there is little direct interaction with the popular youth culture that began in the 1960s in Kinsella's work. The importance of the rock revolution on some poets is vividly described by Dorgan: 'it rocked us into our bodies in a body-denying culture, it rocked us into a global world view out of a culture that had become stultified, insular and inward-looking, it shook and shaped us.'[58] In terms of poetry, the sixties swung without Kinsella.

The popular culture revolution is hardly mentioned, even to discount it. This is further evidence of a modernist artistic sensibility.

Kinsella, although writing decades after the high point of modernism, was deeply influenced by the movement's ideas. In Irish poetry, modernism has not generally been a significant influence on tone and theme. Emer Nolan has written about how the modernist technique of Joyce has not found many true Irish inheritors, 'But it was Thomas Kinsella who turned the Joycean achievement to his own purposes in verse, rewriting Joyce in an idiom that owes a good deal to [Ezra] Pound,' she noted. 'Kinsella's poetry, however, has been increasingly erased from public consciousness by the emergence of a new work that has forsaken the epic ambitions of modernism, making a virtue of the modesty that disclaimed for art the capacity to repair the destitution of the cultural world.'[59]

With Kinsella, modernism came late to the centre of Irish poetry. Whether because of the rural-based economy in the new state, the poverty and internal debates of the 1930s or the cultural isolation caused by World War Two and the stagnation of the 1950s, modernism was not an influential literary style in the period. Kinsella's gradual deployment of modernist methods in the early 1960s was some four decades after the publication of *The Waste Land*. 'Kinsella's adoption of poetic techniques that were groundbreaking fifty years previously does not mean that he is an experimental poet,' concludes Justin Quinn. 'He only appears experimental in Ireland because of that country's overwhelming poetic conservatism.'[60] The majority of the poetry-reading public has been attracted to the more lyrical writing of Seamus Heaney and others, Kinsella's modernist technique having isolated him from many of his contemporary Irish writers. The reputation of inaccessibility in modernist writing, and the actual difficulty of some of the work, has contributed to Kinsella's relative marginality in contemporary Irish literature.

*　*　*

Lacking a literary movement around him, the poet has walked alone. In the absence of contemporaries with whom he felt he could commune, Kinsella has projected aspects of himself and his concerns onto other figures, and through his poetry he has conversed and empathised with them. They include figures of poetic isolation like the Gaelic poet Aodhagán Ó Rathaille (1670–1726), figures of stoic introspection like Roman Emperor Marcus Aurelius (121AD–180AD), and even persons of dark dispositions living on the margins of society like assassin Lee Harvey Oswald (1939–1963).

This poet, with his impression of himself operating on the margins of art, has an affinity with other figures on the edges of society. In 'St Catherine's Clock', as the poet begins a long walk from his house in Percy Place, he sees a *'half stooped image'* through a window across the canal. In lines that have the cinematic effect of an extreme close up, we watch an addict shoot up. The poet's reaction is not disgust or sympathy, but rather a type of creative empathy.

> *The fingers of the right hand are set*
> *in a scribal act on the skin:*
> *a gloss, simple and swift as thought,*
> *is planted there.*
>
> *The point uplifted,*
> *wet with understanding,*

he leans his head a moment
against the glass.

I see.[61]

The analogy between needle and pen, the incision made by the addict and the deep incisions made into the personal psyche by the poet, is clear. It seems that Ireland's leading poet can find more in common here, on the edges of society, than with his fellow writers. Whether it is Ó Rathaille trying to survive on the margins of an Ireland where the Gaelic order has collapsed, or Marcus Aurelius penning his *Meditations* for the closest of audiences (himself), or Oswald, lonely in a city of millions, or an unnamed addict on Dublin's south inner city, here is where the poet finds a community of understanding, and one that he does not experience with his fellow living poets. In terms of artists he admires, it is the most intense and hard-working that attract him. Gustav Mahler in *Her Vertical Smile* is placed on his conductor's pedestal, and is clearly regarded as an exemplary figure. The narrator looks at his great works and thinks: '*If only we could wring our talent out / wring it and wring it dry like that.*'[62]

All these people's lives are not just outside the mainstream of common experience, they are also stalked by feelings of futility, whether it is the desperation of the contemporary addict or the Roman emperor concluding that his power and wealth is worthless in the face of certain death. A modern poet, particularly one who considers himself on the artistic margins, must also grapple with notions of futility: does my work and life matter at all?

The futility of writing in isolation, with a small audience, and seemingly growing smaller by the year, has drawn Kinsella in empathy towards the painstaking work undertaken by Denis Diderot (1713–1784) in researching and writing the *Encyclopédie* in the eighteenth century. The extract of a letter written by Diderot to Voltaire (1694–1778) during this research is published at the beginning of the 1976 *A Technical Supplement* collection. Diderot is in a moment of severe self-doubt during the gargantuan task of collating the *Encyclopédie*, wondering what the point of his work is. 'I cry from morning till night for rest, rest; and scarcely a day passes when I am not tempted to go and live in obscurity and die in peace in the depths of my old country. There comes a time when all ashes are mingled. Then what will it boot me to have been Voltaire or Diderot, or whether it is your three syllables or my three syllables that survive?'[63] The placing of the extract at the beginning of the collection urges the reader to understand that Kinsella wrestles with similar feelings of crisis. In the letter, Diderot wonders if his work will make any impact on the life of man, but despite his awareness of possible futility he does not turn away from the endeavour. He continues to struggle on, with energy inspired by anger more than love. 'That there is more spleen than good sense in all this, I admit – and back to the *Encyclopaedia* I go'.

Similar spleen can be seen deployed less effectively in *Open Court*, but also magnificently in Kinsella's eviscerating political satires, such as 'Nightwalker', or the 1990 collection, *Poems from Centre City*. Kinsella's poetry can hardly be described as possessing a 'punk' ethic, except maybe in one aspect. That 'anger can be power', as The Clash roared out, is something that pumps through the work. For anger is not always a negative energy, but can also be a powerful propulsion towards great artistic works of indignation. The sort of anger in Kinsella's work, however, is rarely communal, and is more often isolationist. It is the furious roar from the midnight prowler on an empty laneway rather than an angry chant from the centre of a mass protest. That this isolation is vulnerable to a critique of unflattering self-indulgence and part of the poet's self-induced marginalisation is apparent to Kinsella.

Since the early 1970s, Kinsella has been publishing his own work through his own *Peppercanister* series. With grandmothers on both sides who ran small shops in their homes, it is tempting to see such a strand of individualistic enterprise in the genes. The poet has always been close to the production of his own work. When he first met Liam Miller, the publisher at Dolman Press in the 1950s, the poet was intimately involved in the setting of his own early published work with 'an old Adana machine that made a noise like a bacon slicer.'[64] This individualistic and close connection to publication has continued with the *Peppercanister* series, brought out in short, limited runs. 'It was a basic irritant which brought it into being: the dislike of poetry being used in journals between articles, stories etc. – poetry as space-filler,' Kinsella said in a 1987 interview.[65] But such limited publication has certainly contributed to the narrowing of readership. In recent years, if you walk into any Dublin bookstore, barring copies of his Gaelic translations, the poetry section will often have no editions of his poetry. Yet his work has remained on the school curriculum, and critically respected, meaning that his name and influence continues to be accepted, despite the shrinking readership.

In section 21 of *A Technical Supplement*, the poet purposely prompts the critics with his own survey of his career to date. Critical of the early work as somewhat *'self-serving, therefore ineffective,'* he is also hypercritical of his later work and allows only that maybe he has written six poems of *'glory / and noble despair'* – hardly the conclusion of a poet interested in self-congratulation. He describes his later poetic persona rather aptly as '*the lonely prowl of the outcast.*'

This self-perception adds evidence to David Wheatley's later observation that Kinsella apparently relished 'his own obscurity.'[66] But the problem with such isolation is that any detached writer, no matter how talented, risks losing their bearings and becoming merely self-indulgent. This danger was all the more potent in the case of Kinsella, who has self-edited and self-published almost all of his work since the late 1960s. He told an interviewer in 1989 that he no longer sent his poetry to others to view before its publication.[67] Even so, and as Wheatley fairly concludes in a muscular 1996 review of Kinsella's *Collected Works*, despite his self-imposed isolation, the poet's intensity and indignation, 'most of the time at least, lift his poetry above self-indulgence.'[68] For Wheatley, Kinsella is a 'stranded' figure associated with an Ireland that existed before the state entered the European Economic Community in 1973[69], which means that Ireland's 'finest unread poet' is a sort of beached figure in an Ireland that no longer exists. This is somewhat unfair, and does not take into account the poet's engagement with social, political and economic developments in Ireland since the 1980s.

Self-confidence may have contributed to making the isolation more bearable. Part of the reason why the reviewers who have criticised Kinsella's work for becoming inaccessible may have had such little apparent impact is because Kinsella is a very honest critic himself. In various interviews, leading poets and critics have been summarily dealt with by Kinsella. Dylan Thomas (1914–1953) was dismissed as sometimes playing the 'role of an entertainer.' Even Patrick Kavanagh

(1904–1967), whom Kinsella admired, is criticised for not entirely fulfilling his great poetic potential: 'Look at Kavanagh still for all the waste there was a handful of very powerful ones.'[70] Kinsella has often dismissed critics and other poets. He wrote in *The Irish Writer* about his fellow Irish poets that: 'I can learn nothing from them except that I am isolated.' In a 1996 interview he said that, with the partial exception of Derek Mahon, 'I can see nothing in common with any of the writers.' In 1990 he told *The Irish Times*: 'It's not one of the lucky times. There's a lot of bad poetry, bad poets, bad critics and bad readers.' Things had not improved much by 2002, when he told an interviewer: 'But at any given time, anywhere, most poets are no good, and in Ireland most of the poets are no good.' The slight to Ireland's poetic egos may have been lessened a little given that their deficiency is not attributed to their nationality, but rather viewed by Kinsella as something shared by all poets across all nations. It is just a numbers game.

Given the theme of death and the tone of disappointment in much of the work, it is also reasonable to speculate on whether the isolation may also be a product of the poetry's at times deeply pessimistic view of existence and consistent flashes of brutal misanthropy. A poet who can tell an interviewer that human beings are a 'worthless and objectionable form of life, [and] I don't see that it is possible, or even desirable, to redeem such a thing,' does not sound like the most communal of people.[71] This reputation had stuck, his wife Eleanor telling an interviewer in 1990 that: 'Oh, everyone thinks Thomas is some kind of ogre who doesn't like talking to people and won't answer the phone.'[72]

The brute fact of death and evil is to the foreground of much of the poetry, like the final lines of 'Drowsing over The Arabian Nights', when the narrator focuses on the *'agonies of death / as we enter our endless nights / quickly, one by one, fire / darting up to the roots of our hair.'*[73] The brutal severance that is death is poignantly portrayed in 'Cover Her Face' when the brother and mother of a young woman who has died visit Dublin from their country home to collect her body. In the room there are priests and friends of their deceased loved one – people they have never met. But despite this, *'these are more their kin'* then their dead relative. The living, even those who have never met, have more in common than a dead family member. The real, tangible connection of life is cut instantly. It could be countered that the memory survives, but the relentless dark logic of the poem continues and crushes any such sentiment:

> *Soon her few glories will be shut from sight:*
> *Her slightness, the fine metal of her hair spread out,*
>
> *Her cracked, sweet laugh. Such gossamers as hold*
> *Friends, family – all fortuitous conjunction –*
> *Sever with bitter whispers; with untold*
> *Peace shrivel to their anchors in extinction.*
> *There, newly trembling, others grope for function.*[74]

The web of family connection is pulled asunder by death. Those that remain alive exist in a sort of conspiracy of the living, but they continue in a trembling state, searching for meaning, trying to make sense of this loss. All living humans experience this shivering fear; they share nothing with the dead. Even this sense of connection, however, does not necessarily make the living show increased love and understanding to one another.

If an unflinching misanthropy formed a constant blanket over the work, it would suffocate it. Thankfully, these are merely peak moments of darkness. Although it is important in the Kinsellian world view to evaluate honestly humanity's bleakest and most evil attributes, the best of his work may not redeem humanity, but it does bring a level of understanding to our actions. We may be beyond redemption, but we are not beyond all comprehension. To understand is not to condone our worst actions, but it is to understand our humanity, and a poet who attempts to comprehend that can never be entirely severed from his fellow human. Kinsella has had close friendships, family and a successful professional life. He is described by his friend Maurice Harmon as a man who is 'most engaging, enjoys good company, fellowship and humour.' The poet on the page is 'often a dramatised self,' says Harmon. 'The things which seem absent from the poetry, especially humour, are very much part of the man's life.'[75] Kinsella has also won the close respect of Irish poets such as Michael Hartnett (1941–1999), who dedicated his poem 'The Poet as Mastercraftsman' to Kinsella, as well as great friends like Seán Ó Riada.

Kinsella has faced questions directly about this isolation. In an interview with Michael Smith in 2002, he mentioned that illness has played a role. The different periods of ill health experienced by his wife, Eleanor, and his own moments of sickness, meant that he was not always in position to be more publicly available: 'On the matter of privacy, there was always an amount of sickness involved – family sickness and sickness of my own.'[76] The illness of his wife has been a constant theme in his poetry, from the early work like 'A Lady of Quality' and 'Phoenix Park'. In the much later 'The Familiar', the young couple is described as being '*Mismatched, under the sign of sickness.*' His own periods of sickness are registered more rarely, but 'Visiting Hour' is one exception where the narrator finds himself confined to a hospital bed, along with more subtle references to the taking of tablets in poems like the 1997 'The Pen Shop'.

The interviewer pressed the poet on what he regards as Kinsella's failure to associate with younger poets from the Republic of Ireland. It is clear in Kinsella's response that illness was not the only reason for not considering himself to be part of such a movement of poets. 'The only encounter that matters is between the individual and the significant ordeal, and I don't find much of that in contemporary Irish poetry,' he said.[77] In an era when top Irish poets can read to hundreds and often thousands at literary festivals, this remains a circuit from which Kinsella is essentially absent. 'Kinsella has devoted himself to primary literary production,' said Dennis O'Driscoll. 'He simply doesn't do marginal activities such as workshops, readings and indeed interviews.'[78]

Kinsella has continued writing and publishing at a regular pace for six decades, but it is writing for the 'closest possible audience,' as Andrew Fitzsimons has commented. Whether by artistic design or critical and public fashion, Kinsella's poetry-reading public has narrowed since the early 1970s, just as his work reached its creative heights.

* * *

If Kinsella has stood on the margins, his admirers have often been attracted by what some regard as an artistic, stoical stance in the face of criticism and ignorance of his work.

With the trees being hacked back in the garden, and his own face displaying the onset of ageing, the narrator of 'Mirror in February' has much to ruminate on as he gazes into his shaving mirror. But despite the gloom, he can rustle enough poise to deliver a riposte of sorts against the passage of time:

> *In slow distaste*
> *I fold my towel with what grace I can,*
> *Not young and not renewable, but man.*[79]

Is Kinsella a stoic, a modern poetic island of the Hellenistic philosophy that was founded in Athens by Zeno of Citium (334 BC–262 BC)? T. A. Jackson thinks so, naming the poet a 'Stoic Virtuoso'.[80] That Kinsella is taken somewhat by an ancient philosophy that preaches an indifference to external or internal pleasure or pain is beyond doubt. One of his later poems, 'Marcus Aurelius', engages with the thinking of the famous stoical emperor. It is clear that the poet empathises somewhat with Aurelius's world view.

In these lines from 'Mirror in February', there is a tense compression of feeling. This is no angry rage against the dying of the light; it is more stoical than that. At least, it is in terms of how modern society regards stoicism: as something along the lines of an ability to take what comes by whilst displaying an inner strength of character. This contemporary sense of stoicism is linked only loosely to the ancient one, and, as Frank McLynn has written, has more 'to do with fatalism, realism and resignation.'[81] What classical stoicism required, however, was for people not only 'simply to accept whatever happens, but to be happy about it.'[82] Whatever happens, no matter if it is pleasurable or horrid, is the natural way, and to live naturally is to live virtuously – the highest form of life. This rather narrowly constructed view of virtue was fatalistic, but also aimed at the elimination of all strong emotions. People should calmly sail through life, taking its peaks and troughs with a simple shrug of indifference and a cool, quiet stare.

The most perfected of human beings in this rather arid philosophy was the sage. This was a state that remained an aspiration, where an individual, through study and concentration, could become a self-restrained ascetic, an island of calm within the stormy seas of life, neither wanting for anything nor fearful of any future disasters that might befall them. 'The would-be sage must live within himself as in a fortress under a permanent state of siege,' and it is clear that Marcus Aurelius for one aspired to such a position.[83]

Kinsella clearly admires an ability to walk alone, and the endurance of what life throws at you is a part of his stoical gait. But there are too many flashes of anger, too much incredulity at man's errors and crimes and too much love in the poetry for it to be called truly stoical. Yes, there is often a stoical poise to Kinsella's tone. His assertion that we must walk on, even if alone, and endure the journey, learning each step of the way, has a semblance of stoical fortitude in it. For the stoics, 'suffering is either long but bearable, or hideous but brief.' But stoicism, as the ancients defined it, is a quietist creed that drains life of much of its colour and passion. All the strong emotions are frozen within the individual, with indifference to both happiness and suffering. But Kinsella's work is anything but indifferent. It crackles and snaps with righteousness at times. It beats with love and burns with frightening flashes of hatred.

Historically, the founder of ancient stoicism, Zeno of Citium, believed in a doctrine of 'eternal recurrence', a conviction that history is cyclical rather than linear. A similar viewpoint permeates much of Kinsella's work: *'I had felt this before'* is said by the first Gaelic settler in Ireland as he steps on the shore in 'Finistère', and lines expressing comparable feelings occur in a number of other poems. In 'A Country Walk', the violence of the Irish Civil War and the Cromwellian invasions of the seventeenth century are placed alongside tales of mythical violence from the Irish sagas to demonstrate a cyclical, recurrent conception of violence. Most things have happened, if not in the exact same way, in a structure that is similar – it seems that almost everything has happened and will happen again.

The journeys of the first voyagers to Ireland is replicated over and over again in many 'first' journeys, such as the young poet's first sleep outside of home, in his neighbour's house in '38 Phoenix Street'. On a more mysterious level, a series of paranormal events takes place in 'At the Crossroads'. A walker returning from work feels strange reactions in his body and sees unusual things near a crossroads; he knows that what he feels was felt in ancient history by his ancestors in the same spot. In 'Morning Coffee', when the Kinsella family comes across the wreckage of a small boat washed up on a beach, the adults tell the inquisitive children that it is the vessel from the journey of the first Gaels to Ireland, the first people never far from the consideration of the poet narrator.

Cyclical history, just as much as linear history, is a way of making sense of the transitory nature of human existence. Timelines are 'models of the world [that] make tolerable one's moment between beginning and end.'[84] Richard Kearney has emphasised the role that narrative, creating a story over time, can have as a catharsis following trauma.[85] The narrative imagination is important in dealing with the little and big traumas of life.

The cyclical conception of history in Kinsella's work seems to emphasise what we all have in common. The stories and incidents in our lives have all happened before, and will happen again to others in the future. That the source of this recurrence is not in an ancient stoical theology, but to be found in a particular understanding of a unified collective unconscious shared by all of humanity, will become clearer in later chapters. For Kinsella, it is not the recurrence of actual events, but the recurring collective archetypal experiences that we all have within our psyche.

That the more recent work since 2000 may demonstrate an increasingly pronounced stoical serenity is mentioned by some critics. Now into the eighth decade of his own life's journey, his 2011 collection, *Fat Master*, includes poems that Maurice Harmon has written possess a 'fresh and positive sense of acceptance.'[86] But this acceptance is not of icy cool stoicism. It is an acceptance of the inherent partiality of man's understanding of life and the apparent meaningless of life. In 'Reflection', the tone is accepting and positive, despite the writer doubting whether his *'contaminated conception'* was of any relevance at all. Despite this apparent fact, he is *'but thankful on the whole/for this ache for even a minimal understanding.'*[87]

Walking alone, the consolations that one finds in life are to be found on the very outer reaches of our journey. But that they are there at all has to be accepted as the best that one can expect.

* * *

Isolation has been regarded as the standard situation for creative artists throughout the centuries, but such an expectation has been particularly strong since the Romantic Movement at the end of the eighteenth and early nineteenth century. Isolation was not to be bemoaned, but expected, as to stand out from the great swathe of man's everyday business was to provide the artist with a detached and thus privileged perspective on life. But if the poet was once expected to walk alone, Kinsella is convinced that the modern plight is that all humans now walk alone. 'After the catastrophe the poet is still isolated of course, but now so is every man,' he has concluded.[88] Existential fear over the meaninglessness of life, and anxiety over the groundlessness of our existence, is no longer merely the preserve of the marginalised artist, but the burden of the everyman. This universalising of isolation means that we can no longer easily be guided by great communal stories. Walking alone has become that most common of experiences. We no longer march together, but in our isolated strolls we can experience what the rest of humanity experiences. This is what it is to be human following the catastrophe.

There is no blueprint, no signpost to tell us where to walk. In 'Death Bed', two sons stand and watch their father die. Their guide has passed on; their 'shelter' is gone. He has left no clear map or plan for his sons. How can they weave this loss into some meaningful narrative? Bluntly, the poetic voice says that it cannot be done:

and try to weave it into our lives
— who can weave nothing but our ragged
routes across the desert.[89]

In the poem 'Morning Coffee' from the 1991 collection, *Madonna and Other Poems*, the apparent aimlessness of our collective lives is again evoked. When the narrator looks at his reflection in the waters of a well, he sees a figure who is contradictory. His face seems '*assured*' in its purpose in life, '*but vague in direction.*' The assuredness is less strident than the weakness, for the section ends solemnly:

We are all only pilgrims.
Travelling the night.[90]

Pilgrims by their nature have some route, but in the dark of the night it is at best groping in a vague direction. If the narratives before the catastrophe had meaning and a destination, whether that was heaven or some earthly utopia, modern man is isolated and unable to weave any easy collective meaning into his life. Our journey no longer has a point, no destination. At best the journey is the point, the destination an illusion. Writing admiringly on the sprawling *The Cantos,* an epic series by American poet Ezra Pound, Kinsella noted: 'the ideal exists not in our achievement of it but in our aspiration toward it.'[91] He could have been writing about his own work, his constant rewriting of old poems and the *Peppercanister* sequence, with its steady reengaging with a series of themes and moments from his own life.

Journeys act as a consolation of sorts for Kinsella. A long walk, a deep dive into the personal psyche, a boat journey, early man's first steps out of the cave or an epic tale of a people in search of a new land – all function as organising narratives that bring a semblance of structure and meaning to life. They chime with the great story arcs of mythical tales told throughout the ages and the world. This is what Joseph Campbell, using Joyce's term, would call the 'monomyth'.[92] For Campbell, however, and to some extent for Kinsella, myth is not merely a conscious artistic act of bringing an element of organisation to our life experience. While T. S. Eliot emphasised the ordering aspect of myth,

Campbell underscored myth's capacity to unconsciously teach and guide.[93] It is not only a narrative barrier to the overwhelming chaos of the world; it is naturally driving up from the unconscious depths of each individual. Myths not only organise, but teach. They are grand repositories of knowledge accumulated by man since the very first. 'It would not be too much to say that myth is the secret opening which the inexhaustible energies of the cosmos pour into human cultural manifestations,' writes Campbell.[94] Campbell recognises the impact the 'catastrophe' has had on collective 'myths', but in its place each of us has the ability to discern personal narrative myths in our dreams and unconscious. 'It is only those who know neither the inner call nor an outer doctrine whose plight is truly desperate,' concludes Campbell.[95]

Mythology is rarely an uncomplicated, happy-ever-after tale, argues Campbell. Unlike some narrow religious world views, the Gods of the myths are seldom all good. The reality is that mythology encompasses the light and dark, hope and disappointment, the totality of experience. Myths do not exist for us to forget about the ordeal of life, but as a way of confronting the difficulty and perishable nature of reality, and how we can grow within that reality. 'Its Olympian laugh is not escapist in the least, but hard, with the hardness of life itself – which we may take it is the hardness of God, the Creator.'[96] According to Julian Young, 'stories create meaning,' and stories of journeys are the most potent meaning-creators of all. Nietzsche, faced by the death of God, felt that one response to such a situation was to create one's own journey, in effect narrate one's own myth.[97]

Kinsella's walking journeys tilt heavily towards desperation, but in the mid 1960s he would discover a pathway inwards into his personal psyche, and outward on a quest for a more balanced personality and poetics. Yet even here, the journey does not render life purely hopeful, or meaningful. It is only through the ordeal of life's journey, and by facing its difficulties, that we can grow and become less imbalanced. Kinsella's poetic quest is 'to find a balance in the violent zone between the outer and inner storms where human life takes place.'[98]

The walking journeys in Kinsella's work are often disruptive and consistently stalked by inevitable disappointment. The consolation here is not complete; no one journey can bring full meaning to our lives. All the great narrative journeys of hope remain unfilled. All hope is shadowed by disappointment. In short – all dreams die.

4
The Dreams that Died

That modern humans may feel uncertain regarding the story of their lives, that they would doubt the existence of a great narrative arc that gives meaning to their presence is, some experts maintain, a relatively recent phenomenon. The ancients of course posed questions of meaning. Since organised Christianity gained prominence in the West, however, any doubt about humanity's role in the universe was, at least publicly, overwhelmed by dogmatic certainty. Julian Young writes that before Nietzsche (1844-1900) announced God's demise in 1882, in the public sphere certainty triumphed over uncertainty. 'For most of our Western history we have not talked about the meaning of life,' writes Young. 'This is because we used to be quite certain that we knew what it was. We were certain about it because we thought we knew that over and above this world of doubtful virtue and happiness is another world ... the "true world" or, alternatively expressed, "God".'[1]

According to Young, traditional thinkers defined the 'meaning of life' as something that we 'discover' rather than something we choose to be the case, arguing that it is characterised by its 'universality and givenness'. The newly independent Irish state was ideologically dominated by Catholic Church dogmatism, and the Church's power was intensified by its strong political, educational and societal influence over the state. Whatever private doubts there were, most people publicly followed the Church's line. In truth, both sides of the Irish Civil War were full of pious men and women, however, the forces that emerged victorious were more right-wing, leading to a period of very conservative rule in southern Ireland during the 1920s. One of the new state's elite leaders, Kevin O'Higgins, proudly declared that they were 'the most conservative minded revolutionaries that ever put through a successful revolution.'[2] By the 1950s the Church was so powerful that writer Seán Ó Faoláin (1900–1991) wrote that the country had two parliaments: 'a parliament at Maynooth and a parliament in Dublin,' a reference to the seat of the ecclesiastical educational college in Maynooth.[3] The attempt by the inter-party government (1948–1951) to introduce state healthcare for mothers and children was thwarted by the Church, which saw evidence of creeping state socialism where there was none. This flexing of ecclesiastical muscle led *The Irish Times* to editorialise in 1951 that the 'Roman Catholic Church would seem to be the effective government in this country.'[4]

This is the Ireland into which Kinsella was born, and from which he emerged as a poet. From an early stage, his poetry hinted at the limitations rather than the possibilities of Catholic religious edicts. It is clear in the poetry that, when it came to providing a comprehensive and satisfactory framework for understanding the world, the teachings of the Church were found wanting. The routines of Catholic observance are depicted as unfulfilling and shallow in 'Dick King'. King marries a woman who *'prayed her life away.'* In another poem in the same *Downstream* collection, 'I wonder whether one expects', the weekly Sunday sacrament is offhandedly referred to as a *'weekly trance at Mass.'* Religion as empty rituals based on cultural routine is scorned; this is not the real, living process of meaning that the poet seeks.

A 1968 poem like 'Ballydavid Pier' is deeply devastating in its rejection of organised religion as a structure for finding satisfying meaning in life. The poet narrator spots the remains of an animal's foetus just off the coast:

> *Farther out a bag of flesh,*
> *Foetus of goat or sheep,*
> *Wavers below the surface.*[5]

As the poem develops, the narrator's mind struggles to locate a structured significance that would allow for examples of utter waste like this. What intentional scheme could incorporate such loss?

> *Small monster of true flesh*
> *Brought forth somewhere*
> *In bloody confusion and error*
> *And flung into bitterness,*
> *Blood washed white:*
> *Does that structure satisfy?*[6]

If the question is not quite rhetorical, it is hard to make a case for any answer that is not in the negative. To pose such a query would hardly be regarded as radical to many Irish or international readers in the twenty-first century, however, in the mid 1960s, when this poem was written, such questions were more controversial. In Ireland there was an official state-sanctioned structure of meaning that was meant comprehensively to answer these queries, but the poet is unconvinced. In the final stanza, the Catholic Church makes a sonic appearance, only to fail to bring reason to this unreasonable scene. It does not satisfy.

> *The Angelus. Faint bell-notes*
> *From some church in the distance*
> *Tremble over the water.*
> *It is nothing. The vacant harbour*
> *Is filling; it will empty.*
> *The misbirth touches the surface*
> *And glistens like quicksilver.*[7]

A poem from *Downstream*, 'Cover Her Face', is set at a tragic bedside scene in Dublin, where a young woman is lying dead. Her family has just arrived from the country to take her body home. The family shows up in their disturbed despair, but the disordered grief that they feel is quickly brought to heel and incorporated into the Church-sanctioned, structured traditions surrounding death. Their passionate, raw pain is restrained by approved ritual.

> *They dither softy at her bedroom door*
> *In soaking overcoats, and words forsake*
> *Even their comforters. The bass of prayer*
> *Haunts the chilly landing while they take*
> *Their places in a murmur of heartbreak.*
>
> *Shabby with sudden tears, they know their part,*[8]

The shabbiness of their raw grief contrasts with the traditional routines of the Church. The routine wins out, and their feelings must accommodate to its structure.

> *The black official giving discipline*
> *To shapeless sorrow,*[9]

A tone of distaste at the Church's attempts to coordinate and dominate people's emotions, particularly at a time of grief, is again visible in the 1968 'Office for the Dead'. The title plays on the organising structure of the working day, as professional mourners go about their business beside the deceased:

> *The grief-chewers enter, their shoes hard on the marble,*
> *In white lace and black skirts, books held to their loins.*
> *A silver pot tosses in its chains as they assemble*
> *About the coffin, heavy under its cloth, and begin.*
>
> *Back and forth, each side in nasal unison*
> *Against the other, their voices grind across her body.*
> *We watch, kneeling like children, and shrink as their Church*
> *Latin chews our different losses into one.*[10]

It is the grinding, homogenising intention of Church ritual to dominate the variety of natural reactions and feelings towards death. This is order imposed on life rather than an order arising naturally from the complexity of lived experience, and so the Catholic Church's rituals fail to provide real meaning to people's lives. The target for the poetic flak is not ritual and symbol per se; Kinsella recognises the importance of ritual and symbol, and it is an almost obsessive theme in his work. Ritual is apparently vital in all societies for rites of passages and for marking moments of individual importance in a communal manner. The Catholicism of the new Irish state, however, did not serve that true purpose. Rather, from its position of power, it provides ritual drained of meaning, leaving an empty shell of dull routine.

Symbolic moments of collective ritual appear to have universal importance. In the 1973 collection, *From the Land of the Dead*, ancient rituals, especially those associated with fertility, are evoked. In later collections, ritual takes on a more domesticated aspect. In section 7 of 'The Familiar', the poet in his dressing gown meticulously prepares breakfast for his sleeping wife. The slicing of the tomatoes *'in damp sequence into their dish,'* the arranging of the toast, the scalding of the tea and the ringing of the bell are all done carefully and good-humouredly. The ritual of preparation, although commonplace, has a veneer of the sacred to it. Once completed, the poet extends his arms self-consciously over the feast he has prepared, and his partner enters the kitchen, praising his work. This is a domestic, self-created ritual, and it has been infused with its own meaning, of a type more real than any of the ready-made meanings provided by the Church.

In 'Model School Inchicore', the young poet hides himself in a shed. His enquiring mind poses questions about life and its meaning. All that returns in response is the direct certainties of the catechism that the young poet has learned by rote, and whose dogmatism he has internalised. In his notes from the *Nightwalker* period, Kinsella is explicit: Church doctrine is inadequate in the modern age, 'the imposed order of the Church will not do in this post-atomic chaos. We must do it out of our own bowels, it is we who have, from our inner wills, brought chaos and we who must, from our own inner wills, bring new order.'[11]

The simmering critique of the Catholic Church develops beyond theological matters into its role in social practice. In a 1990 poem, 'Social Work', a parish priest is depicted in close cahoots with the local authority officials and developers bent on destroying the architectural treasures of Georgian Dublin in the name of modern development. So it is not merely the organised Church in the form of sacraments and service that disappoints; it is also the more socially active, politicised, lay wing that is criticised. In 'One Fond Embrace' (1988), the poet narrator casts his eye across his south Dublin neighbourhood. The Catholic lay organisation becomes involved in social welfare activities in his *'sagging district'*, but the narrator suspects that the motives are beyond any simple Christian urge to do good. The need to be seen to be doing good works, combined with a petty bourgeois nosiness, are the true motives.

> *Catholic Action next door:*
> *the double look*
> *over the half curtain;*
>
> *social workers herding their problems*
> *in off the street*
> *with snooker cues and rosary beads;*
>
> *Knights of Mercedes and the naked bulb*
> *parked at large along both paths*
> *in witness that the poor are being given a party.*[12]

The allusions to real Catholic organisations gives a sense of the disregard the poet feels for the piously stated aims of these organisations, which often conceal deeper and more reactionary political programmes. It may be a stretch to read into the line *'the poor are being given a party'* a more politicised meaning than it holds, but it is not unreasonable to speculate that a latent critique of Catholic social policy can be found here. For many decades the Irish poor and the working class have lacked a strong movement or state to represent their true needs. In its absence, the social activity of the Catholic Church lay organisations has filled the void, speaking and acting *for* the poor, *giving* them a voice that may be expected to be the preserve of a political party, or a movement from the socialist left or trade unions.

The powerful collaboration between the Catholic Church and the Irish capitalist class reoccurs in Kinsella's poetry across the decades. It is a collaboration that does not work in favour of the working class. In 'The Messenger', John Paul Kinsella clashes with the owners of the Guinness Brewery during the push to establish a union, but it was not only the management but also the secret religious organisations, both Protestant and Catholic, which opposed these efforts, the clash taking place against the backdrop of the era's pious popular backing track.

under that good family firm;

formed their first Union; and entered their lists.
Mason and Knight gave ground in twostep,
manager and priest disappeared

and reappeared under each other's hats;
in jigtime, to the ever popular
Faith Of Our Fathers, *he was high and dry.*[13]

Later in the same poem, William Martin Murphy, the leading Catholic capitalist in Dublin at the time, and the nemesis of trade union leader James Larkin during the great 1913 Lockout, also changes his hat, from Catholic to capitalist. The Church has failed, not only in its religious theology and in its role as the leading educator in the country, but also by its close relationship with the economic and political elite in defending privilege.

Whatever its socio-political faults, the thrust of the poetry's assessment of the Church is concerned with its ultimate inability to provide a satisfactory understanding of the nature of life. In the 1990 poem 'The Bell', the poet again hears the angelus bell near his Percy Place home, like he had decades earlier in 'Ballydavid Pier', and in his childhood in the local church:

> *Hauling down on the high rope,*
> *announcing his iron absolutes*
> *audible in Inchicore.*[14]

Across miles of the city, and decades of his life, the certainties of organised religion have failed to chime with the understanding the poet has acquired of the world. The bells, rather than calling him to commune, rather disturb his sanctuary and his thoughts.

In interviews, the poet has spoken about this loss of meaningful religious symbolism, particularly in its importance to his own poetics. 'No, the supports that one might think of finding in organised religion, I found elsewhere,' he has said.[15] In his own notes, he has written of the Godhead figure as something that is located inside the individual rather than in the exterior world: 'All deities reside in the human breast, Good and Evil, Messiah and Devil,' he wrote.[16] In his most recent interview, when asked directly whether he believed in God, he gave the agnostic answer: 'I don't know. When it comes to the point of creation, that is where, it seems to me, where mathematics and physics and religion comes together.'[17] He also acknowledged Charles Darwin as one of 'the major creators' from history 'who are able to answer certain major questions. But they are still not answering the primary question: why?'[18]

Two recent poems, 'Prayer I' and 'Prayer II', he says, are addressed towards an 'unGod, that you aim towards, an imagined end. There is no such thing, but you aim toward it and it gives a kind of direction and impulse to the efforts.'[19] Whatever this is, it is certainly not the Christian God of Kinsella's schooling. The actual objective reality of God is not really seriously considered; it seems that God is in fact more an enabling idea. The concept of an actual God that provides everlasting life is absent from the work. In the same interview, Kinsella was asked about life after death, and said: 'What else can one do except accept that we go back to where we came from, which is nowhere?'[20] This is the acceptance of the post-God sceptical man.

God the father is addressed and essentially pitied in 'Godhead' (1999). It is recognised that his most important creation, man, is deeply flawed. This is a mark against the creator. But what is more, the negative traits with which man is cursed are writ large upon the Godhead figure.

The poem hints that the greatest flaw shared by man and his creator is the ability to have intimations towards totality, while at the same time being unable to reach anything but the pitiful subjective, '*and who also know / how it is possible to grasp completely / while remaining partly incapable.*'[21] We are created incomplete, but with some inherent drive towards a total understanding that we can never achieve. This is a torturous state, a state of perpetual failure. The creator stands accused of bundling its greatest creation. We are a botched job, from a craftsperson of questionable ability. We, with our faults, are created in its image, meaning that the Godhead's understanding is also partial and groping towards an unattainable total understanding. God stands before us as a glorious failure rather than just glorious.

The big dreams of the great religions are not capable of bringing meaning; they do not satisfy the need for structure.

* * *

It is not only religion that falls short when it comes to providing a meaningful structure for life. Other candidates, such as the dream of political progress, also attract Kinsella's criticism.

In the 1973 poem 'The Good Fight', the public persona of John F. Kennedy (1917–1963), whom Kinsella admired, contrasts pointedly with the private individual. The political mythology surrounding Kennedy and his life had reached fantastical levels, even before his brutal end. The use of the shorthand description of *'Camelot'* to describe the wider Kennedy clan captures the sense of royalty and myth that surrounded the elite family. In 'The Good Fight' we witness JFK as the dashing young war hero, senator and presidential candidate. We catch glimpses of him in his bright, public moments on the campaign trail, but also in his dark, private quarters.

The candidate secretly wrestles with the physical pain the campaigning inflicts on him, exasperating old war injuries. These wounds must be kept hidden so as not to sully the public persona of the energetic, youthful contender:

> *Once, he rolled up his sleeve*
> *and looked at the calloused, scratched arm:*
> *'Ohio did that to me.'*
> *(One day in Philadelphia*
> *his hand* burst *with blood.)*[22]

When he takes to the campaign platform, however, the fearless public smile is on show to the crowd. He changes into new and confident clothing that is imperceptible to the audience:

Shock-headed, light footed, he swung
an invisible cloak about him in the uproar
and hunched down from the platform at them,
his hands in his jacket pockets.
A jugular pleasure beat in his throat.[23]

The young Kennedy is the public personification of action and self-will. He is convinced that he can shape the world around him, that he can use rationality to change things for the better, and that he can recruit supporters to help to make this happen collectively:

— Let us make ourselves vessels of decision!
We are not here to curse the darkness.
The old order changes! Men
firm in purpose and clear in thought
channel by their own decisions
forces greater than any man![24]

Kennedy, like any great politician, projects his own strong sense of personal destiny onto the public audience, and onto the nation as a whole. He wraps up the cheering public into the grandest of narratives, a story in which they will all play a role. He is making connections on a large scale, building a story, a dream they can all believe in. His big words clash together like loud cymbals in a cacophony of soaring noise:

'Forward, then, in higher urgency,
adventuring with risk,
raising each other to our moral best,
aspiring to the sublime
in warlike simplicity, our power
justified upon our excellence!'[25]

The energetic and urgent need for progress may, as Kennedy warns his audience, be a peculiarly American compulsion. The 'American Dream' can prove to be an illusion if it is not revitalised by constant forward movement and ever greater success. The nation needs to keep active if it is not to descend into gloomy thoughts over its very foundation and right to exist. There must be vitality in the dream, because if the dream falters then dreary existential speculation over what America is will quickly emerge:

> *If other nations falter*
> *their people still remain what they were.*
> *But if our country in its call to greatness*
> *falters, we are little but the scum*
> *of other lands. That is our special danger,*
> *our burden and our glory.*
> *The accident that brought our people together*
> *out of blind necessities*
> *– embrace it! – explosive – to our bodies.* [26]

It is as if modern neuroses can be warded off only by rigorous action. A healthy, active nation means a healthy national mindset. JFK surrounds himself with the brightest and most talented – a cabinet in waiting, ready to have the world respond to their desire and knowledge. There are many bright, shining cities on the hill to build across the world; the 'American Dream' is for exportation.

> *Inside, a group of specialists,*
> *chosen for the incomparable dash,*
> *were gathered around*
> *a map of the world's regions*
> *with all kinds of precision instruments.*[27]

The excited public campaign beats through the opening section of the poem, capturing the hope that is an important element of any such political movement. The narrator, however, questions the structure of the political process. He wonders aloud whether such lofty campaigning rhetoric and activity helps to generate hope, only to make disappointment inevitable once the politician or party then comes to power.

> *Can we believe it possible for anyone*
> *to master the art of steering while he must*
> *at the same time expend his best skill*
> *gaining control of the helm?*[28]

This is a variation of the political truism that one campaigns in poetry but rules in prose. Of course it also reflects the dialectic of hope and disappointment that Kinsella regards as inherent in life, but there is also a comment on striving. If we expend so much energy in the quest to get the position we want, we may be enfeebled and tired by the time we achieve it. For politicians this is even more acute, with their striving (political campaigns) inevitably involving energetic bombast, compromises and bargaining. James Connolly warned that the greatest problem with the belief that the ends justify the means is that it does not fully account for how the sellouts and questionable bargaining that are part of the means can greatly alter the ends.[29]

If campaigning and striving for power require hope, they are also shadowed constantly by disappointment. On its own, this could be regarded as a rather narrow criticism of politics. At a more substantial level, 'The Good Fight' questions not only the validity of the personal political vision of the young senator from Massachusetts, but whether any political ideology or dream can truly reflect the great complexity of life. A society atomised by modern capitalist development and the legacy of the catastrophe of the twentieth century may not be partial to any encompassing dream. JFK's rhetoric is impressive, his rearticulating of the American dream potent, but in the end it is just another failed attempt at imposing order on reality. It is a doomed experiment in dreaming a story of public progress, when the time for such dreams has passed.

> *The finer the idea the harder it is*
> *to assemble lifelike. It adopts hardnesses*
> *and inflexibilities, knots, impossible joints*
> *made possible only by stress,*
> *and good for very little afterward.)*[30]

Despite these reservations, the public Kennedy of 'The Good Fight' still cuts a heroic figure. He is a dream-weaver par excellence, who through his rhetoric can endow people's lives with a sense of collective meaning and purpose.

But the real 'hero', or at the very least the most authentic character, in 'The Good Fight' is not Kennedy. Much like John Milton's Satan is often regarded as the real hero of *Paradise Lost*, it is the assassin, Lee Harvey Oswald, who emerges best from 'The Good Fight'. As Brian John says, Oswald is the more 'convincing' of the two main protagonists in the poem.[31] Kinsella was an admirer of the young president, and the poem certainly does not celebrate this famous political murder, but the character of Oswald is sympathetically portrayed in his alienated misery. Oswald, like Milton's Satan, gets the best lines. Isolated and inward-looking, Oswald is far more self-aware and self-inquiring than Kennedy. His routine could not contrast more with that of JFK. The severance between the public confidence of the political Kennedy and the aching personal pain of the private man creates a discord in his personality. It does not ring true. Oswald is more authentic, his private, skulking self is not a lie, and correlates with his position as a loner in public.

While the Democratic Party front runner still believes in the dreams of progress and collective salvation, Oswald is the more credible modern man, plagued by doubts and loneliness. He is born into a world where the great dreams have died. He is no longer a part of a collective dream, and as a result his experience is the nightmare of the isolated individual. Kennedy strikes the reader as coming from a bygone era of lost public heroism, while Oswald is the plausible modern man.

> *A lonely room*
> *An electric fire*
> *glowing in one corner. He is lying on his side.*
> *It is late. He is at the centre of a city,*
> *awake.*
>
> *Above and below him*
> *there are other rooms with others in them.*
> *He knows nobody as yet, and has*
> *no wish to. Outside the window*
> *the street noises ascend.*
>
> *His cell hangs in the night.*[32]

While his plight makes him think of suicide, he decides not to self-harm just yet. Because, as if answering Kennedy's earlier clarion call on people to make themselves *'vessels of decision'*, Oswald is set to make his mark.

He could give up.
But there is something he must do.[33]

Oswald's routine resonates with the isolated artist. His room, where he reads, eats and plans, has more than an echo of the Baggot Street flat of Kinsella's early adulthood. In the opening to the collection *New Poems* (1973), the poet in his flat quickly eats forkfuls of scrambled eggs while reading books alone with incessant nervous energy in his small digs. Even Oswald's strange night-time walks are reminiscent in style to the nightfall journeys in other Kinsella poems. Oswald has a private domestic routine:

and reads a long time
with the crumbs hardening and a tawny scum
shrinking on the cold tea, and finally
ventures out for his first night prowl
and takes possession of his neighbourhood,
learning at each turn, and turns for home,[34]

A reading that associates the poet with the assassin is further implied by the reproduction of a John Clellon Holmes quote at the beginning of the poem, which reads: 'Those who are imprisoned in the silence of reality always use a gun (or, if they are more fortunate, a pen) to speak for them.'[35] Like an introverted artist, separated from his audience, Oswald begins to plan his lonely creation. But before he begins, he thoughtfully ruminates and writes out his reflections. His self-awareness and self-criticism diverges from Kennedy's rhetoric on the campaign trail:

I cannot reach or touch anything.
I cannot lay my hand with normal weight

> *on anything. It is either nothing*
> *or too much.*
>
> *I have stood out*
> *in the black rain and waited*
> *and concentrated among*
> *those over-lit ruins*
> *irritable and hungry*
> *and not known what city.*[36]

Oswald is the existential modern man. Wracked by self-doubt, extreme variations of self-loathing and self-regard, he is isolated, pondering how he can make an impact. His stream of consciousness echoes T. S. Eliot's procrastinating anti-hero of 'The Love Song of J. Alfred Prufrock', with similar self-hating notions of crawling along the ocean depths:

> *I have glided in loveless dream transit*
> *over the shadowy sea floor,*
> *satisfied in the knowledge*
> *that if I once slacken in my savagery*
> *I will drown.*[37]

While JFK is on a grand, open, hopeful quest for political power, Oswald believes that his own isolated movements are dependent on continuing with his violent plans. If he were to stop in his scheme, he would perish. The assassin deconstructs his own lingering sense of connection with humanity through a methodical and manic spiral of internal destruction. This *'vessel of decision'* is alienated, and tied up in a series of oxymoronic conceptions of his personality. He sees himself as an actor playing a role, but with a contradictory script. He is ready for action, but devoid of impulse; he is drained of energy, but seized by inspiration; he is manic and depressive.

> *I have watched my own*
> *theatrical eyes narrow*
> *and noted under what stress*
> *and ceaseless changes of mind.*
> *I have seen very few*
> *cut so dull and driven a figure,*
> *masked in scorn or abrupt*
> *impulse, knowing content*
> *nowhere.*[38]

In this culmination of individualistic philosophical speculation, Oswald comes to the conclusion that haunts much of post-Nietzschean continental philosophy: we are alone, there is nothing out there. Crucially, in his own pathway towards annihilation, Oswald heightens this conclusion. Some may locate minimal solace in the fact that everyone else shares this isolation, thus they can empathise with everyone else's plight. Oswald, however, does not share in this understanding. Kinsella's own notes record his belief that after the catastrophe modern man is isolated, but this is all of humanity's plight.[39] We are united in our feeling of disunity; I can empathise with your ordeal because I too struggle with it. But for Oswald, so intense is his isolation that he concludes that even his fellow humans do not share his individual sense of detachment. Oswald does not believe that we are united, even in our isolation:

> *I believed once that silence*
> *encloses each one of us.*
> *Now, if that silence does not*

enclose each, *as I am led*
more and more to understand
— so that I truly am cut off,
a 'thing' in their eyes also —
I can, if my daydreams are right,
decide to end it.[40]

There is a particular narcissism to this that shadows the sense of self-importance in the character of JFK. While the politician clearly regards himself as having a uniquely important role to play in the affairs of his nation, Oswald also regards himself as unique. The extroverted politician is mirrored by the introverted Oswald, both believing that the roles they have in life are uncommon: both men are eager to have an impact on the world around them, and both feel that they hold special positions from which to have that impact, one central and public, the other marginal and private.

Oswald then imagines in detail his own suicide in a highly cinematic manner. He kills himself in the Roman way of slitting his wrists in a bathtub. There is even an accompanying soundtrack with the sound of violins '*as I watch my life whirl away.*' The grandiose nature of his imagined end point is a product of the contradictions of the modern condition. He is aware that society regards him as unimportant and that he lives in a cold and uncaring universe, but he remains doomed to regard himself as having consequence. Oswald is a dangerous cocktail of self-loathing and self-regard. His life is small, but the only way he can visualise his death is with a romantic finale of strings and melodrama.

But these suicidal thoughts are brushed aside. The assassination of the heroic public leader is anticipated. It is clear whose decision will have, if not the greatest, then certainly the final impact. The publicly adored extrovert is no longer in control; his fate is decided by a lonely man looking out from the darkness of a book depository store in Dallas.

> *Or I might reach out and touch.*
> *And he would turn this way*
> *inquiring – Who was that!*
> *What decision was this...*[41]

Oswald is a typical creation of modernist literature, crippled by the pained sense of loss of heroism and a peculiar concern over the role of decision in a world that has become increasingly complex. Like T. S. Eliot's J. Alfred Prufrock, who imagines himself a great lover but spends the length of the long poem criticising himself for approach anxiety, Oswald also hates himself, but secretly thinks himself very important indeed. T. S. Eliot's Prufrock cannot build up enough courage to ask a woman a question, and for this, as well as other cowardly characteristics, he hates himself profoundly. But his internal monologue provides excuses. He lies to himself that he has had many women before, or that she would not be interested anyway. Oswald differs from Prufrock in that his internal monologue says that he is nothing, but externally he is plotting to prove that he is somebody crucial. He is a true vessel of decision that will crash into American history and change it. As psychologists like Alfred Adler (1870–1937) have proposed, an inferiority complex in social settings can often disguise a superior complex in the personal psyche.

The final section of 'The Good Fight' portrays American poet Robert Frost addressing the grieving nation following the murder of its president. The words of Dr Frost are not soothing, but his fantasy speech does find some route between the public optimism of Kennedy and the dire private nihilism of Oswald. Frost, reflecting on Plato, proposes that the world is not reasonable and that anything can happen. Such an observation might be regarded as one of despair, but there is some hope in it. If anything can happen, than maybe even unreasonably good things will as well.

> *That all* un*reasonable things are possible.* Everything *that can happen will happen.*[42]

The actions of an American president are also the focus of an earlier poem, 'Old Harry', from the 1962 collection, *Downstream*. This time the focus is not on potential and hope as part of an electoral season, but on the wicked legacy of a retired politician. The central character is former President Harry Truman (1884–1972) in his twilight years, decades after his period in the Oval Office. Rather than being surrounded by supporters and intellectuals, Truman is now alone, unsteadily stumbling through a forest. Leaning unstably against a tree, he recalls that he was once a reasonable politician, ready to question the military and others when it was warranted – he was not the happy warrior always willing to embrace bloodshed.

But in August 1945, he was to make a decision that was his own personal contribution to the catastrophe, and one of a series of events during the war that would change the perception humanity had of itself. The military leadership gather in the Oval Office and debate whether to unleash the atomic bomb on Japanese cities. Reasonable Truman has entered the realm of the unreasonable, where everything that can happen, will happen.

So long ago ... Assembled like steel children
Around his gleaming table they advised
And were absorbed, as he imposed reason

— A curb to the rash, a pupil to the wise.
Until on a certain day he waved them out,
Thoughtful before his maps. And chose at last

The greater terror for the lesser number.
With rounded cheeks he blew a mortal blast[43]

Truman is a vessel of decision here. Like the ancient gods, he can decide to blow, and across the planet great destruction will be unleashed. The conscious application of decisions arrived at after reasonable calculation makes the inhumane results all the more barbaric. This is carefully considered cruelty on a massive scale. From decisions taken in the reasonable, civilised surroundings of the centre of growing American imperial power, nightmarish scenes engulf cities in the east. Truman is not like Oswald, isolated on the margins. He is at the centre of power. He holds a political position that only exists because of the grand hopes for progress and reason that were legacies of the eighteenth-century Enlightenment, and which greatly influenced the American Revolution. What is progress and political democracy for if it inflicts this amount of inhumanity on tens of thousands?

And the two chosen cities of the plain

Lost their flesh and blood — tiles, underwear, wild cries
Stripped away in gales of light. Lascivious streets
Heightened their rouge and welcomed baths of pure flame.

In broad daylight delicate creatures of love
Opened their thighs. Their breasts melted shyly
And bared the white bone. At that sight

Men blushed fiercely and became shades.
The air in a passion inhaled, and all dissolved
Or collapsed shimmering on black recesses,[44]

The great dreams of political progress like those represented by Kennedy's 'American Dream', or the Enlightenment that gave birth to the United States, are further examples of the dreams that have died, and that can often end in nightmares.

* * *

National dreams that end in disappointment are also part of the Irish experience.

In the 1962 'A Country Walk', the narrator walks along the River Slaney towards the County Wexford town of Enniscorthy. As he meanders, he contemplates the bloody sweep of Irish history. In terms of the modern period, he delivers harsh judgements on the revolutionary generation who '*have exchanged / A trenchcoat playground for a gombeen jungle.*'[45] This is the poet's parents' generation, who were young adults during the period of the Irish Revolution, 1916–22. The trenchcoat is the garment synonymous with the most active IRA volunteers during the War of Independence. The '*playground*' alerts the reader to the childish aspect of the revolutionary struggle – childlike in both its naive imagination and its immature cruelty. But whatever heroic glamour there remained of the revolutionary struggle (despite its childishness), it has been superseded by grubby, small-time middle-men – the gombeen businessmen. The nationalist movement's dream of hope has become by the 1950s and 1960s a disappointing era of the mundane, petty-bourgeois republic. The cynical narrator reaches the town, naming the shopfronts in a mock allusion to W. B. Yeats's famous naming of the rebel dead in his elegiac poem, 'Easter 1916'.

> *Around the corner, in the Market Square,*
> *I came upon the sombre monuments*
> *That bear their names: McDonagh and McBride,*
> *Merchants; Connolly's Commercial Arms...*[46]

These lines have been regarded by some critics as predominately a coruscating attack on the revolutionary generation who pursued their dreams of independence through violent means, but in the end have nothing to show for it but a disappointing state.[47] But such a narrow interpretation seems rather misplaced. Although 'A Country Walk' contains a strong thread of opposition to violence, the specific naming of some of the 1916 leaders carries a more complicated judgement than one that just queries whether the violence of the revolutionary period was justified.

So what if the revolutionary generation has opened merchants and commercial enterprises under their family names in marketplaces across Ireland? Is it not reasonable that, following a change in the political power structure of the country, the familial names of the formerly dispossessed should now hang above shopfronts? In fact, the satire inherent in lines like these arises from a more social and economic critique of the revolution: the revolution has limited itself to the change of names over stores while the underlying economic framework remains in place. This is a classic critique from the left of a revolution that has not gone far enough, in that it was merely political rather than social. The names at the top of the system of political and economic power may have changed, a few extra O's and Mc's added to the cabinet table and boardrooms, but the iniquitous economic structure itself, the financial system that has not worked in the interests of the urban or rural poor, remains untouched. Mass emigration continues, unemployment remains, and the gap between rich and poor grows wider.

This is the poem's primary source of disappointment with the actions of the revolutionary generation. Most of Ireland is independent of British political rule, but the new state is a bourgeois, capitalist republic, a *'gombeen jungle'*, where the law of the capitalist jungle is practised with a local twist. The early radical hopes of a more distributive republic, the more socially equal society envisioned by James Connolly and others, was given a voice in the Proclamation of the Republic of 1916. Later, in the Democratic Programme of the First Dáil in 1919, it was reaffirmed, with that text maintaining that the 'right to private property must be subordinated to the public right and welfare.' But this radical spirit was quenched with the killing of Connolly, the marginalisation of the labour movement in the aftermath of the War of Independence and the defeat of the anti-Treaty forces in the Civil War, to which the most radical left republican element, such as Liam Mellows (1892–1922), gave their allegiance.[48] The Ireland that emerged in the years after the Civil War, under a conservative *Cumann na nGaedheal* government, did not meet these early, radical hopes. One historian of the period has proposed that there was a 'counter-revolution' in Ireland during the period from 1921 until 1936, where the urban bourgeois, farming elite and Church leadership emerged from the pro-Treaty victors and reasserted their power against the more radical forces.[49]

This may be an overstatement, but it is nonetheless true that a left-wing, socialist, republican narrative of the birth of the Irish southern state has remained potent in Irish politics. It is the sort of narrative to which John Paul Kinsella would have adhered, and was sure to have been expressed in the Kinsella home and on election rallies in the 1930s and 1940s, which the poet as a boy attended. It is not that the original republic was the workers' republic to which Connolly had devoted his life, but a radical, significant, socialist, republican strand was active in 1916, and the labour movement was a major part of the War of Independence. This presence was later written out of mainstream history and ignored by the new political and commercial elite. The radical political left in Ireland was small, and the Labour Party was never the majority party in government. Socialism and communism as ideologies and economic theories were regarded with suspicion by the Catholic Church and the political ruling class. Thus, the memory of this labour struggle, and its importance in the revolutionary era, was somewhat lost.

* * *

To turn away is an action of recurrent importance in Kinsella's work. To turn away is to reject or to decide not to assimilate something in front of you. It can symbolise a weakness, an inability to digest matters that need to be faced up to. This is certainly the case in a number of Kinsella's more 'psychological' poems. But in other work of more social and political interest, such as 'A Country Walk', to turn away is an affirmation of sorts; it is a positive rejection of what is in front of you, such as with the poet's father in 'The Messenger', when he turns his back on the parish priest in full flow at Mass.

In 'A Country Walk', Kinsella turns away twice in subsequent stanzas. Firstly, he does so after noting the Irish names along the commercial high street of the town:

> *I walked their shopfronts, the declining light*
> *Playing on lens and raincoat stonily,*
> *And turned away.*[50]

In the following stanza, the narrator looks at a religious building across the town and spots one of the occupants gazing out:

> *Across the silent handball alley, eyes*
> *That never looked on lover measured mine*
> *Over the Christian Brothers' frosted glass*
> *And turned away.*[51]

Whether it is the poet or the brother who is doing the turning away here is not absolutely clear, but that the narrator is rejecting those staring eyes is incontestable. There is both a renunciation and turning away from the disappointing economic conservatism of the present, and also from the strong religious influence in the Irish state. There is indignation that the religious, inexperienced in something as fundamental to life as sexual and romantic love, are in any position to measure the poet. What right do they have to judge from their building, frosted cold by its lack of exposure to love's heat?

Critics have often commented on Kinsella's vigorous critique of the northern state, but less often mentioned is the fundamental disappointment with what the southern state has become. This is in the tradition of critical socialist-republicanism, which can trace its lineage to Connolly's premonition in 1914 that any partition of the island would lead to two sectarian capitalist states and a 'carnival of reaction', from which the working class on both sides of the border would emerge economically oppressed. Connolly believed that a partitioned island could leave a northern state that would have a working-class movement divided (and thus weakened) along religious lines, and a southern, conservative (mainly rural) state where the Catholic Church would have much power.

The great mass of Irish people would remain excluded from the insider dealing of 'official Ireland' in the south. In a series of poems in the 1980s and 1990s, Kinsella would trace the grubby dance between private cash, politicians and development, long before the existence of such practices was proven in court and by investigative tribunals. That the ordinary person had no access to this shadowy insider world, but had to live their daily lives with the consequences of its awful profit-driven planning and development, is depicted in a Kinsellian Dublin of shadows, dark lanes and mounting malevolence.

In the long poem 'One Fond Embrace', there are warnings that '*Dirty money gives dirty access.*' The narrator is raging against what he thinks is the destructive development taking place across his city. The Percy Place area of south Dublin is crawling with malicious shadowy figures in their '*soiled crombie*', representing the worst aspects of commercial progress: '*Invisible speculators, urinal architects / and the Corporation flourishing their approvals / in potent compliant dance.*'[52] This illicit two-step between private profiteering and public administration is ruining Dublin. The tone of incredulity towards local government administrators is harsher than that against the developers. While the pursuit of profit is their *raison d'être*, our civil servants are meant to protect the public good. However, they are willing partners in this dance. Such lines seem prophetic coming years before a series of Tribunals of Investigation into planning matters in Ireland uncovered evidence of corruption.[53] But not only is Dublin being destroyed by ignorance and profit, the gap between its rich and the working class continues to widen, for the former are *'transplanted'* to the foothills of the mountains south of the city, where they live in their new houses and estates with bogus names *'from Kennedy's Villas and Cherryfield Heights.'* To the north of the Liffey, the compromised authorities build *'concrete piss-towers for the underprivileged.'* The best of Dublin is being demolished while the city is becoming increasingly divided.

By the time the *Peppercanister* series entered the late 1980s and early 1990s, Dublin, particularly the district around the Percy Place area of south Dublin, had become a more sinister, dark place, with strange shadows everywhere. Dublin, in the collections *One Fond Embrace* (1988), *Personal Places* (1990) and *Poems from Centre City* (1990) is slowly being destroyed by a dangerous army of profiteering developers, unscrupulous politicians and administrators from local government, and both lay and religious activists in the Catholic Church. The Grand Canal area around the Kinsella home on Percy Place also figured heavily in the late poetry of Patrick Kavanagh, but his depiction of it is very different. While Kavanagh discovered a sense of calm and religious commune along the leafy banks of the Grand Canal, the same area in Kinsella is the scene of creeping corruption and evil shades.

In 'One Fond Embrace', the buildings in the area are regarded as part of the architectural legacy of Empire, *'With a scruffy nineteenth-century / history of half-finished / colonials and upstarts. Still with us.'* Empire may have robbed Ireland of much, but many of its buildings were still worth retaining. In the short three-line stanzas that follow, there is a furious depiction of the meddling, two-faced actions of local Catholic activists in the area running a social club for the local youth. The power and negative role the Church plays in Irish society is clearly as much part of the nation's lingering post-colonial fate as the architecture. But while the religious legacy of interference seems to grow, the architectural gems of old Dublin are being pulled down. Corruption and growing income inequality are also located within this post-colonial context. The historic economic exploitation of imperialism and its endowment of uneven economic development left an independent state mired in financial stagnation and corruption, and heavily influenced by the Church.

The planners are arriving around Percy Place to carry out their discreet operation of ruination. Their impact is great, but their presence is slight. The city elders are *'fumbling in their shadow budget'*. It is an inside job being done in the dark, away from the citizens. It is reminiscent of Yeats's Dublin bourgeoisie fumbling in the greasy till of his 'September 1913'. The administrator stalks the area in his *'soiled crombie'*, Irish leaders no longer wearing the trenchcoats of revolutionary times. This dark individual is a poetic prototype of the type of figure that would wander around poems later in the decade. He is dimly recognised in the community, but his impact is decisive and destructive.

Two years later, and the *Poems from Centre City* collection is crawling with shadow figures. In 'Administrator', a representative for developers is heard of among the neighbours before he makes an appearance. He is *'Seldom seen'*, but finally he is *'Stationed out among the people'* like an early settler, or an imperial officer on a reconnaissance mission, mapping the lay of the land and garnering information from the locals before returning to his masters with a report. The sense of

Dublin experiencing a new invasion is palpable, with an army of developers and politicians with their shadowy foot soldiers out front, ready to conquer and destroy, to free up space for development and profit. In 'Social Work', a neighbourhood meeting breaks up and different parties congregate in knots of conversation around the hall. By the window, corporation workers, an elderly *'very Catholic'* doctor and a parish priest gather furtively. The priest is depicted as an archetypal trickster character, bending the ear of the corporation officials. He had been quiet during the meeting, but now he has them nodding. The narrator is suspicious of his motives.

In 'The Back Lane', the narrator is driven to rage by even the most minuscule examples of what he considers the *'slovenliness'* of the city planners. A little cement indifferently thrown on the ground to cover up digging that had been done by the telephone company is a microcosm for the wider indifference shown by the authorities to the capital. In 'The Stranger', the shadow is everywhere. The narrator spots him across the canal, later turning away along the dark base of the Peppercanister Church across from his home. His face is foreign when the narrator sees it up close on Baggot Street, but another time he looks like a familiar clerk from somewhere in the city. The narrator takes time out from a residents' meeting in his home and looks out of his window. Below, the shade is sneaking around, shadowing the actions of the residents.

> *One evening, when our house was full of neighbours*
> *met in upset, I was standing by the drapes*
> *and saw his face outside, turned up to the light.*[54]

The shadow has a particular meaning in the psychological theories of Carl Jung, by which Kinsella has been much influenced. Its appearance in these poems broadly corresponds to Jung's definition that the shadow is a projection of the darkest, unrecognised and most evil aspects of our own psyches. These unrecognised dark aspects of our personality are ignored but unconsciously projected onto another person or group, who becomes the shadow figure.

The appearance of shadows in these particular collections, however, has an obvious social rather than purely personal projection. The shadow is a manifestation of the wicked results of economic and political corruption as well as unchecked capitalist profiteering. The tendency to view capitalism as 'thing-like', as having a life of its own, separate from human relations, is a phenomenon noted since at least Marx. On a basic level, its legacy continues in the buzzwords of our daily economic news. Markets crash and surge, they are bears and bulls. The government must undertake economic cutbacks to appease the faceless market, which is spoken of as if it were a living organism sitting somewhere and making decisions on our actions. Expert talking heads are rolled into TV studios to inform us of how the market will react to this or that measure. Marx termed it the 'fetishism of commodities', where goods and economic relationships under capitalism no longer look like they are between real human beings.[55] Capitalism has occluded its real structure. It seems like a natural phenomenon like the wind or comets, rather than the consequence of human action.

The dark shadow stalking the streets of inner-city south Dublin is not simply the projection of the negative aspects of the narrator, or his neighbours' psyches. It is not merely the dark underside of Kinsella's generation, the corruption of the leading politicians like former Taoiseach Charlie Haughey (1925–2006), or the underhand dealings between politics and developers. The shadow is not only cast by this generation of *'positive disgrace'*, it is more structural and enduring than that. Rather, the shadow is the dark side of the economic policies first launched by Sean Lemass's (1899–1971) government in the late 1950s and early 1960s. Concern over these policies can be seen as early as 'Nightwalker', published in the late 1960s, where Ireland appears as a mock Statue of Liberty in Dublin Bay, looking for *'Productive Investment'* and promising 'tax concession to foreign capital'.

To this onset of malevolence, Kinsella counters with an individualistic prayer of watchfulness and guidance in 'The Back Lane'. It is an invocation to a greater power to help counsel his attempts at thinking globally but acting locally. The relationship between attempting to understand the totality of his experience and its impact on his actions in his own Dublin terrace is at the core of this prayer.

> *Lord, grant us a local watchfulness.*
> *Accept us into that minority*
> *driven toward a totality of response.*[56]

The original revolutionaries are chided by the narrator in 'One Fond Embrace'. For the poet's generation is the one *'whose fathers, throwing off the chains of bondage / fought the wrong civil war.'*[57] But in this poem, it is the poet's own generation, the first born after independence, who are scolded most. This Irish southern state has been handed to them by their parents, who had shed blood during its bungled birth. This post-revolutionary generation may not have blood on their hands like their predecessors, but they do lack the idealism and probity of their parents. Ireland is now ruled by a political and economic class mired in corruption and ignorance. The dream of Irish independence has been sullied.

The positive dream of independence was weakened by the marginalisation of the radical strand and the labour movement, the injustice of partition, the unwarranted power of the Catholic Church, the barbarism of the Civil War and finally the replacement of patriotism and civility with profiteering and corruption – the actions of some of the elite in the post-independence generation. This is quite a stuffed charge sheet against the southern state, but, while facing its negative aspects, the poet does not reject it entirely. His turning away is not complete. This is because, despite its sins and its sinners, the southern state's existence was still worth fighting for. The narrator may want to turn away from the content of the independent state, but its achievement and the anti-imperialist struggle undertaken to win it, was justified.

And we were the generation also of privilege

to have seen the vitals of Empire tied off
in a knot of the cruel and comic.[58]

This combination of reproof and regard is not a narrowly Irish experience. It is to be expected that the sons and daughters of any revolutionary generation will feel some inherent disappointment with their parents' work. Perhaps in the criticism of the revolutionary generation there also lies a sense of resentment and disguised jealousy? The heroic age of daring is over, and the generation born after liberation must make their way in a more prosaic world. This generation cannot be consoled in dreams of a New Jerusalem to be built on some hill sometime in the future, because this future has already been won by their brave fathers (the mothers' role in this liberation had been largely ignored for many decades). Indeed, any moaning about the new free Ireland could be regarded as ungracious, lacking the requisite respect for the sacrifices of their parents. Such inter-generational friction can be found in many post-revolutionary situations, and the theme of second-generational discontent with the parents' work is a regular one in literature and social discourse. The Israeli author Amos Oz has spoken of the sense of disillusionment felt by his own generation of Zionists, who became adults after the state of Israel was created. He looked back in awe at the leaders of his parents' era who made the state. 'I have seen a dream come true, which is Israel,' Oz has written. 'And I have learned that it is the nature of fulfilled dreams to be somewhat disappointing. The only way to keep a dream intact is to never live it out.'[59] The dialectic of hope and disappointment can be intense in situations of revolution and liberation. In the case of Israel, of course, Oz's dream was the beginning of the modern nightmare (al-Nakba, or 'catastrophe') of the Palestinian people. In a different context, the achievement of the dream of a southern Irish state was the beginning of the nationalist minority's decades-long experience as second-class status in the northern state.

The understanding of the existence of two failed states on the island has existed in the radical tradition since the end of the revolutionary period. Neither state was anything approaching the type of polity envisioned by Connolly, Pearse or most of the leaders of the 1916 Rising. One was a sectarian cold-house, where the nationalist minority was left freezing. The other was a shadow of the proclamation, Church-ridden, philistine, run in the interest of the elite, becoming increasingly conservative as its youth fled in search of work, and gripped by growing corruption.

In a 2001 interview, the poet considers the birth of the two states and the mistakes made by the national leadership. 'It is interesting, but not politically useful, to debate events and analyse responsibilities,' he said. 'To blame De Valera, for example, when Collins had fought the English to the table, for not going to the Treaty negotiations instead of Collins; to blame the South for fighting the wrong civil war, and not continuing the war with England and the North for a United Ireland, as Lincoln fought the South for a United States'.[60]

The consequences of Empire are portrayed throughout Kinsella's work. From the recent nasty brutal war in the north, to the historic loss of the native language, to the basic dispossession of the colonised. In a short poem from 2000, 'Down Survey (1655–1657)', young men are on the side of the road, stripped of their possessions. They begin to chant about their loss:

> *Is there any sorrow like ours*
> *who have forfeited our possessions*
> *and all respect?*[61]

Watching this pitiful scene are the young women of 'Killmainham', who are embarrassed and ashamed to see their men like this. In the six lines of the poem we see the brute reality of colonialism, its programme of dispossession, the turn of the dispossessed to music and chants of anger and the feeling of emasculation among the male colonised. It is all weaved into the short lines. Kinsella has spoken of his time working in the Ordinance Survey Commission in Ireland after he left college as a very important period,[62] and the historic sources he worked with there were windows into the impact of Empire.

Empire and power is not always enforced through constant military application. In a section of 'St Catherine's Clock', the narrator surveys a James Malton painting of Thomas

Street in 1792. The entire scene of old women and men getting on with their business is overseen:

> *a solitary redcoat*
> *is handling the entire matter.*[63]

This is during the period of the United Irishmen, when British concerns over a possible French invasion were very real, yet the *'entire matter'* is overseen by just one soldier. Empire is not imposed by brute force alone; it is cultural, psychological and repetitive. The garrison nature of the original Norman Conquest is reflected in an early poem from the 1950s, 'King John's Castle', where a fortification in County Meath is enough to hold the locality in suppression.

> *This in its heavy ruin. New, a brute bright plateau,*
> *It held speechless under its cold a whole province of Meath.*[64]

The occupation is not purely military. The mission of Empire is articulated by its supporters as one of enlightenment and progress. For the occupiers, their project was not purely one of rapine.

> *King John directs at the river a grey stare, who once*
> *Viewed the land in a spirit of moderation and massacre.*[65]

But the castle is now ruined. In a theme similar to Shelley's 'Ozymandias', what was once great is now a confusing empty shell where *'Views open inward / On empty silence.'*

On a journey to a cross-border northern town, in 'Apostle of Hope' the narrator encounters frail figures as darkness descends:

> *At night, on our own, when the streets emptied,*
> *the terrible number of waifs we met*
> *in a silence of the stunned. The process*
> *as it hath shown its waste to you.*[66]

It is tempting to see these forsaken sickly figures as representations of the relationship between the nationalist northern community and the southern state. They are orphaned and essentially ignored by the southern political elite in particular. Lip service is paid, but nothing practically done. The south turned away from the northern nationalist community.

Much has been written about Kinsella's most infamous poem, 'Butcher's Dozen'. Penned on the occasion of the Widgery Tribunal, it was the first poem in the *Peppercanister* series. The tribunal was established following the shooting dead of unarmed civil rights protestors in Derry on 30 January 1972 – an incident that became known as 'Bloody Sunday'. The tribunal made findings that essentially exonerated the British military from its role in the massacre, and was seen as a whitewash by the nationalist community and many others. Written in punchy lines, the poet himself said: 'That was just an occasional poem and it was as serious as I could make it, but it hasn't affected the larger scheme.'[67] In an artistic sense, it does not hold any significant interest. But in terms of politics, and a moment of angry social commentary, it is devastating. *'I went with Anger at my heel / Through Bogside of the bitter zeal / – Jesus pity! - on a day / Of cold and drizzle and decay.*[68]

'Butcher's Dozen' is a raging explosion of raw anger. It is the poetic equivalent of the young republican socialist MP Bernadette Devlin crossing the floor of the House of Commons and slapping the face of the Tory home secretary,

Reggie Maudling, in the days following the massacre. For, like that moment, 'Butcher's Dozen' is a product of its time. Taken out of context, such an occasion can seem incompressible, and even to some reprehensible, but in its moment, it is an authentic expression of impassioned feeling.

Yes it takes sides – something that many of its critics regard as at best unseemly for a poet, or worse, dangerously indulgent and atavistic. But they are wrong, because 'Butcher's Dozen' takes sides not principally with Catholic over Protestant, nor nationalist versus unionist, but between military force and peaceful protest, between wrong and right, between Empire and resistance.

* * *

If the shadows in Kinsella's poetry came forth from a new economic dispensation in Ireland that began in the late 1950s and 1960s, then that is little surprise. He was at the heart of the operation that changed Irish economic policy in the period. But he then became one of the first literary critics of this economic turn.

Kinsella's position in all this is unique. A civil servant in the Department of Finance during the period of the switch to a more open, liberal economic model, he was for a time the personal assistant to the individual most associated with this change, department head T. K. Whitaker. With Whitaker in the department, and Sean Lemass in the Taoiseach seat, the old economic orthodoxy of protectionism and agriculture was replaced with a shift to more open markets, industrial development and foreign direct investment. A number of writers have quipped that the most important writer in the modern Irish canon was T. K. Whitaker, and the most important text his 1958 economic white paper the *First Programme for Economic Expansion*, and this may have some truth to it.[69]

The popular mainstream historical narrative of mid-century Ireland has now been firmly established. The Whitaker–Lemass-led move changed Ireland, making it a more open society, both economically and socially. This is the standard modernisation theory for the period. A 1963 *Time* magazine cover featuring Lemass was headlined 'New Spirit in the Ould Sod'. A recent review of a book about Lemass called him a 'mould maker a mould breaker.'[70] Valorising everything post Whitaker/Lemass as good, and everything associated with the Ireland of De Valera as bad, is so internalised into modern historiography and the popular imagination that to question it seems the actions of a wanton contrarian. It is also a fundamental aspect of the general 'modernisation' narrative of Ireland, where economic liberalism and EU membership are celebrated as the forces that have propelled Ireland from being an economic backwater to a modern part of the global capitalist system. But this binary mindset blurs contradiction and simplifies beyond what is sensible. As Joe Cleary has written, 'Thus, if one period is conventionally agreed to mean nationalist stagnation and repression, the other, by reflex, comes to mean post-nationalist dynamism and tolerance.'[71]

In the wake of Ireland's recent economic collapse in 2008, critical economists like Conor McCabe have questioned the core focus of the 'Whitaker revolution' on foreign investment, convincingly arguing that the main drive of Irish macroeconomic policy was the attraction of individual foreign exporters to Ireland, with little focus on the creation and maintenance of indigenous export-based business, particularly in the arena of the country's natural resources. Successive government policies since 1959 'typify the dynamics of the Whitaker revolution and the relentless pursuit of exporters over exports.'[72] The shift to more open markets and foreign investment was accompanied by the sale and privatisation of much of the country's natural and economic resources.

Denis Donoghue once joked that no one would expect or want a poem about a bureaucratic institution like the European Community, and Kinsella's 'Nightwalker' is certainly not merely a poem about Irish economic policy.[73] It is a grand epic, dealing with history, violence and the nature of meaning. However, the changing nature of economic policy in the Irish state *is* one of the most important themes in the poem. The narrator walks out to Dublin Bay and sees Ireland personified as a female figure, reminiscent of the Statue of Liberty:

> *Robed in spattered iron she stands*
> *At the harbour mouth, Productive Investment,*
> *And beckons the nations through our gold half-door:*
> *Lend me your wealth, your cunning and your drive,*
> *Your arrogant refuse. Let my people serve them*
> *Holy water in our new hotels,*[74]

Ireland's golden half-door demonstrates that, despite the shiny new economic pretentions, Ireland's cottage past cannot totally be denied. Ireland's central call to the world is financial. This is the gombeen jungle on an epic scale. The dream of Ireland is monetised. We are willing to project this image, maybe any image, to attract foreign money. '*To show them our growing city, give them a feeling / Of what is possible; our labour pool / The tax concessions to foreign capital.*'[75] The tone is judgemental – there is something unsettling and grubby about the new setup.

This is not how the new economic liberal policy is often portrayed in mainstream history. The hold that a straight modernisation theory has over historical and social investigations of the Irish state has become only slightly shaken by the economic collapse since 2008. It is not the triumphalism or lack of self-reflection of many commentators that has most irked those who hold more critical and marginal historical standpoints, but rather their insistence only to see relentless progress where in fact there have been contradictions. 'The musings of modernisation theorists and those within their orbit are also questionable in that they fail to grasp the genuinely contradictory nature of social development. In the course of their evolution, human societies tend to get both better and worse more or less at the same time,' wrote sociologist Colin Coulter at the height of the 'Celtic Tiger'.[76] He charges the mainstream readings of the economic and political progress of the Irish republic in recent decades as not only 'intellectually feeble but politically reactionary as well.'[77] Progress can also be retardation. Walter Benjamin (1892–1940) in the 1920s wrote that the Angel of History 'stares in horror at a pile of debris heaping before him as he is propelled backwards by a storm blowing out of heaven. This storm is what we call Progress.'[78]

Kinsella was there at the centre of the great economic change, but at the moment when the Irish Department of Finance was the engine for new ideas that were shaping the political debate, Kinsella left the department and his career. '1965 was the year of change, resigning from an increasingly demanding and fascinating, but irrelevant, position in the senior civil service and accepting an obscure appointment as poet-in-residence in the University of Southern Illinois,' he has recalled.[79] The description of his former job as 'irrelevant' is devastating. The action can be regarded as an admirable example of someone 'living their dream' and showing some bravery in making such a significant move when they have established a successful career. As a pen-picture of authentic living, it carries weight. But the civil servant post was not just the wrong one for the poet, it was 'irrelevant'. There is a social and economic critique in the use of this adjective. Large numbers of people do work that is not all that vital, but which is made relevant only because the capitalist market deems it so. Meanwhile, huge numbers of people, very often women, do work that is extremely vital, such as the rearing and educating of children, which is not deemed relevant by market economics, or at least not relevant enough to be monetised. With his move from the 'irrelevant' post in the Department of Finance, Kinsella to some extent rejected the priorities of the orthodox capitalist dream, and in the poems 'Nightwalker' and 'A Country Walk', he rejected them on a national basis also.

Kinsella has spoken in interviews about his high personal regard for Whitaker, for his work ethic and his abilities. But although there is undoubted respect for the process involved, the practical consequences of the free market turn under Lemass and Whitaker is subjected to fierce poetic ire. Once he had left the department, he wrote poetry that excoriated the new economic model pursued by a series of Irish governments. Like Jean-Jacques Rousseau (1712–1778), who began the critique of some of the claims of the Enlightenment from the heart of the movement itself, Kinsella began a critique of commercialised Ireland from within its ideological base.

Considering his career, it is no wonder that Kinsella's poetry was largely unmoved by the excess of recent Celtic Tiger years and the subsequent recession. Kinsella's marginality, his modernist artistic form and sensibilities, his apparent lack of interest in delighting a large audience and his isolation from the cultural and political arenas of contemporary official Ireland kept him unscathed from what two critics christened the 'Millenarianism and utopianism in the new Ireland: the tragedy (and comedy) of accelerated modernisation'.[80]

If the dreams of Yeats and de Valera of Ireland as a rural idyll had proved to be disappointing, the new dream of the country taking a fuller part in the world of multinational capitalism did not fill the poetry with much hope either.

* * *

That the dreams of religion, progress and nationalism are exposed as more flawed than their weavers originally believed is not something peculiar to this poet's work, but is reflective of a wider range of critical, philosophical and artistic questioning of theories concerning totality and progress. Such scepticism towards great theories predates the modern period, but the horrors of the modern world, the catastrophes, have made people increasingly distrustful of such expressions of political or social ideology.

For the great 'meta-narratives' or 'true world' theories, life had both a steady object and a subject. For Roman Catholicism, the object was the truth of Christ's resurrection and the message he delivered, the subject of history was the Church of Rome and its flock. For revolutionary socialism, the object of history was the laws of class struggle and historical materialism, the subject was the conscious participation of the working class in active political action. For nationalism, it was the nation and its citizens. All these and other similar 'totalising' theories are damned in the eyes of much critical theory since the Second World War. They stand accused of being all-encompassing in their range, of having a clear goal; they are theories that provide a framework for understanding a 'truthful' view of the world.

The estranged modern man, it is argued, surveying the wreckage of the twentieth century, can no longer believe in an immovable objective truth. The subject is now the isolated individual with no clear path to follow. The object is absent. The loss of that dream of meaning haunts much of modernist literature. It has powerful resonance in Kinsella's work, where if the narrator is not walking, he is often falling, the solid ground of reality disappearing under him. Kinsella's poetics is thus classically modernist not merely because of the fragmentary, evolving form of his work, but also because there is mourning for the loss of meaning.

The poetry groans with the pangs of realisation that the dreams that once purported to make sense of it all have all now proved spurious. But once you have shared this dream, even when its illusions have been dispelled, you pine after its old certainties. One of the significant themes of modernist art is this sense of loss. As Terry Eagleton has noted: 'The typical modernist work of art is still haunted by the memory of an orderly universe, and so is nostalgic enough to feel the eclipse of meaning as an anguish, a scandal, an intolerable deprivation.'[81] And it is from this feeling of it all slipping away from us that modernist writing finds much of its power. 'In this tension between the persisting need for meaning and the gnawing sense of its elusiveness, modernism can be genuinely tragic.' Kinsella's work is absorbed with this tragedy.

In its dispelling of big dreams, the work could also be said to exhibit sensibilities more associated with postmodernism. But unlike the modernist, the postmodernist does not bemoan loss of meaning, they celebrate it.

French theorists like Jean-Francois Lyotard (1924–1998), considering the debris of the twentieth century, concluded that the concept of the inevitability of progress is a sham. 'The idea of progress as possible, probable or necessary was rooted in the certainty that the development of the arts, technology, knowledge and liberty would be profitable to mankind as a whole,' he wrote in 1985.[82] He surmised that both economic and political liberalism had failed in their enlightenment project. That the actions of the German Nazis, in particular, could occur at a state-administered level proved progress to be a delusional dream. 'What kind of thought is able to sublate Auschwitz in a general (either empirical or speculative) process towards a universal emancipation?'[83] Lyotard favours little stories over big dreams.

But how to be a poet in this time of shattered dreams? Adorno claimed that 'To write poetry after Auschwitz is barbaric.'[84] Kinsella does write poetry in the shadow of Auschwitz and the wider twentieth-century catastrophe, but the difficultly of representing its impact is shown in gaps and ellipses through the work. In the poem 'All is emptiness / and I must spin', post-catastrophe man is falling through a universe that makes no sense because in the twentieth century horrific and unimaginable things happened.

I have been in places ... The floors crept,
an electric terror waited everywhere.
We were made to separate and strip.
My urine flowed in mild excitement.
Our hands touched in farewell.[85]

Although divergent on much, on this issue of progress, Adorno and Lyotard take similar positions. Both regard it as foolish and shameful to continue to talk of progress, or the inherent superiority or desirability of western Enlightenment thinking following the administered genocide of Auschwitz undertaken in a 'civilised' western nation. Postmodernism has drawn a direct link between any systematic theories of society and the possibility of slaughter and barbarism. The great dreams, the great, grand narratives that have filled the minds of millions in the modern period, have led to the catastrophes of Western civilisation — the trenches, the camps and the bomb. The big dreams — whether of religions, Marxism, liberalism or scientific progress — have become big nightmares. If we need to dream, they should be as small as possible. Alex Callinicos also links the rise of postmodernist theory to the failure of the 1968 student and leftist movements in various countries. When former student left-wingers grew disillusioned with their socialistic beliefs, and this disillusionment was combined with their entry into the middle class through academia and other routes, many were attracted by some of the conservative political conclusions of postmodernism.[86]

For Kinsella's generation, the events of the Second World War marked a farewell to the apparent certainties that had moved much of European thought since the Enlightenment. Progress is in fact not assured, and barbarism on an industrial scale can be carried out by the most 'civilised' of nations. Denis Donoghue writes that 'Adorno's stricture is too hard to be borne. Nor has it silenced poets or novelists. Life must (if possible) go on. Perhaps the only tribute one can pay to Adorno is to remember him and retain a scruple in favour of his testament, even while one goes on. A scruple is as much as can be sustained.'[87]

Kinsella does not think that the catastrophe means that the reaction to it can only be one of being struck dumb. He continues to write poetry, but evil is present in it, despite the promise of progress. At the time of the Great War, Polish militant Rosa Luxemburg, a contemporary of Connolly, said that the choice for humanity was 'socialism or barbarism'.[88] In the age of dreams, a choice like this could still be made. But in the present period of shattered illusions, some believe that there is no choice – we must make do living under the shadow of barbarism.

None of the great systems of external belief satisfies the quest for order and structure in the poetry. But in his falling though the emptiness of these dead dreams, the poet rescues some semblance of truth and structure that provides him with marginal satisfaction. It is not in the outside world that this satisfaction is to be found, but deep within the individual.

5
The Truth Within?

'Within us is the way, the truth, and the life'

— Carl Jung, *The Red Book*

'Leaf-Eater' is an eight-line poem that on first reading may seem like an arresting yet whimsical description of insect life. A precariously placed caterpillar reaches out in vain from his leaf:

> *On a shrub in the heart of the garden,*
> *On an outer leaf, a grub twists*
> *Half its body, a tendril,*[1]

The struggling insect is analogous to the more fundamental struggle of each individual human. The path ahead is engulfed by nothingness; the solid certainties, from which we used to hang, have now vanished. We, like the grub, turn around rapidly searching for anything to hold onto, before we finally discover that the way of structure and truth may not be outside of us at all.

> *This way and that in blind*
> *Space: no leaf or twig*
> *Anywhere in reach; then gropes*
> *Back on itself and begins*
> *To eat its own leaf.*[2]

'Leaf-Eater' sums up succinctly the poetic turn inwards that Kinsella begins during this period. The leaves and twigs of structure from which it was once possible to hang are unavailable to the grub and writer. The external dreams have withered, and we are all individuals groping in the dark with little option but to turn back on ourselves. The poem is a distillation of what the poet called the 'only encounter that matters ... between the individual and the significant ordeal.'[3]

'Leaf-Eater' is an early indicator of the poet's confrontation with the void of meaning that lies outside. In 'All is emptiness / and I must spin', there is a frightening evocation of this external existential horror, followed sharply with potent examples from the twentieth century. The universe, free of illusion, is empty of meaning and ethics. *'A vacancy in which, apparently, / I hang / with severed senses.'*

In the absence of meaning, the narrator hangs like the grub, unable to grab hold of any external structure. The search for external meaning is answered, in Camus's words, by the 'unreasonable silence of the world,' and within this vast quiet lurks the possibility of administered horror. Left with no positive dream destination outside, and with the horror of the catastrophe facing humanity, the narrator falls inwards and turns back onto his own nutrient leaf of internal consciousness.

> *How bring oneself to judge, or think,*
> *so hurled onward! inward!*[4]

The journey inward is the one of true progression. Kinsella had begun a poetic 'confrontation with the unconscious' that would substantially mark his poetry for the next fifteen years.[5] In this inbound journey, Kinsella was to be guided by one of the most significant and controversial thinkers of the twentieth century, Swiss psychologist Carl Gustav Jung. For Jung, to fall inside your own personal psyche was not to plummet into a vast, self-indulgent swamp; it was to dive into a spacious realm of fear, but one that was also brimming over with enabling knowledge that could assist the individual in finding a true path in life.

'Fall' is one of the most typical of Kinsella's words, and its use often signals a dramatic and deep delving into the personal psyche, or the beginning of a dream. It is also a verb regularly deployed by Jung to describe his internal journeys into the personal mind. A fall captures the lack of control that the poet experiences at the beginning of these inward journeys. The possibility of mental injury is always present, crashing against the anxieties, the memories and neuroses of the psyche. Jung believed that, if not handled correctly, any such inquiring into our internal world had the potential to trigger psychotic episodes in patients. When the Sundance Kid peers over the cliff at the river hundreds of feet below and worries to Butch Cassidy that he can't swim, he fails to identify the real threat. 'Are you crazy? The fall will probably kill you,' Butch replies, exasperated.

The fall in such a confrontation with the unconscious as outlined by Jung, and experienced by the poet narrator of Kinsella's poems, is fraught. The personal consciousness must already be relatively strong for it successfully to engage with the darkest aspects of the deep unconscious. If it is not, it can be shattered into pieces on its contact with the substratum layer of the unconscious mind, resulting in possible psychotic consequences. The narrator in the opening sequences of the 1973 *New Poems* collection is hopeful that his fall can proceed without sustaining any mental cuts and bruises. It is a forlorn expectation:

> *With what joy did I not hope, suddenly,*
> *I might pass through unshattered*
> *– to whatever Pit! But I fell foul at the last*
> *and broke in a distress of gilt and silver,*
> *scattered in a million droplets of*
> *fright and loneliness...*[6]

Broken, but still conscious, the narrator sees '*Dark nutrient waves*', a typical symbol for the unconscious. He walks along the edges of this vast dark body of water, seeking a path. '*How tentative and slack our search / along the dun shore whose perpetual hiss / breaks softly, and breaks again.*'[7] As he moves along this desolate dark landscape, he beholds a cauldron overflowing with archetypal forms, the symbols of the unconscious. The cauldron is surrounded by gargantuan old women – this is the realm of the mothers, the heaving mythical core of the collective unconscious:

> *A pale fume beat steadily through the gloom.*
> *I saw, presently, it was a cauldron:*
> *ceaselessly over its lip a vapour of forms*
> *curdled, glittered and vanished. Soon I made out*
> *a ring of mountainous beings staring upward*
> *with open mouths – naked ancient women.*[8]

In describing his own vivid memories detailing his encounters with the primordial images of the unconscious, Jung echoes many of the symbols found in Kinsella's works. Writing about a series of such experiences, Jung described the scene: 'The action is set in a dark earthy depth, evidently an allegorical representation of the inner depths beneath the extension of the bright space of consciousness or the psychic field of vision. Sinking into such a depth corresponds to averting the mental gaze from outer things and focusing on the inner dark depths. Gazing at the darkness to some extent animates the previously dark background. Since gazing at the darkness occurs without conscious expectation, the inanimate psychic background has an opportunity to let its contents appear, undisturbed by conscious assumptions.'[9]

The poet narrator leaves through the iron grille that he sees above. The rest of the *New Poems* collection enters the world of the poet's childhood, travelling through the grilled shores in the narrow back lanes and into the dark rooms of the grandparents' homes in Kilmainham and Inchicore. We encounter a cast of imposing grandmothers and memorable neighbours. The characters' names add to the mythical sense – 'Hen Woman', 'Jack Rat', 'The Boss', 'Padno Carney' – and there are legendary-sounding places, like the 'Robbers' Den', which is merely a grove of bushes near the poet's home. His early memories of family in his Inchicore childhood, like the ancient past, are full of mythical allusions. Joseph Campbell believed that we still live out these mythical lives, even if we are not consciously aware of doing so. 'The latest incarnation of Oedipus, the continued romance of Beauty and the Beast, stand this afternoon on the corner of Forty-second Street and Fifth Avenue, waiting for the traffic light to change.'[10] For Kinsella, memories of family, especially with grandparents, have a strong mythical component.

'Hen Woman' is set in the back garden of his grandparents' home. The young poet sees a hen starting to lay an egg. The grandmother charges out of the house and grabs the hen, holding it up high. The moment is frozen in comical time, with the bird's open mouth staring at the open-mouthed child, both unsure of what is to happen next:

> *It fixed me with its pebble eyes*
> *(seeing what mad blur).*
> *A white egg showed in the sphincter;*
> *mouth and beak opened together;*
> *and time stood still.*
>
> *Nothing moved: bird or woman,*
> *fumbled or fumbling – locked there*
> *(as I must have been) gaping.*[11]

The egg begins to appear, and finally to fall free from the hen. The egg is falling, like the poet falls in the opening section of *New Poems*. The egg is falling through the empty space without, while the poet is falling through the space within. In both situations, it can end badly:

> *It smashed against the grating*
> *and slipped down quickly out of sight.*
> *It was over in a comical flash.*
> *The soft mucous shell clung a little longer,*
> *then drained down.*
>
> *She stood staring, in blank anger.*
> *Then her eyes came to life, and she laughed*
> *and let the bird flap away.*
>
>   *'It's all the one.*
> *There's plenty more where that came from!'*[12]

The final reaction of the grandmother to the loss of this brief life is comic and brutal in equal measure. Her anger turns to offhandedness, and then swiftly to gallows humour. While hinting at knowledge to come, of a life of inherent unfairness and infant mortality, the reaction of the Hen Woman also recommends a stance of endurance cloaked in black humour. The young boy had much to learn in this momentous moment in a Dublin back garden.

'Hen Woman' is undoubtedly one of Kinsella's greatest achievements. It contains humour (far from universal in his oeuvre), brilliantly realised pen-pictures and a powerful use of allegory, in this case the birth and smashing of an egg echoing wider themes of death and an indifferent natural world. It is also an authentic realisation of how childhood memory lingers in the adult mind, often episodic with a focus on details that later reveal greater meaning. We are made aware that Kinsella has a very particular view on the way childhood memory is processed when he considers this falling egg. For the poet, the image exists as an independent, archetypal memory in his unconscious. As an image and memory it has a life of its own beyond the conscious mind. Its meaning is not specific, it is general, and connected to a wider consciousness that exists beyond the individual memory of the poet:

> *I feed upon it still, as you see;*
> *there is no end to that which, not understood,*
> *may yet be hoarded in the imagination,*
> *in the yoke of one's being, so to speak,*
> *there to undergo its (quite animal) growth,*
>
> *dividing blindly, twitching, packed with will,*
> *searching in its own tissue*
> *for the structure in which it may wake.*

> *Something that had – clenched in its cave –*
> *not been now as was: an egg of being.*[13]

As the egg falls, we all fall through life, birth towards death. The fumbling grandmother may have tried to save the situation, but in the end her efforts are futile. Nothing can stop this ultimate fall to nothingness:

> *Through what seemed a whole year it fell*
> *– as it still falls, for me, solid and light,*
> *the red gold beating in its silvery womb,*
> *alive as the yolk and white of my eye.*
> *As it will continue to fall, probably, until I die,*
> *through the vast indifferent spaces*
> *with which I am empty.*[14]

The unconscious and the dream world are of crucial importance in Kinsella's poetry. In 1996, Kinsella told an interviewer that 'The dream world is every bit as real as the other world that's going on, and every so often it erupts ... and I make no attempt to control or suppress it.'[15] Later, he insisted that the 'dream world has to be represented in poetry.'[16] Whether it is images that develop entirely out of sleep or daydreams, they have emerged and ended up in his work. In 'Nightwalker', the poet narrator opens by saying that he is *'Mindful of the shambles of the day.'* The 'real' conscious world is only part of our experience, not its totality.

> *But mindful, under the blood's drowsy humming,*
> *Of will that gropes for structure; nonetheless*
> *Not unmindful of the madness without,*
> *The madness within – the book of reason*
> *Slammed open, slammed shut.*[17]

In the '*drowsy*' arena of dreaming, there is something stirring – an unconscious will that is reaching for some structure or meaning. Not all meaning is to be found within the everyday goings-on that society prioritises. The opening of the poem is influenced by Jung's belief that our dreams have significant importance and can guide and teach us, and that we can learn much from their analysis. But in typical Kinsellian fashion, there is an instant deconstruction of this claim, for the dream world is not wholly rational either: it is a realm of both madness and knowledge, just like the daylight hours. The poem seems to propose that reason and madness appear and disappear all the time, both inside the psyche in our dreams and outside in our external social world. This understanding of the world of the unconscious and dreams resulted from the poet's own inquiries and experiences, as well as from a thorough engagement with Jungian theories that began in the 1960s. This has developed into a hugely important influence on his work, which continues today.

Jung, for Kinsella, is one of humanity's 'major creators', who has made invaluable contributions to our understanding of the world.[18]

* * *

If a person's importance can be judged by the number of labels that have been stuck on them, then Carl Jung is very important indeed. 'Occultist, Scientist, Prophet, Charlatan, Philosopher, Racist, Guru, Anti-Semite, Liberator of Women, Misogynist, Freudian Apostle, Gnostic, Postmodernist, Polygamist, Healer, Poet, Con-Artist, Psychiatrist and Anti-Psychiatrist – what has C. G. Jung not been called?' asks Jungian expert Sonu Shamdasani.[19] Jung is simply one of the most controversial thinkers of the twentieth century, and a writer that always provokes strong reactions. Jung never compiled his esoteric and expansive theories in a systematic way, unlike his original teacher, Sigmund Freud, from whom he would later split. His writing is thus often entertaining, but infuriating for the reader searching for its core tenets. That the central parts of his theory, however, such as the collective unconscious, archetypes and individuation, have impacted on the work of Thomas Kinsella, can be discerned and explained.

Jung believed there to be a deep layer of the unconscious, inside us all, that was objective and communal in the sense that it exists separately from our own personal consciousness, our 'I'. This contrasted sharply with the Freudian view of the psyche. For Freudians, the content of our dreams and unconscious was the creation of our own self, often the product of wish fulfilment. But for Jung, not everything in our dreams, visions or thoughts was a direct product of our own psyche, but rather it had an objective separate character. Thus, some of the contents of our dreams, or even wakeful visions and thoughts, are not always produced by us. Rather, they are sourced in the substratum of the unconscious, what he calls the 'collective unconscious', which is biologically inherited. This is the layer of common concepts and modes of thinking, often mythical in nature, that are shared by all of humanity. 'I have chosen the term "collective" because this part of the unconscious is not individual but universal,' wrote Jung. 'In contrast to the personal psyche it has contents and modes of behaviour that are more or less the same everywhere and in all individuals. It is, in other words, identical in all men and thus constitutes a common psychic substrate of a suprapersonal nature which is present in every one of us.'[20]

This collective unconscious is packed full of shared forms of thinking and images, which Jung called the 'archetypes'. Some of the archetypes are named by Jung, like the shadow, the old man, the trickster, the hero, etc., but the central thesis is that there are forms of thinking that are common to all of humanity, although their content will be different. 'A primordial image is determined as to its content only when it has become conscious and is therefore filled out with the material of conscious experience ... The representations themselves are not inherited, only the forms,' wrote Jung.[21] These archetypes have a huge hold over us as individuals; we are in awe, whether consciously or unconsciously, of their 'natural numinosity' as Jung describes it. It is here, in this layer of the mind, that people have common experiences and understanding of the world. It is here that Kinsella would attempt to find a common ground with his readership. In 1981, he told an interviewer: 'In any act of communication, if you plunge totally into anything, no matter how odd, you make connections down in the basement.'[22]

'Individuation' is the term used by Jung to describe the personal journey that he and his patients went on during analysis. It expresses the process whereby a person develops their self into a more balanced, functioning whole, and part of this procedure is facing and dealing with the content of the unconscious. The individual must seek to assimilate their 'shadow function' during the process. For example, an extroverted individual must seek to integrate the introverted aspects of the personality that they have denied. 'I use the term "individuation" to denote the process by which a person becomes a psychological "individual" that is, a separate, indivisible unity or "whole",' wrote Jung.[23] The journey, in Jungian practice, can often involve the patient using painting or other creative arts to express themselves and their unconscious feelings.

This notion of approaching totality in Jung's individuation is also important in Kinsella's poetry. Carl Jung was hostile to specialised thinking, and Kinsella's writing, with its eclectic sources and themes, encapsulates a vast swath of history and philosophy. It is the search for totality in psyche, personality and intellect that unites the creative processes of both men. 'Infinitely long paths, paved with thousands of thick volumes, lead from one specialisation to another. Soon no one will be able to walk down these paths any more. And then only specialists will remain,' wrote Jung about his search for totality and his rejection of specialisation.[24] As Thomas H. Jackson has noted regarding Kinsella, 'the ideal of wholeness lies at the core of his poetry.'[25]

Kinsella's poetic content is focused on detailed matter, but is part of a more total response to life. In the poem 'The Back Lane', the narrator is outraged with what he perceives as the destruction of his local Dublin neighbourhood by developers and planners. The poem contains an invocation calling for strength to bridge the particular, local concern with a general, global response:

> *Lord, grant us a local watchfulness.*
> *Accept us into that minority*
> *driven toward a totality of response,*
>
> *and I will lower these arms*
> *and embrace what I find.*[26]

The exposure to Jung in the 1960s was one of the most significant moments in Kinsella's poetic career. As Harmon has noted, 'In Kinsella's notes, the tone of exhilaration is palpable. The Jungian system gave him ideological support and alleviated his feeling of existential disappointment.'[27]

Fitzsimons echoes this: 'The Notes from *the Land of the Dead* are the most voluminous in the Kinsella Papers at the Emory University, and the plan and phrases from these notes recur throughout the *Peppercanister* series, including the work of the 1980s and 1990s.'[28]

Jung described the period of his life when he was involved in the most intense internal exploration as the 'most important time of my life. Everything else is to be derived from this.'[29] The period of the 1960s when Kinsella was first exposed to Jung was to have a similar influence, which would continue for decades. The route of individuation, in which the confrontation with the unconscious forms a part, has been a powerful influence on the poetic persona in Kinsella's work, and has mapped out the most important journey he has taken.

In the 1960s, a student once mentioned to Kinsella that some of his early work seemed to chime with Jung's ideas, and this sparked the poet's interest, which continued until a recent collection, *Fat Master* (2011), where the poem 'Reflection' is apparently directed to both the 'Self' and Jung.

* * *

There is an understandable reluctance to begin such a difficult process of internal investigation. In section 2 of *A Technical Supplement*, the analogy is drawn between dissecting the psyche and the physical dissection of the human body, where at the '*first violation / the body would rip into pieces and fly apart.*'[30] The seat of personal consciousness feels secure in everyday life, but once this security is questioned, for instance through use of hallucinogenic drugs, a major psychotic incident, or in the case of the poet narrator and Jung, a planned confrontation with the unconscious, then the reaction may be violently defensive. So much of everyday social interactions, the commonplace relationships that provide the foundations to our collective civilisation, are based on our perception of our consciousness as a secure totality. But modern science has helped to undermine the belief that the individual is in total conscious control of his or her actions and thoughts.[31]

With the lack of any obvious pathway for heroism available to the second generation of Irish born after independence, this heroic need for adventure could be assuaged by more individualised quests.

But for this poet narrator, the 'turn inward' signals the archetypical initial move in a heroic journey where a 'hero ventures forth from the world of common day into a region of supernatural wonder.'[32] In the case of this poetry, the outside world is the cave, and the internal world the arena for the adventure. This is a major enterprise, not a quick fix en route to psychic perfection. The reader is to understand that this is not some easy New Age 'three-step programme to a new you' self-improvement. This journey is a personal epic, not a weekend retreat organised by a self-help guru. Joseph Campbell called it 'willed introversion', and placed it in the pantheon of other great adventures that comprise his monomyth. 'It drives the psychic energies into depth and activates the lost continent of unconscious infantile and archetypal images. The result, of course, may be a disintegration of consciousness more or less complete; but on the other hand, if the personality is able to absorb and integrate the new forces, there will be experienced an almost superhuman degree of self-consciousness and masterful control.'[33] The world that the poet encounters is the 'zone unknown' that the hero enters on the first stage of the mythological journey. The topology of this zone inside Kinsella's psyche may be different from many classical tales, but in its dark strangeness it fits the bill as a 'place of strangely fluid and polymorphous beings, unimaginable torments, superhuman deeds, and impossible delight'.[34]

In the opening to *New Poems*, the poet has answered the call to begin an internal journey that risks damaging the psyche:

> *Then, getting quietly ready*
> *to go down quietly out of my mind,*
> *I have lain down on the soiled divan*
> *alert as though for a journey*
> *and turned to things not right nor reasonable.*[35]

The willingness to face the unreasonable segments of his unconscious is the 'heroic' aspect of this. In 'Baggot Street Deserta' (1958), there is ample evidence that Kinsella was groping towards what in hindsight could be called a growing Jungian world view. The young poet, reeling from a tiring night of creative work, looks out the window of the small Baggot Street apartment and has a smoke.

> *Lulled, at silence, the spent attack.*
> *The will to work is laid aside.*
> *The breaking-cry, the strain of the rack,*
> *Yield, are at peace.*[36]

The narrator, exhausted like a warrior or torture victim, contemplates the course of the River Liffey, its end roaring into the Irish Sea, its early source in the mountains where it '*Is sonneting origins.*' The reader is swept across the dreamscape of sleeping Dubliners:

> *Dreamers' heads*
> *Lie mesmerised in Dublin's beds*
> *Flashing with images, Adam's morse.*[37]

This dream world is communal and archaic. In a fashion that is resonant of Jung's insistence that the collective unconscious is ancient and mythic in nature, and within us all, these Dubliners see images that share a lineage to humanity's father. Archetypal images, sent like Morse code from the beginning of time, beat through the generations. In a later stanza, the narrator's hand is against a cold window sill and he contemplates this beat, and how it encourages his creative process.

> *Fingers cold against the sill*
> *Feel, below the stress of flight,*
> *The slow implosion of my pulse*
> *In a wrist with poet's cramp, a tight*
> *Beat tapping out endless calls*
> *Into the dark,*[38]

These endless calls are the poems, which are not primarily the creation of individual genius, or even an individual's personal unconscious. They are tapped out from this collective archaic zone, which exists objectively within us all. Negatively, the poet compares this zone in imperialistic terms to an alien encroachment on his personal liberty. Positively, the zone is connected with the greater meaning of life.

> *as the alien*
> *Garrison in my own blood*
> *Keeps constant contact with the main*
> *Mystery, not to be understood.*[39]

This '*main / Mystery*' of archetypal images, myth and knowledge, is the stuff of this collective unconscious, hidden deep inside the individual. Elsewhere in the poem this mystery is called '*the Real*' and a '*single stream*', something inside with which we are connected communally and unconsciously. The poem sees the realm of sleep as most important. Thinking of this '*single stream*', the narrator intends to keep clear-eyed, looking down the water: '*The thousands fathoms, into sleep.*' For Jung, and the therapists who work in the tradition of analytic psychology that he has inspired, dreams were indispensible to knowledge of oneself and society. In contrast to classical Freudian theory, Jung's theory does not regard dreams purely as a repository of forbidden wishes and desires that we are unable to cope with during the day. For Jung, dreams were also a source of knowledge and guidance to a person, they contained symbols that were not always purely the product of the individual's experience, but rather carried a more transcendent function. Dreams were not just compensatory, but had a purpose to them, they could guide us, and in some of Jung's more radical ideas, they had a providential role. They were connected to the main mystery of life.

In his Baggot Street flat, the poet narrator intends to fall deep into sleep, burying himself into his unconscious to locate this communal connection. The poet, like his waning cigarette, must fall down and engage with this layer. The light of consciousness must be willing to fall into the dark realms below, and even risk becoming extinguished on impact.

My quarter-inch of cigarette
Goes flaring down to Baggot Street.[40]

New Poems (1973), which incorporates 'Notes from the Land of the Dead', is a high-concept collection, and signals the moment of an unambiguous turn inward by Kinsella. For the poet, the ground had been set for this move. It was not something that he could have engaged in at the beginning of his career. In an interview, Kinsella described the material dealt with in this turn inward as 'marginal' and nighttime matter, but before he was in a position to face this material he had to undertake a type of daylight apprenticeship. 'Before you allow yourself things like that, poems like that, you have to handle the daylight matter. You have to get ready, to prepare yourself to handle the marginal matter as opposed to the manageable matter ... After the manageable has been documented, you take the lid off and let the random happen.'[41] Latent in observations like this is a hint that delving into the personal psyche too early in a career may be folly, self-indulgent and somewhat dangerous. This is the sort of thing that Kinsella was charged with by critics who were dismayed at this new poetic style.

In an interview in 1981, after this turn inward had begun, but before it had reached its most abstract point with the 1985 collection, *Songs of the Psyche,* Kinsella was in an uncompromising mood. 'I took a dive, rather than a detour. But in retrospect there is an impulse to unify everything ... Anything I'd say would be misunderstood. But there'll be no spoon-feeding – being content to demand the maximum from the audience will be part of it.'[42] *New Poems* is certainly down in the basement, and the later *Songs of the Psyche* would be deeper still.

Like any high-concept work of art, like a concept album, these collections run the serious risk of dividing the audience, being declared esoteric at best and self-indulgent at worst. But such art has the potential to become something like a later 'cult classic' among fans. Kinsella's most opaque collection has fulfilled many of these destinies. Readers were certainly challenged to enter a very strange, personal and dark universe between its covers. It is mesmeric and challenging, leading the reader on a strange journey within.

But what we have in the opening of *New Poems* is a description of preparation for a confrontation with the unconscious. This is something that is evidently an epic internal journey into the depths of the psyche for the writer, but in the external world it can take place in the most ordinary of situations. As Ulrich Hoerni has written of similar actions taken by Jung, 'His children, for example, were not informed about his self-experiment and they did not notice anything unusual.'[43] While Jung was heavily involved in the creation of *The Red Book* through elaborate wakeful fantasies, his 'real' life continued unaffected. 'Each year, he continued his military service duties. Thus, he maintained his professional activities and familial responsibilities during the day, and dedicated his evenings to his self-explorations.'[44]

This gap between a tranquil, bourgeois exterior and the apparent convulsions in his interior life can lead to some questions of authenticity. Some would say that the gaping gap between pen and persona was proof that Jung was 'mad'. Summing up Jung's period of confrontation with his unconscious as a long-lasting intense period of psychosis has been a familiar diagnosis of many (particularly Freudian) critics. Jung himself was incredibly self-conscious and aware of this charge. The main reason he never published *The Red Book* in his lifetime was because he was sure that it would be derided by critics, and would further discredit his wider theories within international psychology. 'To the superficial observer, it will appear like madness,' he wrote in the Epilogue.[45]

A poet by and large gets a by on the madness charge. Certainly in the traditional Romantic view of the poet, the creative artist is expected to delve into the internal realm. There is of course the constant hazard of partaking in self-indulgent nonsense. As Harold Bloom has written, an ability to delve deep inside oneself and to remain disciplined enough to create artistic structure is the sign of a great writer. 'Self-awareness sought entirely for its own sake is a significant journey into the interior if you happen to be Hamlet or Paul Valery, but it is likely to collapse into solipsism for most of us.'[46] If the great artist reaches into his own psychic substratum and pulls out opaque and unique images, all the better it is for the poetry. At the beginning of *New Poems*, we are left in no doubt about the deadly serious nature of it all:

> *At such a time I wouldn't thank*
> *the Devil himself to knock at my door.*[47]

With an often deserved reputation for difficulty, erudition and exactitude in his poetry, and a career as successful civil servant and academic, Kinsella is not often portrayed as a starry-eyed poet with his mind engrossed in dreamy landscapes. He is not often included in the more mystical tradition of Irish poetry. Although he respects science, there is a sense, echoing Jung, that rationality can only explain so much of life's experience, and that modern society has turned its back on less quantifiable knowledge that is gleaned from custom, intuition or the internal psyche. In section 11 of *A Technical Supplement*, the so-called progress made by man is gently praised, although it is heavily qualified:

> *We have shaped and polished.*
> *We have put a little darkness behind us,*

we are out of that soup.
Into a little brightness
That soup.

The mind flexes.
The heart encloses.[48]

Man has developed far from the primordial soup, but the consequences of this development are dialectical, not unquestionably positive as the more one-sided celebrants of progress would make out. In section 10 of the same collection, the need to delve deep into this enclosed heart is expressed. A visit to an aquarium leads to an analogy with a visit to the dark underworld of the personal psyche, where ominous shadows may be found. But it is a place where knowledge and renewal can also be sourced, the type of positives that cannot be found merely in the rational, conscious mind.

We have to dig down,
sieve, scour and roughen;
make it all fertile and vigorous
– get the fresh rain down![49]

The poetry often compares the pen to a knife when describing the dissection of the psyche. The pen as scalpel, making incisions into the human body, is an important motif running throughout the often bloody descriptions of slaughterhouses and natural violence found in *A Technical Supplement*. In section 4 there is a detailed account of a physical incision and the wound it creates. The bloody image jumps to a wider evocation of the need for deep incisions into the psyche:

Blood welled up to fill the wound,
bathing the point as it went deeper.

Persist.
   Beyond a certain depth
it stands upright by itself
and quivers with borrowed life.

Persist.
   And you may find
the buried well. And take on
the stillness of a root.[50]

The incision into the psyche takes on a life of its own, as the objective contents of the collective unconscious, the *'borrowed life'*, begins to affect it. As with any incision or surgery, this carries risk, but however difficult this may be, to persist brings its rewards, in this case a more rooted sense of your own life. There is a prize to be found deep down through these incisions into the psyche. A *'buried well'* contains sustenance for the traveller on an internal quest. Finding the well allows the individual to become rooted, to have a deeper understanding of themselves and the forces that move them. A deep perspective of self-awareness allows the individual to find their feet.

In his collection most concerned with intense personal assessment, *Songs of the Psyche* (1985), the journey inwards reaches such obscurely personal realms that it is difficult for even the most sympathetic of readers to keep pace. Again, similar to sections of *A Technical Supplement*, the intention is set out. The narrator is to dig deep into himself, carefully facing the forgotten and ignored contents of his unconscious, with the hope of learning from this excavation.

But even in this difficult process, the prize at the end is marginal, not total:

> *There are certain*
> *ill-chosen spirits*
>
> *that cower close*
> *on innermost knowledge*
>
> *and must burrow with special care*
> *to find the shallowest peace.*[51]

Songs of the Psyche is an odd and controversial book in the *Peppercanister* series. Kinsella has rightly defended the collection from the criticism that it is wilfully and entirely obscure. Indeed, the opening 'Settings' section of the collection contains some of the poet's most evocative and accessible poetry about his childhood. However, the poet himself admits that *Songs of the Psyche* is a 'special book, dealing in intimate psychic things.'[52] He views the collection as an 'addition to accessible work. They don't replace it.' But the thirteen individual songs that make up the central series in the collection are obscure, as is to be expected from poetry that is unforgiving in its dealing with 'intimate psychic things.' Kinsella told an interviewer that three songs, at least, were accessible to the reader, but even if that is true, that leaves almost ten with various degrees of inaccessibility.[53]

Song nine, for instance, has a number of foxes at night in a city: '*a cistern hiss / in their erect ears / they are dreaming / one another.*'[54] Song three describes leaving meat outside an unidentified person's door, and '*then when you wake / rat small, rat still / you will carry her life / in our palms, rat self.*'[55] There is not enough detail in many of the songs to allow the reader to communicate sufficiently with their theme and tone. They seem to be a series of vignettes of the psyche, thrown up by the narrator's unconscious, but they are so individualised that it is difficult to connect. As a case study in proving the Jungian theory that deep personal psychological matter can have communal resonance, it seems that we may have reached the limits.

Some critics were confused by and disliked *Songs of the Psyche*, but the most intense of the criticism was unwarranted. The thirteen songs in the collection are prefaced and followed by a series of far more accessible poetry. In the songs themselves there are intriguing images and rhythms, not all of them easily communicable to the reader, but interesting nonetheless. The songs within the *Songs of the Psyche* collection are not representative of the poet's five-decade-long career. However, its difficult content, along with some other obscure poetry in earlier works, has become part of a familiar narrative surrounding the poet's development. Simply put, he wrote beautiful, elegant, accessible poetry in the beginning, and then, with his turn inward, the poetry became deliberately obscure and wantonly self-indulgent.

Such a timeline has, as the poet noted himself, become 'a fixed idea' among many critics.[56] But for it to be sustained, it needs to ignore much of Kinsella's output in the 1970s and 1980s, and to give undue primacy and importance to his most opaque poems. *Songs of the Psyche* is exceptional rather than typical in the work. For all that, it remains intriguing, brilliant in parts, enigmatic in sections and at times frustratingly impenetrable, the literary debris left from a full-frontal impact with the unconscious, fragmented and obscure.

Whatever the legacy of *Songs of the Psyche* in Kinsella's career, it does mark a moment when intimate psychic matter was to become a less overt part of the poetry. Beginning with *New Poems* in 1973, and ending with *Songs of the Psyche* in 1985, the work had often, though not always, had an overt interest in facing, digesting and dealing with the mythical and personal matter of the personal psyche of the poet. The 1985 collection represented a high point, or rather a deepest low dive in this Jungian confrontation with the personal consciousness. Personal psychological matter has remained in more recent editions to the *Peppercanister* series, but never in this uncompromising, almost systematic, manner.

It is interesting to speculate as to why this is. It seems reasonable to reject any suggestion that the poet felt that he had gone too far and had become too obscure for the critics and his tight readership. Negative criticism of his work since the early 1970s had not brought a halt to the pace of psychological speculation in his work. By 1985 his active readership was not large, and although *Songs of the Psyche* would have tested the capabilities and patience of readers, they had long been conditioned for challenging work from the poet.

The source of this change may well be found in the later pages of the collection itself, where there are hints at both a questioning of the fundamentals of Jungian psychology, and an almost contradictory sense that this psychological journey has resulted in some element of partial success.

In the thirteenth and final song, the narrator speaks positively of the benefits that such intimate psychological evaluation can bring to the individual:

> *Yet it* is *a matter*
>   *of negative release:*
> *of being thrown up*
>
> *out of a state of storm*

> *into a state of peace, or sleep,*
> *or a dream, or a system of dreams.*[57]

The '*state of storm*' is the social world we inhabit each day, and the thoughts that fill our conscious ego every moment. But through this process of individuation we can release some of the negative aspects of that world and find peace in the system that lies deep in our unconscious. This system of dreams, as the song later tells us, is full of mythical knowledge ('*dragon slayers; helpful animals*'), and finally, for the western mind at least, ends in the symbol of the cross. This is a concise outlining of the classic map of Jungian individuation and the hope for personal improvement that is to be found in the process.

But immediately following this hope, in the final three-lined stanza of the final song, the poem almost offhandedly questions the whole basis of this theory – and the whole basis for the songs themselves:

> *Unless the thing were to be based*
>   *on sexuality*
> *or power.*[58]

The sexuality focus of Freud and the power focus of various theorists including Adler and Marx may hold as much validity as Jung's theories, the poet narrator now seems to be contemplating. If the poet narrator applied their theories, would the poet get a different result?

Despite this questioning, predominately the tone is one of affirmation of the process. The journey in the collection ends in the poem 'Self-Renewal', which as the title suggests celebrates the marginal personal progress the narrator has made after his '*negative release*'. Sitting in front of his shaving mirror, the narrator's experience of individuation is set within the history of all private moments of self-reflection in human experience. Unlike the Oswald character in 'The Good Fight', who felt himself unique in his isolated plight, the narrator here knows that he is just another in a long historical line of solitary humans. Just like millions before him, he is facing his inner demons and trying to make life easier by gathering himself in a moment of silence before going out to face the day:

> *I peered into these*
> *and their velvet stirred*
> *with the pale secrets of all*
> *the lonely that had ever sat*
> *by their lonely mirrors*
>
> *studying the shame*
> *that had brought them to sit there*
> *and kiss the icy glass*
> *and recover themselves a little*[59]

Such a process is clearly open to a critique as unduly narcissistic and self-involved, but that the people kiss the glass and find only '*a little*' recovery provokes feelings of empathy rather than scorn in the reader. To learn to love oneself and what goes on within oneself is something that does not necessarily lead to overwhelming perceptions of self-importance. We are all united in our varying degrees of psychological maladjustments and problems. None of us is born complete; we are porous and puny. Some of us, like the poet narrator, may be on an individuation quest towards a more total response to life, but the journey is difficult and lonely. This moment of self-renewal in front of the mirror allows individuals to steady themselves alone for one moment, to make it that little bit easier to step forward into the world around them and face its ordeals:

> *with icy brow on brow,*
> *and one eye cocked at itself,*
> *until they felt more able*
> *to slip off about their business*
>
> *with the glass clouding over*
> *a couple of fading eye diagrams.*[60]

That this moment marked a change is given further evidence in the later *Peppercanister* edition, *One Fond Embrace* (1988), released three years after *Songs of the Psyche*. The opening of this long poem seems to indicate a change in direction: '*Enough / is enough / pouring over that organic pot.*'[61] The organic pot is associated with the cauldron and the cup of ordeal that have made appearances in some earlier work dealing with the internal psyche and mythology. The poet narrator has had enough of that for now, and the rest of *One Fond Embrace* turns to issues of political and economic change in Dublin and short appraisals of friends and enemies of the poet. It is focusing on matters in the external world. Later collections *Personal Places* (1990) and *Poems from Centre City* (1990) also, though not wholly, deal with matter outside the personal psyche. The centre of the city has an association with the totality that Kinsella says he was seeking in his numerological system, a centre point of observation with four points coming out from this home at the city's core.

If the inner journey has not stopped completely, it has become the main highway of literary pursuit for the poet to a lesser extent. It is a turn back to the world around rather than inside. As the narrator of *One Fond Embrace* pulls back from his work over the organic pot, he rubs his eyes and looks about his family home, full *'of prides and joys / bicycles and holy terrors / our grown and scattered loves.'*[62] His change of mood brings lightness to the surroundings, *'where, it occurs to me / I never want to be anywhere else.'*[63] That this thought only 'occurs', as if unexpected, signals to the reader that the narrator may have had his mind more focused, perhaps *too* focused, on other matters. The focus on what was within may have led to an imbalance in the poetry, and maybe life, with an undue neglecting of the world outside the personal psyche.

This uplifting appreciation for the life around him may have resulted from a turning away from the vigorous encounter with the material of his unconscious. As hinted in the final poems of *Songs of the Psyche*, however, the improved mood could also be part of the marginal benefit that such deep psychological investigation has brought. *One Fond Embrace* is not free of seething anger: developers, the local authority and politicians are all lashed at for their unthinking destruction of the architectural heritage of old Dublin in the pursuit of progress and profit. The unwanted developments around his area act as a call to action: *'It alerts me to knock my head.'* The poet will knock his head against the walls of his *'sagging district'*. Rather than lying down and going inside his head, the poet is now facing his skull outwards to encounter the malevolent figures doing damage in his neighbourhood.

But alongside this renewed outflung anger at society, reminiscent of much earlier poems like 'Nightwalker', there are snatches of warmth in *One Fond Embrace* that had been absent in Kinsella's work for some time. During the long poem, the narrator imagines calling up many of his ageing acquaintances for an impromptu lunch, and, despite their many faults, the host is feeling momentarily forgiving. '*Here's a hug while the mood is on me / Take your places around my table.*'⁶⁴

From the grub groping through empty space to the narrator hugging his guests and feeling content in his family home, it seems that some truth and help have been found in the many years spent searching what was within his psyche. It was now time to appreciate the daylight world a little more.

* * *

So what is one to make of the incredible influence Jung has had on the poetry of Thomas Kinsella? Has it been of benefit or a hindrance to the work?

Clearly, the adoption of Jungian psychological categories for the poet is not simply a new or innovative way of *interpreting* the world. Rather, it serves two major purposes in the writing.

Firstly, with the collapse of any meta-narratives or great dreams in which the writer can share a world view with his readership, the journey inwards has apparently provided a solution. What is ostensibly an individualistic, self-centred 'turn inward' actually proves to be a road to a more communicable mode of writing. For despite its deep focus on the individual as the primary focus of interest, Jung's theories claim to possess a universal and communal core. The collective unconscious is shared by all of humanity; in it resides a storehouse of knowledge and forms of thinking that everyone can access. It is independent of the individual. With the breakdown in the 'exterior' forms of collective ideology – organised religion, socialism, nationalism etc. – Jung postulates a point of ultimate collective experience in the very deepest core of the individual. It is easy to understand the attractiveness of this for isolated artists working in the era when great dreams are dying. Access this collective unconscious, and you reach across the void and write in a way that connects with your reader.

In the poem 'C. G. Jung's "First Years" ', from the collection *Songs of the Night and Other Poems* (1978), there is a telling poetic description of the collective unconscious: '*Dark waters churn amongst us / and whiten against troublesome obstacles.*'[65] The use of the phrase '*amongst us*', to describe the connectedness of this universal unconscious layer of myth, emphasises its communal aspect. For although the Jungian turn to deep personal matters may be seen to be the route of potential individualistic ruminations, it is rather a path that will eventually take you to a new form of connectedness with your fellow man. It is this eventual goal of commune through an individualistic search that is attractive to Kinsella, both as a poet and as a man living after the catastrophe. As a poet, it allows him to connect his audience with a shared heritage of mythical forms and archetypes. If we cannot march together as a class, a nation, a tribe or a religion, we can locate this lost dream of solidarity in the collective unconscious.

Secondly, the deployment of Jung's concepts is not just a literary device for making Kinsella's poetry understandable to the reader. Despite some doubts (expressed at the end of 'Songs of the Psyche'), Jung's theories seem to approach the same truths as the poetry - truths that more or less correspond to people's psychological reality. It is not merely a way of looking at the world, it *is* the world. You therefore do not have to read Jung or study his theories to understand his central concepts.

All of this has disappointed some of Kinsella's critics. Many of the more hostile responses amount to little more than expressions of disappointment that the days of the perfectly crafted sonnet have gone. However, there have been, and continue to be, perfectly reasonable, cogent questionings of whether Kinsella's 'turn inward' was ultimately successful.

Some say that this 'turn' unduly influences the tone and content of the poetry, making it work in service of a theoretical system (in this case, Jungian thought) rather than working according to its own rules. In fact, this is a problem of which Kinsella himself has shown awareness. In a 1996 interview with Ian Flanagan, Kinsella was honest about the appeal of hanging his art upon the structure of Jungian thinking. 'The temptation is to make maximum use of ideas from Jung,' he said. 'For me, the idea of making use of Jung's ideas is as fascinating as the original ideas themselves, encountering or dipping into Jung. The unconscious as such can't be fitted into a scheme. If you're trying to fit reality into a numerological construct, it can't be done.' Later, when discussing his poem 'Ely Place', Kinsella laughed at how easy it could be to retreat to a Jungian interpretation: 'I could make sense of it by falling back on Jung if I wanted to [laughs], but I'm not going to.'[66]

A second reasonable criticism is that Jung's theories and this confrontation with the unconscious contributes to some of the alleged incomprehensibility of the poetry. This is harsh when it comes to collections such as *New Poems* and *One,* which I suggest can be comprehended with thoughtful reading. With regard to later collections, however, like *Songs of the Psyche,* the case could be made that the poet narrator has entered his own psyche so deeply that it is hard for even the most motivated of readers not to lose connection. When questioned on the difficulty of this collection, Kinsella once answered rather unhelpfully: 'Well, they are quite clear to me.'[67]

Thirdly, it must be asked frankly, is this not all a bit too dramatic? Is this confrontation with the unconscious rendered in such melodramatic fashion that it is unbelievable? Is it really as hard as we are led to believe, when compared for instance to the hardship in the external world? Justin Quinn's questioning reflects the suspicion that there is an incongruent gap between the heightened drama of the poetry and real life. The poetry may be full of heroic drama and symbols of the pain and ordeal of the poet, but does this reflect the reality of life? 'What are these beasts symbols of? Which exact forces of historical change do they represent? This is never stated. Instead of helping us to gaze into the murky depths of national history and distinguish various agencies, the Jungian bestiary and locales only serve to heighten our awareness of the bravery of the poet in facing these things. And in the case of the artist we must ask, what exactly is the ordeal he undergoes when trying to comprehend history? It is clear that the politician who would change the course of a nation must face physical danger, but less clear in the case of the artist, especially one not living in a repressive regime.'[68]

In Kinsella's defence, he seems conscious of this possible critique, indeed his poem 'The Entire Fabric' from *One* works as a comic send-up of some of the gothic and heroic symbolism he deploys in his poetry:

A tableau rattled up from the crypt:
a man, sporting a striped jacket,
posed in confident quackery, bearded;
a woman, drawn up like a queen,

rouged and spangled. A round pot
bubbled on a stand between them
leaking a phosphorescent mist.[69]

Later in the poem, this bearded man, most likely the narrator himself, steps forward, ready to pronounce his poetry in this ridiculous setting:

He paced forward. A spotlight struck:
he peered in mock intensity,
a hand cupped behind an ear,
out of the waiting dark, as if
searching the distance. He made to speak.
Above the temple, in the flies,
a mechanism began to whirr.[70]

Kinsella has mentioned Joyce's *Finnegan's Wake* as an exemplary work, where readers and critics have often complained of becoming lost in the density and opaque writing. But the poet argues that if the material requires the writing to be superficially strange and inaccessible, then so be it: '[*Finnegan's Wake* is] a splendid example of a person staking their all on peculiarities and making it all function. It's all done with significant detail again. The lesson is to be content, to be as odd as you have to be, and all manner of things will be well again.'[71]

For Kinsella, the importance of Jung has been in helping to provide some sort of structure to art and communication with an audience.. It is part of the resistance when facing life's ordeals.

6
Resistance

The 1962 poem 'Chrysalides' from the *Downstream* collection evokes that period of light, yet bittersweet, timelessness experienced during the dusk of youth – timeless because it occurs in the period when time does not dominate, bittersweet because the nagging sense that change is coming has begun to pull a little. Two teenage brothers spend a summer holiday together in an era of personal history where nothing of lasting significance seems to happen. It is episodic rather than purposeful, and there is little occurring except for the smooth process of lazy fun. This is all remembered later in maturity, when nostalgia is needed to contrast with the daily difficulties of adulthood:

> *Our last free summer we mooned about at odd hours*
> *Pedalling slowly through country towns, stopping to eat*
> *Chocolate and fruit, tracing our vagaries on the map.*[1]

Time is not animated here. It is not being fought against; rather, the young brothers are unconstrained by it. It does not rule the young, as their day, free of routine, denies any rhythmic schedule '*Sleeping too little or too much, we awoke at noon.*' Late nights are still youthful, time to eat, not sleep, as the possibilities of early hope momentarily overwhelm the driving certainties and social customs of time:

> *To the unique succession of our youthful midnights,*
> *When by a window ablaze softly with the virgin moon*
> *Dry scones and jugs of milk awaited us in the dark,*[2]

There are long cycles, late-night dances and '*the lurch of melodeon music.*' This is more than the remembrance of an unforgettable last summer: what is presented is the evocation of a different style of life – a style of life lived, however momentarily, by the young people in their '*last free summer*' before their freedom was overwhelmed by the accruements of adulthood, careers, families, mortgages.

It is the inclusion of the word '*free*' that moves the early stanzas of 'Chrysalides' from mere pleasant description into the more philosophical realm. Like Camus with his celebration of his home coastal city in his 1936 essay 'Summer in Algiers', 'Chrysalides' contains a strong identification between an aimless life unconstrained by time-sensitive duties and a vision of ultimate freedom.[3] It is active resistance against time restrictions. For Camus, 'In Algiers whoever is young and alive finds sanctuary and occasion for triumphs everywhere: in the bay, the sun, the red and white games on the seaward terraces, the flowers and sports stadiums, the cool-legged girls ... every summer morning seems to be the first in the world. Each twilight seems to be the last.'[4]

'Chrysalides', like Camus's 'Summer in Algiers', conjures a world that is prelapsarian, with all the positive and negative aspects that this entails. While the paradise of youthful freedom sings with unfettered aimlessness, it also lacks struggle. This absence of struggle means no ordeal, which also entails no learning or history. But it would not be Kinsella's style just breezily to evoke an idyllic and hopeful time without the shadow of disappointment casting itself ominously over proceedings. The dialectic of hope and disappointment is at the core of his world view. So, after the young holidaymakers happily tuck into their late-night feast of milk and scones, the final stanza groans:

> *Or to lasting horror, a wedding flight of ants*
> *Spawning to its death, a mute perspiration*
> *Glistening like drops of copper, agonised, in our path.*[5]

The evocation of sweat, agony and death on the path points to the struggles ahead. There is an echo of the lost youth in 'Chrysalides' in snapshots of other poems. In the 1985 'Phoenix Street', rooting through his father's old cupboard, the poet comes across paraphernalia from optimistic young adulthood. He finds a collection of books from his father's book club (Ruskin, Engles, Carlyle, Shakespeare), and beside them an old photograph of the archetypal band of brothers. The image is of hopeful friendship, a group of men ready for the adventure ahead:

> *a brown photograph*
>
> *with four young men*
> *dressed up together*
> *and leaning together in laughter.*[6]

The correlation between the possibilities of childhood education and an innocent belief in the capacity to understand everything is found in 'Model School, Inchicore', also published in 1985. In the poem, the poet reminisces about the opening stage of his educational journey, with his high hopes in its possibility:

> *In the second school we had Mr Browne.*
> *He had white teeth in his brown man's face.*
>
> *He stood in front of the blackboard*
> *and chalked a white dot.*
>
> *'We are going to start*
> *decimals.'*
>
> *I am going to know*
> *everything.*[7]

In the mind of this eager child who is thirsty for education, the future is an expanse to be conquered. It is the locus of future adventure, of coming wisdom. It is not to be feared. Even the seasonal changes that demark the cycle of birth and death do not strike fear into this young child and his friends. In the schoolyard they gather the debris of annual autumnal loss, and vault over it, fearless:

> *When the Autumn came*
> *and the big chestnut leaves*
> *fell all over the playground*
> *we piled them in heaps*
> *between the wall and the tree trunks*
> *and the boys ran races*
> *jumping over the heaps*
> *and tumbled into them shouting.*[8]

In 'Artists' Letters', a mature poet searching in old boxes for something stumbles across early love letters penned to his beloved. The sight of these early epistles first provokes embarrassment, but on closer inspection the poet begins to have some respect for his youthful self, admiring the energy and sense of importance that comes with inexperience. *'Letter by letter the foolishness / deepened, but displayed / a courage in its own unsureness.'*[9] The spirit of breathless pursuit of his beloved is linked to the innocence and passion of youth. Extracts from the lines in the letters read as well-intentioned but bombastic dramatic statements. *'There is one throw, no more'*, *'There is / a poverty of spirit in the wind / a shabby richness in braving it.'*[10] The big, confident pronouncements on such matters belie his youth and echo similar language in the poet's early poetry. There is an unironic seriousness resembling the educated air of boredom of Stephen Dedalus in Joyce's *Ulysses*. That there is a positive to this budding enthusiasm is noted, however, that it is fleeting and flawed is also confronted in 'Artists' Letters'. Such early youthful confidence, not based on experience, is something familiar to many writers. The British author Zadie Smith has noted that, when surveying her early multi-award winning writing, 'It is full of aphorisms, full of moral little sentences. Young people are full of that kind of stuff, they are very certain, they think they know what is going on. As you get older in my experience that all disappears, I don't write aphorisms anymore because I have no idea what is going on.'[11]

But, as is to be expected in the Kinsellian world view, the enthusiasm of youth is not one-sidedly celebrated as comprehensively resistant to the ordeals of life. A more malevolent, atavistic side of childhood is recalled in 'St Catherine's Clock', where the night's darkness is brightened by the children's fire on the street. These piles of leaves are not leaped over playfully, but gathered together with other rubbish and set fire to. The light illuminates occasions of bullying and brutality:

> *The Night crept*
> *among our chalk signs on the path*
> *and trickled down into the shores.*
>
> *The moon hung round and silver*
> *out over the empty Back*
> *between the backs of the peoples' houses*
>
> *where we piled the rubbish up*
> *on the clay in the dark*
> *and set it on fire and talked into the flames*
>
> *and skipped around in wickedness*
> *with no mercy on the weak or the fat*
> *or the witless or the half blind.*[12]

Childhood does not offer a refuge from the difficulties of life. It has its own cruelties, its own shadow side. The chalk signs, remnants of innocent daytime games, give way to a more savage scene. The deployment of words like *'shores'*, *'half blind'* and the colloquial *'backs'* accumulate to produce a wicked psychological hue to the setting. Childhood has a nasty nighttime, which is analogous to the dark aspects of our unconscious. It is not all optimistic learning and fun times in the playground.

Thus, hopeful youth is mirrored by its cruel shadow side in the poetry. Indeed, in the sense that youth is celebrated at all, it is always within the constant shadow of decay and death. 'The Messenger' contains some of the most heartbreaking contrasts between the heroism of youth and the decay of old age. The poet's father is showing off in front of fellow Guinness workers with an act of bravery by walking across a steel beam high above his work floor. But that image immediately bleeds into the onset of illness that would eventually kill him – the heart-stopping, extroverted excitement of his daredevil feet in the racking shed becomes the final internal heartbeats of his life:

and dared with outstretched arms
what might befall.

And it befell that summer,
after the experimental doses,
that his bronchi wrecked him with coughs

and the muffled inner
heartstopping little
hammerblows began.[13]

Towards the final section of the poem, John Paul Kinsella is a young boy with '*bright*' eyes and '*all excitement: arms akimbo*', energetic and brimming with vigour as he begins his job as a messenger boy, '*shoes polished, and a way to make in the world.*' He gets on his Post Office bicycle and turns to depart the scene with a burst of vitality:

through the shop and into the street.
It faces uphill. The urchin mounts. I see
a flash of pedals. And a clean pair of heels![14]

The '*uphill*' is the cautionary word here, as this is the topography of everyone's life, even if the young are unaware.

For as the teenage John departs the poem on wheels in a blistering blast, he reappears a few short lines later, rolling in on his final set of wheels:

He rolled on rubber tyres
out of the chapel door. The oak box
paused gleaming in the May morning air

and turned, sensing its direction.[15]

In 'The Secret Garden', the narrator looks down at a young child and wonders how he is to prepare for the uphill battle of life: '*How set him free, a son, toward the sour encounter?*' The child is unaware of the topography of life ahead, but this ignorance is not celebrated. The bloom of youth is darkened by the '*sour encounter*' – how best to let him freely face this unavoidable destiny? The youth cannot live in the protective cocoon of the secret garden. Even the dew of the early morning is destined to experience the ordeal of the day:

The sun climbs, a creature of one day,
And the dew dries to dust.
My hand strays out and picks off one sick leaf.[16]

Youth is conflated with the unexamined life in 'The Little Children' from the *Songs of the Psyche* collection. Much like an adult who has yet truly to examine their personal psyche and to begin the individuation process, a child does not possess a rounded conception of what makes them act. Rather than seeing life as a process of ordeals, where one learns something from each confrontation with difficulty, childhood is often experienced as a series of new engagements, each leaving little legacy:

> *Incurious about his own*
> >   *breaking and renewing energies,*
> *his developing and abandoned purposes,*
> >   *he fixes the pieces in and upon each other*
>
> *in a series of beginnings*
> >   *with feathery touches and brutal fumblings,*
> *in stupefying waste, brooding and light.*[17]

But childhood innocence does not make it more authentic than adulthood. For out of the mouth of youths, Kinsella does not hear truth, but often an aspiration towards a false unity, a naivety that is not so much charming, but embarrassingly confident. In 'Baggot Street Deserta', the poet criticises his own youthful artistic attempts at writing *'a private masterpiece'*, but is honest enough to say that its source is *'doctored recollections'*. The young writer's musings on the great issues of truth and beauty are faintly ridiculous, for he has not yet endured enough of life truly to understand; he has not dissected enough the complexity of life. The bravado of his early life, like the morning dew, will evaporate as experience grows:

> *Truth*
> *Concedes, before the dew, its place*
> *In the spray of dried forgettings Youth*
> *Collected when they were a single*
> *Furious undissected bloom.*
> *A voice clarifies when the tingle*
> *Dies out of nerves of time:*
> Endure and let the present punish.[18]

Looking back on his early career, Kinsella has said: 'I think at the beginning my poems were influenced by literature more than by fact.'[19] When only the early period of life has been lived, acquiring knowledge from art rather than experience is often the only route available to the young writer. In Ireland, for a young poet in the 1950s, with Yeats as a 'looming shadow over all our works and days,' the influence of Yeats and his contemporaries was very strong.[20] All writers, critic Harold Blooms claims, suffer from some element of anxiety of influence – the anxiety is 'achieved in a literary work, whether or not its author even felt it.'[21] Kinsella's early poems do not read like Yeats, and they lack any overtly Irish theme, but he is influenced by the Yeatsian legacy even by reacting against it. Kinsella, in much of his early poetry, 'strives to go beyond' narrow Irish experience, as Augustine Martin has written.[22] In this conscious striving to resist the influence of the Irish tradition, we can see the symptoms of Bloom's influence anxiety. Thus, the most crucial early poetic influence was not an Irish poet like Yeats or even Austin Clarke, whom Kinsella came to know personally and admire, but the English poet Auden. Kinsella has said that the influence of Auden was not 'an escape, but an entry into poetry.'[23] But it is hard not to conclude that locating an influence outside the modern Irish canon was some act of resistance by a young poet finding his literary legs. That the influence was colossal on the early poetry has been admitted by Kinsella: 'For a while, I wrote only imitations of Auden,' he said in 1989.[24]

In 'Baggot Street Deserta', the River Liffey works as a metaphor for the journey of the artist and his life:

> *Tucked in the mountains, many miles*
> *Away from its roaring outcome, a shy*
> *Gasp of waters in the gorse*
> *Is sonneting origins.*[25]

The association of youth with sonnets mirrors the poet's own career, where structured poetic metre, deeply influenced by Auden, marked his early work. Borrowed literary convention rather than real, lived experience is the most important influence on much of his first poetry. As the poet becomes more confident and experienced, he reaches a greater level of authenticity; no longer 'shy', his work is confidently 'roaring' out to the world.

What amounts in Kinsella's work to a rejection of youth as resistant to life's ordeal is not merely because of the obvious fact that youth passes and death closes in. Rather, it is to be found in the deeper philosophical and psychological approach the poet has made towards adulthood and growth. The poet's oft-quoted declaration in 'Mirror in February', *'for they are not made whole / That reach the age of Christ'*[26] encapsulates an important mindset that guides his poetry. Rather than regarding growth and individual development as primarily a process confined to childhood, Kinsella sees growth as the central task of adulthood. A person who reaches 33 is not a 'whole' adult, and still has much to be getting on with when it comes to individual growth. Kinsella rejects the perception, held by many, that childhood is a process and adulthood merely a final state.

It was not long before Kinsella's poetry broke free of pure literature and turned to face reality around him. 'Baggot Street Deserta' is a work that can already be described as mature, and it was published early in his career. It is with mature adulthood that a more nuanced art and life can come, and if you are not 'made whole' by 33, then there is plenty of becoming to be done, much dissecting to do.

Thus, Kinsella's poetry rarely suffers from an unbalanced sentimentalising of childhood, nor is it burdened with the all-knowing arrogance that can grip and entrap many adults. Like Jung, the poet regards the second half of life as the most important period for the individual. Rather than solidifying your notions and world view, it should be a time of challenge and flux. Cynics may say that this is intellectualising the common mid-life crisis, but Jung built his most important theories of psychological development upon his studies of the adult mind rather than the child's. Jung once wrote that two-thirds of his patients were in the second half of life, and many were suffering what he termed 'the general neurosis of our age', which was a sense of ennui and aimlessness.[27] This understanding that much of an individual's personal development will take place in the second half of life can lead to an understandable element of bemoaning of what could have been. In the opening song of *Songs of the Psyche*, the narrator is regretful that in his youth he did not understand the need for deep personal growth, and how it was essential for all humans to investigate their own psyche.

> *Why had I to wait until I am graceless,*
> *unsightly, and a little nervous of stooping*
> *until I could see*
>
> *through those clear eyes I had once?*[28]

But there is no point lingering on this. Youth, in the Jungian view of personal development, is by its very nature less reflective. People spend the early part of their life establishing and differentiating themselves, getting educated, finding love, building a family and home. The focal point for the child and young adult is out rather than in. It is in middle age when the narrator realises the importance of confronting the personal psyche, '*But I settled back and / turned inward.*'²⁹

In the 1973 'Tear', the poet as a child has refused to kiss his dying grandmother because of a mixture of fear and disgust. His youthful refusal is contrasted sharply with the actions of old age. While the child cannot face death, the older family members, like his grandfather sitting in the kitchen, are more capable of assimilating the grim faith.

> *Old age can digest*
> *anything: the commotion*
> *at Heaven's gate – the struggle*
> *in store for you all your life.*³⁰

But the irony is clear. Although by the time of old age a person may have accumulated so much knowledge that they can '*digest / anything*', what is '*in store for you all your life*' is already, mostly, over. The kiss is not given in 'Tear' more out of childhood fear than any expression of will. But in a poem decades later, 'Dura Mater', from the 1990 *Personal Places* collection, the adult narrator refuses to kiss his elderly mother on the lips or cheek as she implores him in Dublin dialect to '*Come here to me. Come here to me, my own son.*' In this case, the narrator wilfully withholds the kiss to lips or cheeks to the chagrin of his imposing mother. Instead, he plants his lips on the hardness of her forehead. In both poems, kisses are withheld. But it is only after the narrator has become an adult in 'Dura Mater', and reached such a level of self-assuredness, that the decision is made from a position of strength.

Not all middle-aged people realise this. Unchecked by individuation, the older person can develop one-sided characteristics – they become stuck in their ways. In

'Breakdown' from the *Littlebody* collection (2000), an elderly person has become irritated and coarse. Although the onset of some mental illness like Alzheimer's is hinted at, the central character is an extreme example of a one-sided older person, whose personality now displays *'infantile stubbornness.'* There is *'the exaggeration of established traits'*, personality development has halted, and irritation has become *'the dominant mood.'* This is a personality as solid state rather than growing development.

By implication, the poet is almost promoting an active adulthood/retirement policy to resist the onset of unhealthy established traits. An active mind as well as body is helpful in resisting the unwanted solidification of a negative psyche. But things do not have to be as extreme as 'Breakdown' for problems to become apparent. In 'Brothers in the Craft', the poem looks at the inter-generational relationships between the young promising writer and the older, established artist. There is mention of Kinsella as a younger poet in the 1950s, and how he and his contemporaries looked up to Austin Clarke. The poem warns of the pitfalls of *'the imbalance of growth'* in the older person. The ageing artist grown solid and unquestioning in his ways can become slightly destabilised by the presence of younger writers with fresh ideas. The elder's reaction to this may be defensive, but in the more perceptive older person, such interaction should be regarded as an opportunity for growth and renewal:

> *In the elder, an impulse against the settled state*
> *when the elements work in balance against each other*
> *in worn stability, no longer questioned,*[31]

Thus, interaction between the generations can help to prevent the old person from becoming stuck in their ways, youthful companionship acting as a source of fresh impetus, helpfully destabilising the world of the elder. The one-sided elder will react defensively, but the understanding elder will regard the youth as an enabling figure, providing an opportunity to learn afresh. The relationship is dialectical, with the youth also finding an archetypal 'old person' figure from whom to learn, much like the young poet did in 'Dick King'.

If youth is flawed, middle to old age is not pristine either. Even the individuated person, the older individual who has confronted his psyche and has learned much, cannot escape the process of mutability. The well-rounded individual must face the end, even if they are on surer footing than their contemporary who has lived the largely unexamined life. In the opening lines of 'The Messenger', when Kinsella's father has become old and is dying, it is as if his once-pulsating masculinity has been replaced. We are told: '*His mother's image settled on him*' at the end, and he was now '*unmanned*', walking around '*corded*' into his dressing gown.

In section 20 of *A Technical Supplement*, there is an image of old age, chilling in its simplicity:

Loneliness. An odour of soap.
To this end must we come,
deafened with spent energy.[32]

But this stark truth does not lead the narrator to despair, for after a further description of creeping mortality, there is a defence of the potential of individuation to make the whole thing that little bit easier:

And so the years propel themselves onward
toward that tunnel, and the stink of fear.

> — *We can amend that. (Time permits*
> *a certain latitude. Not much,*
> *but a harmless re-beginning.)*

> *'And so the years propel themselves*
> *onward on thickening scars toward*
> *new efforts of propulsion...* [83]

The narrator's claims for individual development, for individuation, are therefore humble. The process of facing your internal psyche and developing as an individual cannot halt the inevitable process of deterioration and death, but it does allow a certain freedom, a little bit of resistance, with the '*harmless re-beginning*'. A concept of a second life, a rebirth in adulthood, is an almost playful response to the slender sliver of latitude that time grants us. By using this opportunity available to us, we can launch a rejuvenated beginning and experience new '*efforts of propulsion*'. We will still be propelled in the same direction towards the inevitable end, but at least the experience of that journey will be slightly fresh, and new learning can take place.

* * *

Thomas Kinsella's early ornate and structured poetry is predominately love poetry. His first collection was written as a wedding present to his wife, Eleanor. In poems like 'A Lady of Quality', although his partner's illness sets the scene, the tone and theme is of the ability of love to be resilient:

> *In hospital where windows meet*
> *With sunlight in a pleasing feat*
> *Of airy architecture*

> *My love has sweets and grapes to eat,*
> *The air is like a laundered sheet,*
>   *The world's a varnished picture*
>
> *Books and flowers at her head*
> *Make living-quarters of her bed*
>   *And give a certain style*
> *To our pillow-chat, the nonsense said*
> *To bless the room from present dread*
>   *Just for a brittle while.*[34]

The wordplay on '*brittle*' for little says much of Kinsella's conception of love and life. But in this poem, and other early work, the potential of love to defeat life's difficulties is characterised in a relatively traditional manner.

By the time of the 1968 collection, *Wormwood*, however, there has developed a devastating honesty towards the practice of love, especially love based in a long-term relationship. Admirable, cringeworthy and naked, the poet poured his brutal honesty into a series of poems in *Wormwood*. Eleanor Kinsella has publicly spoken about her own sadness and anger at the content of some of the poems.[35] The poems dealing with married life are far from the wondrous idyll of the early work. There is a common domestic ordeal here, with much to be learned with each difficult incident. In the final section of his epic 'Nightwalker', the poet concludes that love is as much about what you learn from struggles together as it is about passion.

> *I believe now that love is half persistence,*
> *A medium in which from change to change*
> *Understanding may be gathered.*[36]

In the opening poems of the *Wormwood* collection, the draining nature of domestic rows gives an eternally autumnal tone to the poetry, as in 'First Light':

> *A prone couple still sleeps.*
> *Light ascends like a pale gas*
> *Out of the sea: dawn-light*
> *Reaching across the hill*
> *To the dark garden. The grass*
> *Emerges, soaking with grey dew.*[37]

The '*Lover and beloved*' have '*raved and wept*' into the night with a regular and unwanted '*vigil*'. The next morning the child upstairs begins to cry loudly:

> *– A child enduring a dream*
> *That grows, at the first touch of day,*
> *Unendurable.*[38]

In 'Mask of Love', a conflicted couple are: '*Face to face / Across the narrow abyss.*'[39] But the so near but yet so far nature of their division makes the anger and stresses all the more intense:

> *That our very bodies lack peace:*
> *In tiny darknesses*
> *The skin angrily flames,*
> *Nerve gropes for muscle*
> *Across the silent abyss.*[40]

In 'Remembering Old Wars', there is a violent snap in the poem's first question. The reader is left reeling from its directness:

> *What clamped us together? When each night fell we lay down*
> *In the smell of decay and slept, our bodies leaking,*
> *Limp as the dead, breathing that smell all night.*[41]

The final stanza of the poem contains the darkest, most demoralised lines within the collection:

> *And so on, without hope of change or peace.*
> *Each dawn, like lovers recollecting their purpose,*
> *We would renew each other with a savage smile.*[42]

If these poems outline in painful honesty the nature of the ordeal of love, there is also much that can be learned from this, not least of which is a new understanding about how love can be strengthened, or at least persisted with. In a short prose introduction to the *Wormwood* collection, the poet tells his 'Beloved' that they must drink from the bitter cup if they are to transmute and allow their love to persist. Ordeals by their nature are horrible, but if dealt with and digested, they can be a source of renewal and resistance. 'This bitter cup is offered, heaped with curses, and we must drink or die,' writes the poet. 'And even though we drink we may also die, if every drop of bitterness – that rots the flesh – is not transmuted.... Love also, it seems, will continue until we fail: in the sensing of the wider scope, in the growth toward it, in the swallowing and absorption of bitterness, in the resumed innocence.'[43]

This concept of love as process and endurance is certainly celebrated in the long poem, 'Phoenix Park', which brings the *Wormwood* collection to a close. While it has been judged by one critic to be one of the 'great love poems' of twentieth-century Irish literature, you may not find 'Phoenix Park' in any of the many selections of Irish love poetry that are to be found on bookshelves.[44] For this is no easy lyrical celebration of Eros, it is rather a long, grinding exploration of the difficulties inherent in long-term love, and how its positive factors are hard-won, but precious – not only as a source of balm and comfort within a difficult life, but also as a type of weapon to help a person deal with the ordeals of life. Love itself here is a form of resistance.

The poem is certainly among Kinsella's greatest, and opens at an important point in his life. Eleanor's continuing health difficulties haunt the poem, and at its core the couple have to make a life-changing decision on whether to move full time to the United States. On a trip to hospital in the Phoenix Park, Eleanor wonders why the poet no longer writes her love poems. There is a conclusion in the poem that loving companionship demands the giving of some of your own self, but this must be done carefully, because to give can rip you asunder. Early in the poem, the narrator writes: 'I had learned / Giving without tearing is not possible.'[45] Later in the poem, the logical conclusion of this tearing is outlined:

> *Giving without tearing*
>
> *Is not possible: to give totality*
> *Is to be torn totally, a nothingness*
> *Reaching out in stasis a pure nothingness.*[46]

This is not merely a defence of the autonomy of the individual, and it is also more than a reluctance to surrender totally to another, an act often valorised in romantic discourse. Rather, the poet narrator concludes that the giving of oneself totally is both bad for the individual and the relationship – it leaves nothingness. Jung wrote that a satisfactory relationship with others, including your lover, could only come about after the individual had truly come to terms with their own psyche. 'Companionship thrives only when each individual remembers his individuality and does not identify themselves with others.'[47] What the male poetic voice wants from woman is contradictory, and at least partially patriarchal. In 'Artists' Letters', as the narrator reminisces over the early love letter he sent to his partner, he approvingly sees his muse look with '*shocked and shining*' eyes at his advances. This combination of innocence and knowledge is an important part of the female figure in Kinsella's poems. Eleanor has been his great muse throughout the decades of his output. 'More often than not, the prevailing notion of a muse is that they are women. Usually they are beautiful, commonly they are mute and impossibly and perhaps unselfconsciously graceful.'[48] In the poetry, Eleanor fits this classical definition of the muse, but her role as the inspiration behind the work is often more nuanced than that.

Love, like most other things in Kinsella, is hard-won, or at least it is presented as much as a matter of persistence as it is passion. This poetic mythologising of personal life is conscious, but does not stem from a feeling of grandiosity. By incorporating the everyday and ordinary into the language of the mythic and extraordinary, Kinsella is sketching the private realm of love and family onto a much larger canvas. By doing so he links the particular to the universal, making what may seem petty in a narrow sense come alive with much wider significance in a universal setting. As Maurice Harmon observes, this method 'validates personal experiences by relating them to archetypal actions so that particular incidents become part of a universal tapestry of events.'[49]

In 'Phoenix Park', the couple leave a pub in Lucan village. As they stand in the Main Street, the poet watches as his partner fixes her scarf. The movements are specific, and apparently of little note, but the poem places the actions in the overall structure of the female anima, the muse:

> *You wait a minute on the path, absently*
> *— Against massed brown trees — tying a flimsy scarf*
> *At your neck. Fair Elinor. O Christ thee save.*
> *And I taste a structure, ramshackle, ghostly,*
> *Vanishing on my tongue, given and taken,*
>
> *Distinct. A ghost of that ghost persists, structure*
> *Without substance, all about us, in the air,*[50]

She is the unconscious mythical image of womanhood that man has within him, in Jungian terms, the anima. The structure of the anima is inherited, but its substance and content changes in different circumstances. Here, it is Eleanor moving her scarf. In the Ashling poetry of the Gaelic poets it is in the form of the female ghost figure appearing in front of the poet. In the opening sequence in 'The Familiar', Eleanor as the female figure of *'Comely Wisdom'* is an image of understanding and knowledge, again wearing *'a scarf around Her throat.'* The capital 'H', in 'Her' points to the general rather than merely personal meaning behind this vision. This is not just his wife, this is womankind, looking back at man from outside, and inside as his anima.

As Thomas H. Jackson has written, those seeking some easy resolution in this poetry will be disappointed, for resolution is 'not an aspect of Kinsella's outlook.'[51] But if love through resolution is not apparent, then love through endurance is. In the final lines of 'Nightwalker', the midnight suburban prowler returns to his home. He sees the shadow of his partner in the kitchen. It is an image both positive and threatening:

> *Her dear shadow on the blind.*
> *The breadknife. She was slicing and buttering*
> *A loaf of bread. My heart stopped. I starved for speech.*[52]

The shadow is not just his beloved, but his own female psyche, as well as female archetypes representing Ireland and the Great Mother. The shadow holds a knife, which can both create and enable ('*buttering*'), but also threaten ('*slicing*'). The female figure is not wholly enabling; she carries threats within her. But the combination of positivity and negativity means that any long-term, real relationship with your lover will always be complex and difficult. There is no happy, uncomplicated tale of romance that endures without glitches. 'Nightwalker' comes to a somewhat stuttering stop with a sincere appraisal of long-term love as a place where '*Understanding may be gathered / Hesitant, cogitating, exit.*'[53]

The long-term prospects of love are faced in Kinsella's art. There is a focus on the early formative moments between the lovers, but it is to his credit that the process and grind of making a relationship work are dealt with. This is the period when a relationship has long established its rhythm, a time that is often neglected in art. The passionate openings and the destructive endings of relationships have been the more typical historical focus of the writer, but in Kinsella's work the long-term relationship, in this case in the form of a marriage, is the subject of close appraisal and the inspiration for so much of his poetry. Catriona Clutterbuck has said that Kinsella 'celebrates marriage as a lifelong accumulating act of invitation and response, of offering and answer. Where the consensual, the repeated reopening of yourself to another, as of the dark to the light, is one of our truest names for creativity. The art of Thomas Kinsella is, for me, a marriage art.'[54]

The female is not just the object and source of romantic love; she is also an important enabling figure in terms of art. In a later collection, *The Familiar* (1999), the poet reminisces about his bachelor days where he lived in his 'cell' in Baggot Street, '*on my own, fumbling at the neglect.*' The early, pre-Eleanor poet is often portrayed in unflattering images in the poetry as almost lost and dishevelled. But in this sequence of vignettes, which transcend the early period and later period of married life (before children and after children had left the home), Eleanor's impact is vital.

The narrator reminisces over the early sexual intensity of young love: '*Bending above me / with busy neck / and loose locks / my mind black,*'[55] but it is the later, mature love that is also articulated and given prominence. The older couple, now living in the countryside, share a breakfast prepared by the poet. The slow, methodical, caring creation of the meal ('*I sliced the tomatoes in thin discs / in damp sequence into their dish*'[56]) wins the gentle affection of his partner: '*You are very good. You always made it nice.*' Husband and wife, sharing a life over decades with the simple ritual of breakfast.

It is interesting to note that children are absent from both scenes – in the early one they are yet to make an appearance, and in the later one they are not in the family home. It is the horizontal relationship between the lovers, not the vertical one between parents and children, that is the poetic focus here. More often art that deals with established marriages does so with the family as a whole unit, but in 'The Familiar' the relationship between poet and beloved retains its own separate validity throughout the decades.

Love, it seems, cannot conquer all, as its most impassioned supporters preach. Kinsella, particularity in the *Wormwood* collection, displayed incredible honesty in laying bare the often torrid difficulties that many couples experience. But he concludes that love is often to be found in the endurance and learning from the struggle. By doing so, the poetry portrays romantic love as a form of resistance to the difficulties of life. Whether intensely physical or a more laid back form of companionship, romantic love cannot defeat the ordeal, but on the margins it can help to 'make it nice'. That in itself is a form of resistance.

* * *

Another form of resistance to the ordeal of life proposed in Kinsella's poetry is Eastern philosophy, particularly the Tao.

In section 18 of *A Technical Supplement,* there is a sweeping overview of the breadth of eastern thought:

Asia: great deserts of grass
with poppies and distant cities trembling
in the golden wind. Whole centuries
(if I have it even partly right)
valuing passive watchfulness – not to fuss.[57]

However, following this slight engagement with the history of Eastern religion, it seems to be immediately contrasted with the rationalist tradition of 'Western' scientific thinking.

Ah well.
  Grind it up, wash it down,
stoke the blind muscular furnace,

> *keep the waste volatile*
> *— sieve it: scoop and shake, shiver and tilt.*
>
> *Reach up expertly in your shiny boots,*
> *tinker and trim, empty your oil-can*
> *into the hissing navels, tap the flickering dials,*
> *study the massive shimmering accurate flywheels.*[58]

The traditions are laid out in stark divergence with the Western mode of thinking — one that is full of action, measurement and intervention, while the Eastern way is one of inaction, not fussing and sitting back. Kinsella may share with Jung, Arthur Schopenhauer (1788–1860) and other Western thinkers a belief that the Eastern way can provide at least some respite from the incessant ordeal of striving and its resulting disappointment. For Jung, the Tao was analogous to the search for a psychic whole within the individual. Tao is thus a sense of contentment that can only come from a perfect balance between the unconscious and conscious parts of the person's psyche — the calm, rounded personality. 'To rest in Tao means fulfilment, wholeness, one's destination reached, one's mission done, the beginning, end and perfect realisation of the meaning of existence innate in all things.'[59]

In the poem 'Downstream', the opening line contrasts the violent complexity of the western world with the apparent harmony (represented by a pearl) of the east. The poet narrator and a companion then begin to paddle slowly downriver.

> *The West a fiery complex, the East a pearl,*
> *We gave our frail skiff to the slow-moving stream,*
> *Ruffling the waters. And steadied on a seam*
> *Of calm and current.*[60]

The river symbolises the simple, organic flow of nature, the way of the Tao. The companions talked of poetry and *'drifted in peace'*, but the soothing early evening begins to give way to darkness and *'gathering shades beginning to deceive.'* Their small boat ruffles the water, and the tone is relaxed and flowing. It all feels natural, with a lulling sense of hope that things will always be this smooth. But once the decision is taken to make land, things become grimmer and disappointment welcomes the first footfall.

The easy river flow of nature is replaced by obstacles that must be negotiated, such as thorns and bushes. No longer just pulled along by the current, the companions *'clambered out'*, holding onto a branch with difficulty. This landing scene is far from auspicious. The thorns speak of coming danger, and the easy flow of the boat along the water has been replaced by the unsteady exit onto the river bank.

> *He coughed,*
> *Standing against the sky. I took my turn,*
> *Standing on the earth, staring aloft*[61]

The ominous cough speaks of disease to come. It is as if illness is in the soil, as if the ultimate point of the sea or river journey brings with it inherent diseased disappointment. The ultimate destination of life's journey is death, preceded often by increasing illness. The woods on the river bank are dark, unwelcoming and a place of active death and decay – the opposite of the Tao. The night is *'The black cage closed about us,'* and the land is full of dangerous animals. In this dark place, the poet narrator recalls a story of a dead body that was found in the woods. This sparks further contemplation about the deaths of millions in the twentieth century's major wars. The flow of the river is gone, and replaced by earthbound death. It is as if the earth itself is intervening to feast itself on human life:

> *The soil of other lands*
> *Drank lives that summer with a body thirst.*[62]

The river allowed non-interference; the men were taken along its natural way by its own energy. The earth is different, violently consuming human life with a basic dichotomy between water and land, east and west, the Tao and interference. The flow of water is an exceptionally important concept in Taoist thinking.

In 'Tao and Unfitness at Inistiogue on the River Nore', Kinsella deploys the teachings of the Tao in a practical way as a form of resistance to the passage of time and the violence of history. Set during a family holiday, the poet and his family visit the ruins of an old *'Big House'* owned by the Tighe family. The centuries of history of empire, resistance, rebellion and horror that surround the building are all brought to mind in a myriad of historical snapshots:

> *Black and Tan ghosts up there, at home*
> *on the Woodstock heights; an iron mouth*
> *scanning the Kilkenny road: the house*
> *gutted by the townspeople and burned to ruins.*[63]

History is interference, it is the *'fussing'* and the actions of humans affecting the normal flow of nature. The results of this interference are rarely pretty, often brutal, and sometimes architecturally incongruent:

> *The ghosts of daughters of the family*

> *waited in the uncut grass as we drove*
> *down to our mock-Austrian lodge and stopped.*[64]

It is clear here that the unfitness the poem notes is not only associated with the Tighe family's position of ascendency within the old colonial system. Although the Tighes did not live harmoniously with the locality and the locals, when independence was won, things did not alter much. The architecture and society does not become particularly more harmonious with a mock-Austrian bungalow built in a small Kilkenny village. The new state does not fit in with nature any more than the previous colonial system did.

The Tao preaches non-interference, and throughout this long poem the actions of history are interspersed by some of the axiomatic sayings from the *Tao Te Ching*.

> *Be subtle, as though not there.*[65]

If you must interfere or do anything, the Tao tells us to do it in the most natural way possible: '*Move, if you move, like water.*' In the poem, the figure of a local poacher is depicted as the closest human to the Tao tradition. From generations of poachers in the locality, he smoothly sails by the poet and his family along the river. The poacher is living the flow of the river:

> *The flat cot's long body slid past effortless*
> *as a fish, sinewing from side to side,*
> *as he passed us and vanished.*[66]

While the Tao and eastern philosophy is proposed in the poem as a potential source of resistance to change and suffering, frankly it does not work on a thematic level. One does not have to agree entirely with critics like Douglas Dunn, who, albeit a fan of Kinsella's early work, saw in this poem 'imported mysticism' that led to the poem becoming 'preposterous' in parts.[67] But there is something to this critique, for the short interjections of Taoist teachings give the poem an unsettling rather than calming tone. They are parachuted in, and read as being rather redundant in the work. This, of course, may be partially the author's intention, to display how inapplicable Taoist instructions are to real life with all its messy history. But despite this, the repeated interjections from the Tao, the focus on water in the poem and the detailing of the horrors of interventionist history all make the poem sympathetic to the Taoist principle of action by inaction.

For the poet narrator, the Taoist symbols of opposites (Ying/Yang) and the natural way of things, symbolised by flowing water, have freshness that the symbols of the leading western Churches do not. Jung, writing on the symbols of eastern religion, mentioned this phenomenon: 'What is more, these images – be they Christian or Buddhist or what you will – are lovely, mysterious, richly intuitive. Naturally, the more familiar we are with them the more does constant usage polish them smooth, so what remains is only banal superficiality and meaningless paradox.'[68] Thus, if the symbols and rituals of Roman Catholicism or other Christian Churches do not fulfil a need in western man, there is a tendency to believe that the spiritual garden is greener on the other side of the world. There is something exotic and unfamiliar in the east that the western intellectual in search of esoteric structure may find attractive. The poem does not enter the realms of embarrassing orientalism, but it is open to a very critical reading because of its adoption of eastern philosophy as possibly faddish and indulgent.

Adorno for one was disparaging towards the type of bourgeois intellectual in the west who was quick to 'scuttle into Indian temples'.[69]

While the poet narrator must state the Taoist aphorisms to guide him, the animal world does it unconsciously. Whether it is the flies on the cow dung, the midges over the river or the natural flow of the river, they all fit in. Humans do not seem to fit properly into the scheme of things – we are incongruent and awkward. The Tighe family did not fit in with the locality, and their wealth and privilege created resentment. Their attempts at benevolence, like the funding of a water pump in the town green, was *'with an eye to the effect'*. The village itself is rather underwhelming, described as *'perfectly lovely / like a typical English village.'* Even this does not fit in.

Going with the flow, as the Tao instructs, is never easy. There is an overarching sense of historic unease and violence surrounding the ruins of the house, and no amount of Taoist affirmations can soothe it. The Tao proposes that we do not interfere in life, that we sit back and let it happen. But we do interfere, and are forever destined to. Not all interventions, however, are bad.

* * *

Thomas Kinsella has been active in a series of campaigns during his life. As we know from 'The Messenger', he began leafleting for the political left at a very young age, watching his father address Labour street meetings from the back of a lorry. In adult life he was a participant in civil rights marches in Northern Ireland, a leading campaigner in the fight to prevent the Wood Quay development, and active with neighbourhood opposition to development plans in the Percy Place area of south Dublin.

He went leafleting with his father in his school days, and it is said that he 'would vigorously defend his father's Connolly socialism whenever such defence was needed.'[70] In later life he strongly articulated a position on the Northern Irish conflict that was clearly anti-imperialist. He visited the streets of Derry days after the Bloody Sunday massacre, and gave an angry poetry reading in the city.[71]

The icons and personalities of the Irish labour and republican movements often figure in his poems. A description of stepping out under the Larkin statue on O'Connell Street in the 'The Pen Shop' (1997) is instructive on his contradictory thoughts on the tradition:

> *Under Larkin with his iron arms on high,*
> *conducting everybody*
> *in all directions, up off our knees.*[72]

There is reverence and respect here, but there is also a troubling incongruity between this leader of a communal cause and the individuals around him. What is Larkin conducting? Is he getting us up off our knees as atomised individuals going around in a myriad of different directions? Whatever he is conducting, it is not a mass of people united in a collective struggle. It is not a working class following his political lead. His figure seems merely to be able to raise individuals up, not a class. Is this the message – that liberation or progression may be possible, but only as individuals and in different directions?

But the collective was never a very strong force in Kinsella's poetry, except in the sense of the internal psyche and the collective unconscious. This is an internal rather than external collective. Indeed, the crowd is sometimes regarded suspiciously as sinister and animalistic. In 'The Good Fight', the mass electorate is looked upon as a wild beast that needed to be placated. The visionary speeches of JFK try to shape the *'swaying mass,'* but without this leadership they would be wild. In Platonic terms, the mass is an ignorant beast whose desires demand satisfaction. In Jungian terms, the mass is a carrier of the most violent aspects of the collective unconscious, for the artistic modernist high art must be protected from the swamp of popular, commoditised culture.

The educated, conscious leadership of JFK must resist being *'swamped / and swept downstream'* by the power of the mob. And when the leader is killed, the mass of people reacts in embarrassing and deranged ways. A collective psychosis violently emerges into the public sphere:

> *Everybody started throwing themselves down*
> *and picking themselves up and running*
> *around the streets looking into each other's face*
> *and saying 'Catastrophe' and weeping*
> *and saying 'Well! That's that.'*[73]

People felt anxious and saw visions of the dead president. There was collective apprehension that this assassination was to herald a period of even worse trauma. Insomnia was rampant, and children watched their parents weep for the first time. This moment of mass hysteria erupted, only to disappear almost as quickly, leaving a lingering sense of embarrassment:

> *It was unhealthy – a distortion of normal attitudes.*
> *Things had been exalted*
> *altogether out of proportion. Afterward,*

> *when the shock was over, matters settled down*
> *with surprising swiftness, almost with relief.*[74]

Such moments of collective trauma that spark individual and collective psychic problems are recorded throughout history. Political deaths in recent decades such as that of Nasser in Egypt and Diana, Princess of Wales are examples that have sparked mass reactions that demand a psychological reading. In 'The Good Fight', the message is clear: the collective mass is untrustworthy at best, and dangerous at worst.

But in terms of the poet's entire work, this is not the whole story. Kinsella was brought up in a home that had reverence for Connolly, the author of the line: 'All hail, then, to the mob, the incarnation of progress!'[75] The socialism of Kinsella's father and grandfather was built on the belief that the mass of the labourers under capitalism not only had the political clout to end capitalism through collective action, but that collective action could reshape the economic and political world into a more equitable and just system. As was noted in Chapter 2, there is recognition of the importance of collective political struggle in Kinsella's poetry. In 'The Messenger', the focus is on the often neglected narrative of the history of class struggle in Dublin and the particular form of working-class politics in which his father and grandfather participated.

In 'Night Conference, Wood Quay: 6 June 1979', the subject of the poem is a struggle that the poet participated in as a leading activist. In 1979, an active campaign and series of protests were mounted against plans to build a Dublin Corporation building and car park on an ancient Viking burial site and settlement along the River Liffey. The poem is rather exceptional for Kinsella as it opens with the collective '*Our*' – it is clear this is a poem of struggle, defiance and collective action. The battle is depicted as an almost mythic fight between light and dark, with imagery that is gothic, science fiction-like and nightmarish. The forces of good are huddled together around the fire at an encampment built on the proposed building site. It is their collective action that is the source of enlightenment, a flickering flame of resistance:

> *Our iron drum of timbers blazed and sparked*
> *in rusty tatters at the mouth of the shed,*
> *apples and bread and bottles of milk flickering.*[76]

Both '*blazed*' and '*sparked*' are positively associated with resistance. The activists are gathered in the half-dug pit on the site, but despite the darkness of their scene, they are the people who produce light. A debate over strategy takes place around the drums – it is democracy and organisation in action, activism as a process that can counter the ordeal of destruction. The protestors speak in very moralistic tones; this is not just a skirmish over a specific issue, this is a black and white struggle. '*You couldn't trust their oath,*' one warns.

While the protestors are glowing on the side of righteousness, the '*white-cuffed marauders*' look down upon them, behind their digging machines of destruction and their development plans. They have no voice, but force. In scenes of machine-age horror, those behind the controls are undoubtedly the forces of evil:

> *A high hook hung from the dark: the swift crane locked*
> *– and its steel spider brain – by our mental force.*[77]

They have the physical power, but the activists have the ideas and passion, the '*mental force*'. This collective mental force proved not to be enough in the real struggle, but this short poem remains a strong evocation of the intoxicating sense of righteousness and collectivity that any participation in active struggle brings.

'Night Conference, Wood Quay: 6 June 1979' appeared in an activist newsletter during the Wood Quay struggle, but was not published in an official Kinsella book until the *Personal Places* collection in 1990. Speaking about the poem in late 1996, it was clear that the high passions of that event still moved Kinsella some sixteen years after the controversy. He recalls meeting future Irish President Mary Robinson in a tent on the protest site, and seeing a priest 'almost offering himself up for crucifixion, throwing himself in front of one of those smaller bulldozers.' The poet told the interviewer that he remains 'bitter' about what happened in Wood Quay.[78]

As a writer and translator, much of Kinsella's work has been focused on the careful retrieval of the past – on a poetic level, an often dark but honest recalling of his childhood; on a collective level, a carefully nuanced resuscitation of a lost Gaelic tradition. But what he witnessed in Wood Quay was not careful, but rather a brutal exhuming of an ancient history in the name of progress, carried out with modern mechanisms. 'We were just standing and this small bulldozer passed by our settlement, where we were camped out protesting, and its pickup container was full of medieval remains, shoes, things like that. And that moment, we knew it was all over, that everything had been destroyed. The events at Wood Quay were in a way the destroying of a birthplace,' he said in 1996.[79]

In 'One Fond Embrace' (1988), the poet imagines a bombing operation against the city fathers – it is part comic, part burning with intense anger. The corporation has dug up a sacred ancient Viking burial site for an underground car park. The narrator explodes: *'May their sewers blast under them!'*

Despite such anger in verse, when asked if he was still fighting this Wood Quay battle in his writing, the poet replied no. 'I wouldn't say that I have accepted it, but things have to be endured.'[80] This is something close to Reinhold Niebuhr's (1892–1971) famous serenity prayer, with its appeal to the almighty to 'grant me the serenity to accept the things I cannot change, the courage to change the things I can, and wisdom to know the difference.' But while the content of the prayer may chime with Kinsella's position, there is no sense of serenity in the poetry. Endurance, rather than stoical serenity, is the key theme in his work – endurance as the last stand of resistance. It may possess no obvious positivist programme of its own, yet its refusal to yield finally to despair and acceptance gives it a grim majesty. Nearing 70, Kinsella's feeling of continuing bitterness at the Wood Quay events echoes his ageing father in 'The Messenger', who in his retirement still bristled with anger at the injustice he suffered in the Guinness Brewery.

Joe Cleary has been highly critical of Irish literature for being quiet on social and political struggles, particularly those of the working class or rural poor. 'While a lot of writers have offered eloquent indictments of the oppressiveness of Irish society, one will search their work in vain for any equally compelling or memorable depiction of the many who have collectively struggled with the resources to hand to transform that society, or at the very least to mitigate its ills.'[81] This observation is undoubtedly true, but leads to the obvious question: do the writers reflect a lack of major social struggle that marked much of the history of southern Ireland in the 1920s until the present time, or is it the artists' inherent conservatism that makes them ignore the battle raging under their nose?

The truth, I would propose, is somewhere in between, and Kinsella's work reflects that.

There is no forced glorification, no overstating the real influence or impact of such struggles. But there is also no ignorance of it, of which the official narrative of the Irish state and its leading writers may be guilty. Unthinking celebration of the downtrodden is not part of Kinsella's poetics. Adorno warned of the reactionary problems inherent in such knee-jerk solidarity, 'In the end, glorification of splendid underdogs is nothing other than glorification of the splendid system that makes them so.'[82] Historically, popular Irish verse and song is full of celebration of the underdog (most often on a national rather than class basis), and with it an often unconscious celebration of the system that makes them an underdog. Both Kinsella's father and grandfather in 'The Messenger' do not wallow in their deprivation, but strive to do better, individually and collectively. There is a rugged realism in Kinsella's depiction of solidarity and resistance in politics.

The tension between physical power and grim peaceful resistance is also evident in 'Apostle of Hope' from the 1990 collection, *Personal Places*. The poet narrator is accompanied on a group trip to a northern town across the border. Their steps in the market town are stalked by young occupying British forces, *'with deadly undernourished faces.'*

> *kneeling and posing with their guns.*
> *Our polite faces packed with hate.*[83]

The tension is balanced, and there it shall remain, because in Kinsella's work there is no unbalanced glorification of physical-force resistance. Indeed, revulsion towards violence permeates his poems, even those most castigating against power and empire. Resistance and political activism of a peaceful nature are displayed in a positive light, despite the fact that they often lead to failure, but militarist actions are not seen as favourably.

When considering the bloody way in which the modern Irish state won freedom, there are competing impulses in the poetry. On the one hand, the violent beginnings of the Irish state are depicted as an original sin that the modern state forever carries. The Civil War in particular is regarded as a repulsive waste of life that marks the character of the Irish Republic. In a poem from the early 1960s like 'A Country Walk', a visit to the grave of a fallen republican leads to a damning recollection of how blood was followed by more violence:

> *— For one who answered latest the phantom Hag*
> *There he bled to death. And never saw*
> *His town ablaze with joy; the grinning foe*
> *Driven, in heavy lorries, from the field.*
> *And he lay cold in the Hill Cemetery*
> *When Freedom burned his comrades' itchy palms,*
> *Too much for flesh and blood and, armed in hate,*
> *Brother met brother in a modern light.*[84]

The volunteer who answered Ireland's (*'the phantom Hag'*) dubious call died before he saw the British leave and before the Civil War. There is nothing glorious here. In the much later 'One Fond Embrace', this revolutionary generation is castigated as having *'fought the wrong civil war.'* Violence in itself is shown to be a wrong. In the poetry there is an attitude to violence that comes close to Martin Luther

King's rejection: 'The ultimate weakness of violence is that it is a descending spiral. Returning violence only multiplies violence adding deeper darkness to a night already devoid of stars.' But in Kinsella's poetry, violence, it seems, is inherent in humanity. Violence in restricted circumstances, however, can be understood, if clearly not celebrated or condoned. In a 2002 interview, where the poet restated his basic position that the northern statelet was founded on injustice, the poet addressed the violence of the recent Troubles. 'And I reject violence as a means towards anything. In most of its aspects – the masked expression of provincial bigotry and religious prejudice, for example – it passes my understanding. But I would understand it as a defensive last resort in certain circumstances, and if I were a brutal bigot pushing hard I would always be mindful of that aspect.'[85] The poet understands the source of some of the violence.

But to understand is not to condone. The great failure of the revisionists has been their inability, often apparently wanton, to understand the sources of rage, and the roots of political violence in modern Ireland. In *One Fond Embrace* (1988) a long-established enemy of the narrator is seen making a name for himself in journalistic and intellectual circles in London. Although not overt, the figure closely resembles a leading figure of the revisionist school, Conor Cruise O'Brien(1917–2008). But despite this figure's intellectual gift, the rigidity of his thinking towards republican violence makes him unable to understand the actions of republicans and others; he is *'Baulked in Redmondite bafflement at human behaviour.'*[86]

Although Kinsella is angered at some of the violent actions of the revolutionary generation, there is also regard. For although the freedom that was won was partial, mishandled and violent, the poet regards his generation as nonetheless blessed to be born after independence.

> *Not to misunderstand*
>
> *– the English are a fine people*
> *in their proper place.*[87]

Political resistance and activism, encapsulated by his father in 'The Messenger', is never disregarded or disrespected. Kinsella himself has involved himself in activism, but its positive nature is consumed within the poet's overarching conception of inevitable disappointment in life. There is a beautiful loser's quality to this – the resistor as tragic figure, courageous yet comic. A three-line pen-picture of an unnamed acquaintance in 'One Fond Embrace' goes:

> *You with your bedtime mug of disappointment*
> *– the loser in every struggle;*
> *always on the right side.*[88]

The character may be on the side of righteousness, but he inevitably fails. But the disappointment that results from this failure provides nourishment. He finds meaning in the struggle, although the struggle is never-ending defeat. This is the core contradiction of Kinsella's sentiment towards political resistance and activism: it is righteous and ridiculous, meaningful and useless. There can be no stirring rebel songs that do not also contain a comic moment, no celebratory activist meeting that does not also murmur with concerns about further struggles ahead.

But it is those who struggle in the name of justice who are in the end the most heroic. Those who seek material wealth or power will also experience inevitable disappointment, but it will not have the positive heroic struggle within it.

David Wheatley has written; 'Like Ezra Pound, there has always been something of the consigliere about Kinsella, keen to bend the ear of the nearest prince or Irish government minister.'[89] But it is hard to sustain such a conclusion. In real life, Kinsella was in a position to bend the ear of ministers and top civil servants, but turned away from such a career in the mid 1960s. His subsequent poetic career has been low profile compared to other leading Irish poets, and it has hardly been conducive to capturing the attention of those in power. Yes, Kinsella has written about powerful figures, like John F. Kennedy and Marcus Aurelius, but these pen-pictures of power have served only to undermine some of the claims that these icons publicly made. They are not hagiographies.

There is certainly none of what the Russian critic Mikhail Bakhtin (1895–1975) termed the 'carnivalesque' in Kinsella's poetry. This is the radicalism of the popular celebrations and culture of the people that mocks, subverts and turns upside down the normal power relations. Popular culture is not regarded as an effective instrument of change or resistance to power in these poems. There is a partial exception in the case of Irish traditional music, on which Kinsella focuses in his two collections about his close friend, Seán Ó Riada, 'A Selected Life' (1972) and 'Vertical Man' (1973). In the later poem, the appearance of Ó Riada's spirit in the poet's Philadelphia home on the one year anniversary of his death leads the poet to reminiscence about his late friend's career. Ó Riada is shown to have connected with the wider public through his music, *'That there can be a sweet stir / hurrying in the veins.*'⁹⁰ This stir in the individual performer connected with his wider audience.

> *That you may startle the heart of a whole people*
> *(as you know) and all your power,*⁹¹

But even this moment of connection between individual artist and mass public is fleeting. The mass appeal of the work can mean that its quality decreases and *'is soon beating to a coarse pulse.'* Music in 'Her Vertical Smile' (1985), this time by Gustav Mahler, provides the score to the descent into the madness of the Great War. The aristocratic and bourgeois couples under *'chandelier after trembling chandelier'* dance to Mahler's music. But its beauty, which the poet believes to be a great artistic creation of civilisation, is no bulwark to the descent into barbarity. Even art at its highest achievement cannot stop wickedness. The high hopes inherent in great art are quickly followed by the disappointment of the *'muttonchop horror'* of the trenches.

Even the moments from the Great War that seem to provide shards of hope do not provide respite from the barbarity. A picture of the famous fraternal moment when German and allied troops met in no man's land on Christmas Day is not a glimpse of hopefulness. Rather, the poet narrator does not linger on the fraternity of the troops, but on the hand of a dead man that can be seen in the corner of the picture. Mahler's music is the overture to this incomprehensible horror on a continental industrial scale. Music, even when popular or worthy, cannot resist the worst that life inflicts.

Kinsella is not a socialist or socialist-republican poet, at least certainly not an unambiguous one. In 'The Back Lane', he sees the symbol of Irish labour in the night sky, and recognises it as his own:

> *The Moon had set.*
>   *And the Plough, emblem of toil.*
> *And my own sign had descended.*[92]

It is the plough, more symbolic of hard craft rather than the political icon of working-class struggle, that is evoked here. This contrasts with a more overtly class-conscious reflections on the night sky by a writer like Paula Meehan in 'A Child's Map of Dublin' *(1991)*, who saw the constellation clearly as '*I wanted to find you Connolly's Starry Plough / the flag I have lived under since birth or since / I first scanned the nightskies and learned the nature of work.*'[93] Meehan's reflection is more the voice of Kinsella's father.

Since leaving university, Kinsella has not lived the life of his father or grandfather. There is not a hint of triumphant, unbalanced honouring of collective action or political belief in his work. However, class consciousness and a lingering respect and even affinity for the progressive cause permeate much of his work. The poems may not be an expression of a clear class consciousness, or the Connolly socialism of his father. It is closer to the Italian communist Antonio Gramsci's (1891–1937) notion of the 'pessimism of the intellect, optimism of the will.' Too much rumination on the possibility of major political and social change can lead to pessimism over the huge challenges involved. But in the gut, when there is raw admiration for those who fight the good fight, there is a hard-won and marginal optimism. The fact that it is hard-won, and not built on fiery, empty rhetoric, makes it all the more authentic.

It is in these places where the poet is very much his activist father's son. It is here that collective resistance provides some relief.

* * *

Can answers to life's difficulties be located in the ancient past? Can antiquity provide the insights needed to resist life's ordeal?

Jung certainly believed so: 'I became aware of the fateful links between me and my ancestors,' he wrote. 'I feel very strongly that I am under the influence of things or questions which were left incomplete and unanswered by my parents and grandparents and more distant ancestors.'[94] That the ancient world may have possessed solutions to modern life's difficulties had been a strain of belief even during the Enlightenment as Rousseau valorised the 'noble savage' as an authentic expression of man living in the 'state of nature'. The modernists regarded myth as a way of bringing order to a disordered modernity, so the 'mythical method' became an important part of the modernist project. In a seminal review of *Ulysses*, T. S. Eliot praised 'Mr Joyce's parallel use of the *Odyssey* as being of great importance. It has the importance of a scientific discovery. It is simply a way of controlling, of ordering, of giving a shape and a significance to the immense panorama of futility and anarchy which is contemporary history.'[95]

But while Kinsella's work has been influenced by Eliot in stylistic elements, his deployment of myth is not the same as this. Kinsella's use of myth chimes closer to the Jungian-inspired theories of Joseph Campbell, who argued that myths are a universal insight into deep-rooted knowledge. For Campbell, unlike Eliot, myth is not primarily a strategy for organising reality: 'For the symbols of mythology are not manufactured; they cannot be ordered, invented, or permanently suppressed. They are spontaneous productions of the psyche, and each bears within it, undamaged, the germ power of its source.'[96]

Thus, Kinsella's use of myth is not principally as an ordering mechanism. It is not to impose a meaning and linear progression on the history of Ireland or man's understanding of the meaning of life. If anything, it is mythology deployed as a disordering principle. It displays a link between our present concerns and those of the past, because both modern and ancient man suffer from doubts and angst in Kinsella's work.

In Ireland during the Literary Revival, the distant Gaelic past was a key foundational influence. The ancient sagas featuring Cuchulain and other characters had a massive impact on Yeats, Lady Gregory, Patrick Pearse (1879–1916) and others. The original source of these tales was questionable. Compiled in the Middle Ages; its content was contested and compromised from the start. 'The story of the origins of Gaelic Ireland from the time of creation was first set down as a definitive account by an unknown author of the *Lebor Gabála Érenn* or *Book of Invasions*. Compiled in the late eleventh century from a number of earlier poems, this great prose and verse narrative attempted to accommodate native origin tales with Biblical word history as expounded by the medieval Church,' writes John Waddell.[97] Another writer has noted that the book was an amalgamation of writings from different eras. 'All of this points towards a huge cooperative effort at bringing together material that was in danger of being lost forever.'[98]

The Celtic gods in these tales were really ancient superhuman heroes, not all-loving, all-knowing deities. They exhibited many human emotions like anger, jealousy, hate and love. The original mythological tales served a particular function in Celtic Ireland. As Carmel McCaffrey has written about the 'Song of Amergin', the poetic invocation supposedly recited by the first Celtic settler on the island, 'The poem is similar to other "foundation" poetry uttered by the mythological founder of other peoples. The mythmakers who first wrote this story knew what they were doing. They were giving validity to the lineage of the Irish.'[99]

The original mythologies reflected the mores and political needs of twelfth-century Ireland. Thus, a narrative of waves of invasion, including one massive Celtic arrival, was pushed, although 'archaeology shows no indication of large-scale movements of people into Ireland from overseas; immigrants trickled in over hundreds or thousands of years.'[100] One writer has compared the authors of the mythologies to 'public relations officers for one tribal grouping or another ... trying to prove how noble their tribe's ancestry was, and how long established its supremacy.'[101] For those looking for an uncomplicated source of knowledge and understanding, the ancient Irish past was already compromised.

Examples of Kinsella's creative engagement with the ancient Irish past is found throughout the decades of his work, but most intensely in two poems from his *One* collection. 'Finistère' and 'The Oldest Place' work as twin poems written with the ancient sources as the broad blueprint. The characters in these poems from Ireland's heroic, mythical age, however, are not those familiar in the early manuscripts or the writings of Yeats and Lady Gregory. They are individuals full of doubt rather than daring; they are fumbling rather than fearless. Their dark musings and hesitant progress are the theory and action of a modern man rather than a superhuman from the mythical cycles. Rather than bright, sweeping tales of victories, early life in Ireland is presented as hesitant, cruel and dark.

The character in 'The Oldest Place' is less a warrior with an archetypal mission of daring ahead of him, and more an angst-ridden and hesitant individual. The famous druid Amergin in 'Finestere', when he lands in Ireland and recites his poem, is not confidently declaring the nature of things like he does in the original ancient sources. There is no pumped-up machismo talk. Rather, he poses a series of bewildering questions. Doubt rather than swagger marks his words; this is a very different 'Song of Amergin' than the one found in the sources.

Who
    is a breath
that makes the wind
that makes the wave
that makes this voice?

Who
    is the bull with seven scars
the hawk on the cliff
the salmon sunk in his pool
the pool sunk in her soil
the animal's fury
the flower's fibre
a teardrop in the sun?[102]

Rather than the mythical tales providing a structure to modern man's sense of angst and meaninglessness, rather modern man's plight is here imposed on the ancients. Looking to Amergin or other ancient figures for insights into meaning thus seems foolhardy. There is not much wisdom in the dim past; they are as clueless as we are, maybe even more so. In answer to Amergin's scattergun quizzical searching, modern man would probably answer his questions with 'nobody', and the suspicion while reading the poem is that Amergin may concur. His description of a religious congregation is humorous in its depiction of human ignorance:

> *When men meet on the hill*
> *dumb as stones in the dark*
>   *(the craft knocked behind me)*
> *who is the jack of all light?*
> *Who goes in full into*
> *the moon's interesting conditions?*
> *Who fingers the sun's sink hole:*
>   *(I went forward reaching out)*[103]

Amergin does not stride off the boat onto Erin confidently kick-starting the era of Celtic Ireland. Rather, he steps forward, reaching out with no clear direction, his head full of riddles. Neurotic rather than heroic, he needs to lie down on a coach rather than erect the first standing stone.

While Cuchulain and others of the Yeats, Pearse and Lady Gregory plays and poetry are in some sense heroic exemplars, in the Celtic mythology poems of Kinsella, the ancients serve more as a mirror. The ancient world may be a location of alternative living, but ancient man is apparently just as doubt-filled as his modern descendent.

In 'The Clearing' in *Notes from the Land of the Dead*, a solitary ancient man is '*A troubled figure*', muttering to himself between the small fire he has created and the vast gloom that surrounds his small encampment. But the fear of animals and darkness around him changes when '*He stops suddenly and straightens*', his teeth growing sharper. The way to face ancestral fears is to become fearsome yourself, to compensate for your weaknesses. If anything, the ancient world is darker and may be a more dangerous place than the contemporary world. In 'His Father's Hands', Kinsella goes back deeper and deeper into family history, eventually reaching the outer limits of inherited knowledge with ancient relatives on the side of hills, nameless and scraping a level of survival from the land.

> *Littered uplands. Dense grass. Rocks everywhere,*
> *wet underneath, retaining memory of the long cold.*
> *First, a prow of land*
> *chosen, and wedged with tracks;*
> *then boulders chosen*
> *and sloped together, stabilized in menace.*
>
> *I do not like this place.*
> *I do not think the people who lived here*
> *were ever happy. It feels evil.*
> *Terrible things happened.*
> *I feel afraid here when I am on my own.*[104]

These are no noble savages as envisioned by Rousseau; this is no way of life to be emulated as proposed by some of the most radical rejectors of modernity, and there seems to be little wisdom here to be rescued, as those who celebrate the ancients as the carriers of great knowledge would claim. While there is no unbalanced celebration of the ancient, there is a strong and important feeling of historical continuity. Kinsella looks at his grandfather and traces the accumulation of historical and familial generations:

Dispersals or migrations.
Through what evolutions or accidents
toward that peace and patience
by the fireside, that blocked gentleness...[105]

While much of Kinsella's work calls into question any uncomplicated progressive view of history, in these lines there is a lingering belief in progress and hope. For while the ancient hillside is cold and dark, and the generations that follow experience war and dispersals, one of the results of all that history is accumulated into the gentle, sympathetic figure of his grandfather by the fireside. It is not an easy, flowing calm – it is still blocked – but that the blood lineage full of such difficult history can result in this imperfect but still decent humanity is something to be positive about, even in a limited way.

In 'Finistère', the sons of Mil, the mythical original Celtic warriors to arrive in Ireland, strain their eyes westward from the Spanish coast:

We hesitated before that wider sea
but our heads sang with purpose
and predatory peace.[107]

There is an internal dialectic of doubt and hope, not a monologue of onwards and upwards.

Mythology, including the Celtic mythological cycle, is predominately a celebration of individualistic endeavour and valour. In 'Finistère', however, Amergin and the other Celtic explorers are not portrayed as rugged, atomised individuals, but rather as weak and scared ones, reliant on their fellow man to provide protection from the elements:

At no great distance out in the bay
the swell took us into its mercy,
grey upheaving slopes of water
sliding under us, collapsing,
crawling onward, mountainous.

Driven outward a day and a night
we held fast, numbed by the steady
might of the oceanic wind.
We drew close together, as one,
and turned inward, salt chaos
rolling in silence all around us,
and listened to our own mouths
mumbling in the sting of spray:[106]

Rather than being at one with nature, the explorers turn their back on its worst elements, relying on each other for support. Unified (*'as one'*) as a small settler society, they *'turned inward.'* This is not an ancient people living in perfect harmony with the natural world, but rather living at uneasy odds with it. This is not a selection of brave, rugged individuals ready to face anything on their own, but rather a rudimentary society making do as best they can. It is society and civilisation, created as a bulwark against the worst that life and nature can throw at us. It is a far from perfect society; there is no flowing communication for one thing, but rather *'mumbling'* between the sailors.

There is a communal questioning of why they remain unsettled. What pushes them onwards to sail the sea, to build religious monuments, to create art? The questions are posed as a people, not as a person:

who gave us our unrest
whom we meet and unmeet

*in whose yearning shadow
we erect our great uprights
and settle fulfilled
and build and are still
unsettled,*[108]

In other poems we have encountered this exploration of what moves us forward on an individual basis, but here there is a marked communal context. This communal context exists elsewhere in the work, such as the solidarity of political struggle in 'The Messenger', but also most importantly in Jung's concept of the collective unconscious. If thoughts are communally accessed as Jung maintained, should it be surprising that actions are communally accomplished? It is not a matter of what makes me do anything, but what makes my community, nation, class do anything? In 'Finistère', the Milesians do not have a clear answer. They lack any assuredness, as one might expect from ancient people. Their querying is not truly modern, however, because it concerns the identity of the being that propels the community's progression and drive, not the question of whether or not such a being exists. It is the sex of the God or Gods that they question, not whether such a celestial being or beings exist.

*in whose outflung service
we nourished our hunger
uprooted and came*[109]

They are tying themselves up in theological knots, something that is reflected in the circular nature of much of the art they produce. The poem's allusion to the famous spiral designs of the Newgrange burial ground and others shows how their feeling of no fixed point of assuredness was scratched into the walls and religious stones around them:

> *unsettled, whose google gaze*
> *and holy howl we have scraped*
> *speechless on slabs of stone*
> *poolspirals opening on*
> *closing spiralpools*
> *and dances drilled in the rock*
> *in coil zigzag angle and curl*
> *river ripple earth ramp*
> *suncircle moonloop...*[110]

To this day, the precise meaning of the distinctive spirals of this type of ancient art baffles experts, but the questioning collective mindsets of the travellers from Finestère points to confusion rather than assuredness as the source.

The early settlers in 'The Oldest Place' begin the process of constructing a society, attempting to impose their collective will on the land with deforestation and rudimentary agriculture. Following the initial creation of a coastline outpost, they are unsatisfied and forge ahead deeper into Erin:

> *We fished and fowled and chopped at the forest,*
> *cooked and built, ploughed and planted,*
> *danced and drank, all as before.*
> *But worked inland, and got further.*[111]

However, the Ireland of 'The Oldest Place' is not a welcoming land of milk and honey. There is little sense of an accepting fertile paradise; rather, the land has an ominous feeling from the start. It will not yield unquestioningly to the settler's whims. This growing atmosphere of evil is linked to the settlers forging further ahead:

And there was something in the way the land behaved:
passive, but responding. It grew under our hands.
We worked it like a dough to our requirements
yet it surprised us more than once
with a firm life of its own, as if it
used us.[112]

Things get worse, as the earth itself begins to reject the settlers' most sacred rituals.

Once, as we were burying
one of our children, the half-dug grave
dampened, and overbrimmed, and the water
ran out over the land and would not stop
until the place had become a lake.[113]

This flood is followed by sickness and death, with settlers falling ill after developing skin blemishes. This image of the soaking, sodden earth is like the soft foundation upon which Ireland is being built. It is a place where it is hard to find your footing, even to bury the dead. It is the 'foundationless foundation' in Sartre's phrase, but it also has a more narrowly Irish meaning, with Daniel Corkery's reflection on Irish literature where the 'national consciousness may be described, in a native phrase, as a quaking sod. It gives no footing. It is not English, nor Irish, nor Anglo-Irish.'[114]

The land, of which its people talk of so lovingly, can betray you. People begin to die, one by one, but no heroic individual comes to the fore to save the day. There is no great intervention by a God, or any supernatural force.

Rather, the weak and fading society tries to gather together to provide support. The misery breeds unity. The society retreats to the original settlement closer to the coast:

> *We thought of the bare plain we found first,*
> *with the standing stone: miles of dead clay*
> *without a trace of a root or a living thing.*
> *We gathered there and the sick died*
> *and we covered them. Others fell sick*
> *and we covered them, fewer and fewer.*
> *A day came when I fell down by the great stone*
> *alone, crying, at the middle of the stinking plain.*[115]

Despite the unity, notwithstanding the reversal of the earlier thrust into the centre of the land, disease and death grows apace. What is left is nothing but the wretched individual, despairing at death while standing beside a silent stone. Nothing remains but the physical remnants of his faith – a faith of which he is unsure. But the dying society projects meaning out of itself and into the standing stone, the fearful settlers placing gifts for the Gods around the rock:

> *With each gift, the giver*
> *sighed and melted away,*
> *the black stone packed more*
> *with dark radiance.*[116]

The rock as a symbol pulsates with the hopes and fears the humans have projected onto it. It is an emblem of important human experience, and as such is a portal into a collective experience. 'There are not many truths, there are only a few,' wrote Jung. 'Their meaning is too deep to grasp other than in symbols.'[117] While the pulses of the settlers stop one by one, the symbolic rock seems to increase in strength, beating with growing potency as the human hearts stop all around it:

> *And its glare*
> *gathered like a pulse, and struck*
> *on the withered plain of my own brain.*[118]

The rock's symbolic power is created by humans; its mystery is a projection of human will, but its inscrutable potency is not delegitimised by this. Just because it does not come from the heavens, it does not follow that it does not carry meaning. Man made God, not God man – but God exists in man's eyes.

In section 3 of *A Technical Supplement*, a mysterious process of human growth from unconsciousness to consciousness is narrated. A human figure breaks out of his unconscious shell and decides to depart:

> *And so he departed, leaving a mere shell*
>   *– that serene effigy*
> *we have copied so much*
>   *And set everywhere:*[119]

The shell that is left is the symbol from the unconscious that we have left behind through evolution, or that we leave behind every morning after we arise from our beds and forget what we have dreamt. These unconscious remnants remain with us principally in the forms of symbolic shells. They are littered everywhere in cave drawings, *'perched on pillars in the desert / fixed in tree forks / on car bonnets, on the prows / of ships and trains.'*[120] But these symbols are not manufactured, or cannot be permanently suppressed. 'They are spontaneous productions of the psyche, and each bears within it, undamaged, the germ power of its source,' as Campbell observed.[121] It is a communicative link to our ancient predecessors, and even our unconscious antecedents who existed in a dark world, untouched by the light of human consciousness.

Kinsella is the modern poet, tracing the lineage, this time of his own paternal bloodline in 'His Father's Hands'. The family history is not evoked here to valorise a claim to power or wealth. This is not a Gaelic aristocratic clan making a power grab; it is a working-class family in twentieth-century Dublin, grounding its history. Kinsella shares a concern with the Gaelic poets that the historic generations of the family should be acknowledged. It is more to do with place than power.

There is a mythologising, a reliance on oral tradition, just like the synthesising historians of the eleventh and twelfth centuries. The narrator pieces together the family history from stories rather than research from written sources. The strength of the oral tradition is in the vivacity of the narrative that is told – it has to be that way to help with the process of memorising. But the weakness is in its tendency towards error, exaggeration and the inevitable creation of black holes in memory.

> *Your family, Thomas, met with and helped*
> *many of the Croppies in hiding from the Yeos*
> *or on their way home after the defeat*
> *in south Wexford. They sheltered the Laceys*
> *who were later hanged on the Bridge in Ballinglen*
> *between Tinahely and Anacorra.*

> *From hearsay, as far as I can tell*
> *the Men Folk were either Stone Cutters*
> *or masons or probably both.*[122]

As well as the vital bardic function of tracing lineage, there is also the Gaelic tradition of *dindshenchas* ('lore of sacred places'). According to Muireann Ní Bhrolcháin, 'In Irish tradition, the names of places are crucially important and the stories are set in the physical landscape of the country even if their physical characteristics are not described in detail.'[123]

> *They lived in Farnese among a Colony*
> *of North of Ireland or Scotch settlers left there*
> *in some of the dispersals or migrations*
> *which occurred in this Area of Wicklow and Wexford*
> *and Carlow. And some years before that time*
> *the Family came from somewhere around Tullow.*[124]

This attention to bloodline is a common thread in the poetry. The concern over a broken past on a national and cultural level is echoed in more intimate family history. Lineage is important, and in the final, elusive sections of 'St Catherine's Clock' there are hints of hidden family stories of broken and questioned bloodlines. The poet narrator gets confusing intimations from his father and other family members of stories untold. A sense of apprehension and concerns that maybe the bloodline is not clear permeates the second half of the long poem:

> *His voice, empty and old,*
> *came around to it more than once:*
> *something about the family*
> *he had to tell me sometime.*[125]

But the moment when the *'something'* is to be revealed never seems to come:

> *I leave you a few faint questions*
> *and good and bad example*
> *and things I have not told you,*
> *and who and what you are.*[126]

This final line jars with an earlier line in the poem when the narrator as a young boy recalls: *'And I always remembered / who and what I am.'*[127] Doubt, it seems, haunts not just the ancestral lineage of our nation, but also all our own families. In his introduction to the Oxford Anthology of Irish Verse, Kinsella writes about 'past heavy with loss.' Later, in the essay 'The Irish Writer', it is referred to as a 'gapped' inheritance.'[128] But in the poetry this gap reflects itself on a number of levels — there is a linguistic, national, cultural and personal rupture. In a 1996 interview, the poet stated baldly that his poetry and his translation work was not a matter of trying to bridge the gap, for it 'can't be closed. The most you can do is attempt to understand it, to put it in its place as a gap, as fracture, as rupture. The failure of these ideas is as important as any success. Significant experience has to allow for failure.'[129] But it is clear that the poet feels this gap viscerally. In the same interview he spoke of its geographical legacies: 'I live in Killalane; in the past this was someone's "kill", someone's sanctuary, but we don't know whose. There's a palpable sense of loss ... even of living physically with this sense of loss, around where I live now.'[130]

While the project of the generation of the Irish Literary Revival may have been to resuscitate or even reconstruct this lost tradition, Kinsella's project may be more modest, but it is also modernist. In Eliot's *The Waste Land*, the allusions to historical mythology and classical tales only serve to confuse the modern reader – this may be part of the point. According to Nick Mount, Eliot is attempting to show in his fragmented epic that we have lost touch with that old tradition of learning, that there has been a rupture in the modern world, particularly after the Great War, and the past in its totality has become irretrievable. As Mount has said about the poem, 'it's bits of culture, broken up by war and reassembled into a new frame.'[131] That we as contemporary readers must consult secondary sources to make sense of the many classical allusions in the poem speaks to this rupture. The past is not present to us. It exists on the far side of a colossal trench that we cannot traverse. In Kinsella's poetry and translation work, it is not the Great War that is the moment of rupture, but a series of historical events that resulted from the island's position within British colonial expansion. The crushing of the Gaelic order had its most important cultural impact in the loss of the Irish language as the island's predominant mode of communication.

This world, in Kinsella's eyes, is lost to us. Mythical references to the Gaelic cycle tales or the sagas from the *Book of Invasions* and other medieval documents occur often in the poetry, but although some of the stories might still be taught in school, most modern Irish readers will find the references difficult, and will need to consult some guide to Gaelic and Celtic history. These tales that were known by heart in the past, and told to generation after generation of Irish people living prior to the destruction of the Gaelic order, have now become distant. It is not a past easily accessible to most of us. The references in Kinsella's work serve to remind us of how much we have forgotten and lost rather than of any continuity that may still exist.

But if the ancient sagas and myths are gone, it is principally because of the loss of the native language. This theory cannot be rejected as sentimentally nationalist, or as part of an aggressive anti-imperialist cultural agenda, for two reasons. Firstly, Kinsella has carried out very important work in translation, and knows well what has been lost.[132] Secondly, the proposition that a loss of a language is not merely something to be bemoaned as a sad fact of history, but represents the disappearance of the repository of a whole psychological and cultural history, is backed by modern science. One of the world's leading cognitive scientists and linguists, Professor Steven Pinker, regards the disappearance of a language as something that should not merely be thought of as an inevitable product of globalising trends towards greater linguistic uniformity. When we lose a language, 'We are losing something very precious. It is like losing a species. Each language is an astonishingly rich and beautiful system that captures something about the culture of the people who speak it, and it is a great tragedy for the species.'[133]

The Irish language has been of utmost importance at different points in the poet's life. In his youth and early adulthood it was actively used and promoted, and he made trips to the Gaelteacht. He, like the Gaelic Leaguers before him, believed the resurrection of the language to be an important part of the national project, a part of the dream of independence. But there is a characteristic coolness and objectivity in the attitude of the mature poet to the language. Any hint of early romanticism has ceased. He has coolly looked at the legacy of rupture and sees a dual tradition in its place.[134] He also has been honest in how his own poetic voice was not articulated in Gaelic, telling an interviewer in 2002 that his first expressions 'of real feeling' were in English, although his first writings 'of any kind' were actually written in Gaelic.[135]

As the narrator wanders towards Dublin Bay in 'Nightwalker' he sees a seagull, which passes over his head *'whingeing'*. In this rather ridiculous sound of persistent complaint, he hears the voices of the ancients from the beginning and end of the Gaelic era. At first it is Amergin representing the first Celtic voyagers to Ireland, and latterly the voice of Aogán Ó Rathaille, the great bard who chronicled the collapse of the Gaelic order in the seventeenth century. The voices are not strong, but squawking peevishly – it is sad what the language has become. Even the ghosts cannot communicate in the language any more:

> A seamew passes over, whingeing: *Eire*
> *Eire. Is there none to hear? Is all lost?*
> *Alas, I think I will dash myself at the stones.*
>
> *I will become a wind on the sea again.*
> *Or a wave of the sea,*
>   *or a sea sound.*
>
> *At the first light of the sun I stirred on my rock.*
> *I have seen the sun go down at the end of the world.*
> *Now I fly across the face of the moon.*[136]

The night prowler lingering on the suburban streets of the 'free' modern Irish republic can only listen sadly to the voices from the past. For the narrator, the new Ireland is not a continuation with the Gaelic past as its modern mythology would like to insist. Rather, it is a republic of rupture, the disappointing debris of historical failure:

> *A dying language echoes*
> *across a century's silence.*[137]

The acknowledgement of a gap, a loss between the historic Gaelic world and complex Irish modernity haunts Kinsella's work. In his book *The Dual Tradition*, Kinsella argues that because of the historic cultural impact of colonialism, Irish literature and Irish writers work within a dual tradition – part in Gaelic, the other part in English.[138] Irish literature exists in both, and any literary movement or critical consideration that ignores one does not capture the whole – a dual approach is necessary. Such a duality can be enriching, but can also create a sense of displacement and exile within the Irish writer's experience. In an early poem like 'Baggot Street Deserta', there is despair in how the poet glances back at Irish history. In contrast with many of the leading figures of the Irish Revival, the island's past is not a place for creative sustenance for the poet. It is distant, irretrievable and a faintly ridiculous place. The momentary empathy felt towards the ancient monks comes to nought as the poet can find no track on which to meet them:

> *Looking backward, all is lost;*
> *The Past becomes a fairy bog*
> *Alive with fancies, double crossed*
> *By pad of owl and hoot of dog,*
> *Where shaven, serious-minded men*
> *Appear with lucid theses, after*
> *Which they don the mists again*
> *With trackless, cotton-silly laughter;*[139]

There is a faint mention of *'midnight mutterings'* being taken away – a reference to one of the final great works of Gaelic

Ireland, *The Midnight Court*, by Brian Merriman (1749–1805). Midnight has also struck for Gaelic Ireland, and Erin, who appeared so beautiful in the high period of Gaelic poetry, has now disintegrated:

> *The goddess who had light for thighs*
> *Grows feet of dung and takes to bed,*[140]

This break with the past has also contributed to the 'blocked' nature that Kinsella witnesses in his father and grandfather. It is as if the nation's natural path of growth has been broken by colonialism and the cultural loss of the native language. Ireland is not made whole, and neither are the Irish. When the two languages 'interchanged', as Kinsella writes euphemistically in his 1987 poem 'Entrance', it ended a conversation the Irish were having in their own language. It closed off a whole cultural and psychological tradition mid-flow.

> *We came to a halt*
> *with our half-certainties:*[141]

Gaelic Ireland was not fully formed, much like a middle-aged person in the Kinsellian and Jungian view of adult development. There was much work still to be done, but it could no longer be done in the Irish language, which had been taken by the British Empire. The Irish tongue had been caught, its people left to mumble partial sentences.

Kinsella, like Yeats and others, found literary stimulation and intellectual sustenance in the ancient texts and in the stories of Gaelic Ireland. But while Yeats tended to idealise this past in an attempt to provide a vivid alternative to what he disparaged as the 'filthy modern tide,' Kinsella's past is a far more earthy and brutal location. There is a lack of the superior, isolated, heroic individual as an icon to be emulated. History is more collective, with some victories of sorts to celebrate, but then also many defeats to endure. It is not a place where resistance to life's difficulties can easily be sourced.

* * *

Nature has long been associated in poetry with escape from the difficulties of life, a refuge, resistant to the worst aspects of civilisation. The importance of it for the Romantics is well recognised, but some recent writers have also argued that in the modern world nature can still act as a portal into the sublime. As Julian Young writes: 'For post-death-of-God humanity, nature represents one of the few avenues to the experience of awe that still remains open.'[142]

Kinsella, the hard-nosed, urban poet, may seem an unlikely source for paeans to rural life, but especially in his later poetry there has been an increasing contrast made between rural and urban life, with the urban faring badly. 'Glenmacnass' from *Littlebody* (2000) is an entertaining escapade across the Wicklow Mountains. A comical magical realism quality is provided when the poet narrator encounters a leprechaun playing his pipes behind a rock. The little musician stays in the hills to perfect his personal art. He shuns Dublin, where he would be expected to play for popular tastes and perform for economic rather than artistic reasons.

> *'I thought I was safe up here.*
> *You have to give the music a while to itself sometimes*
> *up out of the huckstering*

> *— jumping around in your green top hat*
> *and showing your skills*
> *with your eye on your income.*[143]

The link is made between rural solitude and artistic integrity. It seems that the poet feels a sense of affinity with this magical creature who toils away at his art, to no large audience, but with greater integrity. Probably intentionally, the poem opens with a personal declaration that resonates with a series of famous lines from T. S. Eliot's 'The Love Song of J. Alfred Prufrock' (*'For I have known them all already, known them all…'*). But while Prufrock's series of declarations of experience of women and life contrasts pathetically with the reality of his life of bourgeois fear and loneliness, this is not the sense of 'Glenmacnass'.

The poet narrator opens up by lashing out at the phoniness of urban life:

> *I have known the hissing assemblies.*
> *The preference for the ease of the spurious*
> *— the measured poses and stupidities.*[144]

This is the inauthentic world of Prufrock, where he has *'measured out my life with coffee spoons.'* It is the artistic arena on which the narrator has turned his back. The narrator looks down towards Dublin, and is repulsed by what it represents:

> *On a fragrant slope descending into the smoke*
> *over our foul ascending city*
> *I turned away in refusal,*
> *holding a handful of high grass*
> *sweet and grey to my face.*[145]

This *'refusal'* is a conscious act of resistance to what the narrator believes the city represents. In contrast, the rural hills of Wicklow and the nature that lives there is genuine and organic:

> *A light deer sailing back and forth*
> *up the hill through the long grass*
> *on his accurate feet*
>
> *stopped to look back at the mess*
> *scattered at our back door,*
> *and disappeared in among the trees.*[146]

The narrator is at one with the deer and the leprechaun in their refusal to partake in urban social life. That the deer is more at ease in his natural surroundings than the teeming mess of humans in the city is clear. In a much earlier poem like 'The Route of The Tain', it is not a deer but a swift fox who *'ran at full stretch out of the bracken,'* perfectly finding its footing at great pace across the hillside. His sense of direction and sure-footedness contrasts with the human party, of which the poet is a member, who wander directionless across the mountainside trying to find the route of the great Irish saga. The group breaks up, *'We ourselves irritated,'* with one person studying a map, and others making their own way towards the river. The poet goes back towards the car *'the way we should have come.'* The humans *'Scattering in irritation,'* have no natural route, fussing, following and fumbling their way across the land.

In the 1978 'Song of the Night', the noise of the Philadelphia streets breaks into the narrator's home and disturbs the personal silence. The cacophony of traffic creates *'exhalation without cease / amplified / of terrible pressure / interrupted by brief blasts and nasal shouts.*'[147] The noise of the city is unnerving and relentless. The poet, in an attempt to distract himself from the din, lets his mind wander east over an open atlas, across the map of the Atlantic Ocean. A family camping holiday in the Irish countryside is recalled. The family finish up their meal at the Carraroe campsite and head down to the beach to wash their utensils. The family are close to the natural environment, the tone calm as the children play by the sea's edge. Enlightened by the poet's lamp, *'They splashed about the stark red basin.'* As a storm forms in the distance over the Connemara plains, there is not the same uncomfortable pressure of the noise from the American city. Rather, the winds pick up local Irish music, bringing pleasure to the poet's ear. *'The bay – every inlet – lifted / and glittered towards us in articulated light.'*[148] The contrast between city and countryside is starkly made.

It is not that Dublin, or urban life in general, was ever really celebrated by the poet. In 'Phoenix Park' the capital is damned as *'the umpteenth city of confusion.'* During the 1960s, the city had its fair share of huckstering, nastiness and destruction.

> *A theatre for the quick articulate,*
> *The agonized genteel, their artful watchers.*
> *Malice as entertainment. Asinine feast*
> *Of sowthistles and brambles! And there dead men,*
> *Half hindered by dead men, tear down dead beauty.*[149]

In the early 'A County Walk' the rural town towards which the narrator is walking is *'Blocking an ancient way with barracks and brewery.'* This man-made barrier is unnatural, and stops the natural flow – the town *'received the river.'* Later in the poem, however, the surrounding countryside is contrasted to the town, but not as an uncomplicated location of sweetness and light – the fields, mountains and hills around the town have hosted numerous acts of horror and death through the centuries. The narrator recalls the battles of the Cromwellian invasions, in which locals were murdered:

> *Then melted into the martyred countryside,*
> *Root eaters, strange as badgers.*[150]

The odd final image here leaves a disconcerting sense of the countryside as a place of weirdness and death.

In later poems, the poet returns to a biting critique of city living. In 'One Fond Embrace' (1988), the poet snarls at an alliance of local government, the Church and private enterprise for the negative impact they have on his city. It is the era where *'Dirty money gives dirty access.'* The actions of men and women gives the narrator cause to despair:

> *And I want to throw my pen down.*
> *and I want to throw my self down*
> *and hang loose over some vault of peace.*[151]

This *'peace'* is found in a series of simple, natural vignettes, united by their lack of humanity. The misanthropic mood is lightened by the pleasant hum of nature getting on with its processes, avoiding or ignoring humanity and its stupidities:

> *Bright gulls, gracefully idling*
> *in the blue and wholesome heights*
> *above our aerials;*
>
> *fatted magpie*
> *big and bold*
> *in the apple shade;*

> *grey maggot, succulent*
> *underfoot, inexorable*
> *on your invisible way;*[151]

But the evocation of the natural world in contrast to the doings of humanity is partial, never reaching the point of an overarching world view. Kinsella's later work is never enwrapped in a warm, pastoral philosophy like the later work of Patrick Kavanagh. While Kavanagh found a religious numinosity to the scenes around the Grand Canal in Dublin, Kinsella, living close by, was never as entranced.

While later poems have deer and gulls participating effortlessly in the peaceful process of nature, earlier works from the 1970s, such as 'A Technical Supplement', never let the reader forget that life in the fields and plains is far from passive. For instance, section 23:

> *(Tiny delicate dawn-antelope that go without water*
> *getting all they need in vegetation and the dew.*
> *Night-staring jerboa.*
> *The snapping of their slender bones,*
> *rosy flesh bursting in small sweet screams*
> *against the palate fine. Just a quick*
> *note. Lest we forget.)*[153]

Nature, like youth and the ancient world, is an arena of shadows. There is no purity to be found here; brutality and death exists on the natural plains as much as it does in human interaction.

The belief that the natural world provides a route towards the sublime or towards authenticity has a long lineage. In the modern period, the Romantic poets turned their backs on the rising stacks of industrial Britain and faced the lakes and countryside. From the heart of the Enlightenment, Rousseau began the counterargument against reason, urban life and progress, valorising the rural, simple life and the authentic 'state of nature'. As capitalist development progressed, the countryside became a less stable location of the authentic. With the enclosures and the creation of private land, the imprint of man's economic relations has arguably as much a role in the shaping of the rural world as the urban. Eric Hobsbawm has noted that 'The reality is that we have already changed the environment.... Our landscapes are for the most part man-made. Everywhere in the developed world, and without doubt in Europe, the environment has been transformed ... above all by agriculture.'[154]

Kinsella's later poems display a growing affinity towards the natural world. He finds its greatest strength in the isolation it provides to the writer, a place where the poet can escape from the testing nature of human interaction. It also provides tiny snatches of moments where, for that fleeting instant, all can seem well. We should snatch what we can as we negotiate the ordeal. Weekend trips to the countryside, or holidays on the outskirts, may be more than mere interludes from the ordeal, they are strategies of resisting it.

* * *

The most sustainable form of resistance to life's ordeal in Kinsella's work is persistence and endurance, particularly when it comes to the artistic act.

Writing and creating are often described as tortuous horrors by the poet. Thus, the young narrator in 'Baggot Street Deserta' has just laid down his pen having suffered *'the strain of the rack.'* But with all the punishment, the narrator comes to the conclusion that nothing can be done but '*Endure and let the present punish.*'

In the third section of 'I wonder whether one expects', the poet struggles to begin his work, and his imagination brings forth a wondrous '*bored menagerie*', who file past, all representing the aspects of the ordeal involved in artistic work:

> *Once more emerges: Energy,*
> *Blinking, only half awake,*
> *Gives its tiny frame a shake;*
> *Fouling itself, a giantess,*
> *The bloodshot bulk of Laziness*
> *Obscures the vision; Discipline*
> *Limps after them with jutting chin,*
> *Bleeding badly from the calf:*
> *Old Jaws-of-Death gives laugh for laugh*
> *With Error as they amble past;*
> *And there as usual, lying last,*
> *Helped along by blind Routine,*
> *Futility flogs a tambourine...*[155]

The creation may be futile, replete with error and slowed by laziness, but this can be resisted with energy, discipline and routine. It is in this process of resistance that something worthwhile is created.

This persistence gives meaning on a communal rather than personal level. While the narrator struggles to find meaning on the level of the individual, it can reside at the level of the entirety of humanity. There is a sense of something important and structured in nature, and in the prospects of the human race. As far back as 'Baggot Street Deserta', the poet felt some faint sense of order in the universe with an ambiguous *'main / Mystery'*. In the opening text of 'Wormwood', he writes: 'Certainly the individual plight is hideous, each torturing each, but we are guilty, seeing this, to believe that our common plight is only hideous. Believing so, we make it so.'[156]

There is something in the wide sweep of humanity's history, in the story of our collective lives on the planet, where meaning can be found, but what exactly this is remains unclear. In section 21 of *A Technical Supplement*, the poet narrator writes:

> *Somehow it all matters ever after – very much –*
> *though each little thing matters little*
> *however painful that may be.*[157]

The narrator, who has embarked on a journey into the individual psyche, is surmising that the plight of the single person may not be of much importance. But it is in the deep psyche, where Kinsella found the communal connection with the rest of humanity, where meaning resonates. The poetry seems to indicate a belief that there is something in this collective unconscious, something in the dark depths of each individual, where the collective reason for humanity can be sought. It is here where the narrative makes sense for the poet narrator. In the fourth section of *Nightwalker*, following a long series of negative vignettes, a clear voice of hope steps forward, booming out in an effort to halt despair in both the reader and narrator:

> *From time to time it seems that everything*
> *Is breaking down. But we must never despair.*
> *There are times it is all part of a meaningful drama*
> *Beginning in the grey mists of antiquity*

> *And reaching through the years to unknown goals*
> *In the consciousness of man, which makes it less gloomy.*[158]

Does this ring true? I have my doubts. The urging never to despair sounds like pleading based on little foundation of fact. The follow-up attempt at outlining a structure is heavily qualified, for even if this is a *'meaningful drama'*, it is only at *'times'*, not all the time. And if there is a grand, progressive narrative hidden deep in an unconscious layer of all our psyches, it does not banish disappointment or death, merely making the whole thing that little less gloomy. The rejection of despair and the inherent need for hope feels wilful rather than hard-won here. That hope is needed to create movement and growth is part of Kinsella's poetic philosophy.

Although the stated theory for his work has been to elicit order from reality, not the other way round, there has been a strand of Kinsella's writing that has attempted to impose some progressive structure on reality. Catriona Clutterbuck has written of the 'general agreement among the critics upon the fundamental element of this revolutionary aesthetic: Kinsella's famously dual technique-cum-ethic of eliciting order from experience rather than imposing order upon it.'[159] Kinsella's career, however, has never been entirely free from attempts to organise his art into a coherent whole. From his early poetry's formalism, to the structure provided by Jungian theory, to the use of numerology and the interaction and self-referential nature of some of the later poems, the poet has often attempted to provide structure.

His use of a numerological system in his poetry during the 1970s and 1980s was part of this structural urge. Kinsella saw the central importance of numbers in how we view the world, and as an archetypal form that could connect with readers. In this regard it was successful; its use in *Notes From the Land of the Dead, One* and other collections was not overwhelming, and worked as part of the imagery of the series. But the poet had greater hopes for the structure, and consciously outlined a system for the scheme at the beginning of the *Peppercanister* series. Counting from zero to five, Kinsella believed that reaching five would provide some totality of understanding. 'Five then would be the ultimate solution where totality would be understood. Five would be the Quincunx or Mandala, both of Jungian theory and Taoism, the four-pointed figure with the observer in the centre, making the five and making totality.'[160] Such high hopes for the project did not last, and poems outside the numerological structure began to appear, like 'The Messenger' and 'The Good Fight'. The scheme was abandoned. It was explained by the poet 'in very simple terms: ordinary experience began to take over.'[161] Although briefly and intensely fascinated by the system, the poet believed that it was an important enabling concept, and its abandonment when it proved redundant is another example of the poet's artistic honesty. Life is not as easy as one, two, three, and the imposition of even the most basic artistic structure on it is fraught with difficulty.

Claims are made about life's meaning in some poems, like the lines from 'Nightwalker'. There is a leap of faith here, but maybe not as wide a leap as one into the intricate theology of the world's great religions. In a recent poem, 'Elderly Craftsman at his Bench', from the collection *Fat Master* (2011), there is an incredible image of an arm reaching out from the past and appearing before the poetic narrator at work. If the narrator feels little connection with his contemporaries, there is a connection to this mysterious arm from the past, reaching out to the poet through the collective unconscious. There is something connecting all of humanity through this main mystery, with which we all have some contact deep down in our unconscious.

But this Kinsella, the poet of the main mystery that cannot be understood, is not as convincing as the writer of the fall. His poetry is more authentic when it deals with the loss of meaning, the absurdity of life, its happenstance, and in the traditional sense, its absolute meaninglessness. In 'Hen Woman', as the poet remembers himself as a boy, watching the egg fall from the hen's sphincter and crash against the grate, he understands why the image is recurrent:

As it will continue to fall, probably, until I die,
through the vast indifferent spaces
with which I am empty.[162]

In 'All is Emptiness / and I must Spin', man is spread out over a reasonless existence that is *'A vacancy in which, apparently / I hang / with severed senses.'*[163] That this is *'apparently'* the situation in which we find ourselves adds an absurdist tinge, for it seems that the way we are made is to seek meaning 'out there', even though we exist in a universe where none exists. It is a quest that we cannot but make, but the destination is nowhere. Man here is depicted as isolated and puny, helplessly falling through the vast uncaring spaces of existence. In the paintings of the Romantic period, man is portrayed as small in the foreground of the canvas, with a large, sweeping backdrop of natural beauty. The epic vastness of the pastoral backdrop compared to the smallness of man was meant to provoke a sense of wonder and awe in the viewer. A positive feeling of our own small role in the vastness of beautiful nature, this is the feeling of the sublime. Man falling in Kinsella's poetry is also set against the incomprehensible hugeness of the universe, but rather than filling one with a sensation of positive wonder, we feel scared. In place of Romantic awe, there is modern sterility. In the place of natural birth, there is ash:

> *I was lying in a vaulted place.*
> *The cold air crept over long-abandoned floors,*
> *carrying a taint of remote iron and dead ash.*
> *Echo of voices. A distant door closed.*
>
> *The sterile:*
> *it is a whole matter in itself.*[164]

Ultimate resistance to the 'ordeal' of life, it seems to me, cannot be found in the adherence to a belief system based on life as an unfolding universal story hidden in our collective unconscious. This may be what the poetry espouses, but even if this psycho-historical thesis were true, it would not bring happiness or comfort, it would at best make things a little less 'gloomy'.

This is the closest that Kinsella's Jungian world view comes to a religious set of beliefs. Jung wrote that 'man cannot stand a meaningless life,' and this insight made him formulate the question he believed most pertinent to humanity. For Jung, the 'decisive question for a man is: is he related to something infinite or not?'[165] To answer that question in the negative is to risk, according to Jung, mental collapse. Søren Kierkegaard (1813–1855) sketched the spectre of such a negative response in dramatic language: 'If man has no eternal consciousness, if, at the bottom of everything there were merely a wild seething force producing everything, both large and trifling, in the storm of dark passions, if the bottomless void that nothing can fill underlay all things, what would life be but despair?'[166] The Danish philosopher looked at the void, and decided he did not like what he saw. He leaped into Christianity to provide meaning. To leap into faith is to jump headlong into 'the substance of things hoped for, the evidence of things not seen.'[167] But it would be wrong to say that Kinsella dives deep into this substance in the way Kierkegaard did. Kinsella looks at the meaningless void and writes about it with passionate, dark honesty, but in response he makes, if not a leap, a skip towards something eternal. It is a skip too far for this reader at least, but it is of importance in the poetry.

Does the stripping away of all illusions signal inevitable despair? Karl Marx did not believe so. Specifically writing about religion, but having a much broader target than that, the young Marx claimed that 'The abolition of religion as the illusory happiness of the people is the demand for their real happiness. The demand to give up the illusion about their condition is a demand to give up a condition that requires illusions.' For Marx, God was a projection of real humanity, 'for the more man puts in God, the less he retains of himself.'[168] To deny all illusions is thus not to experience loss for the Marxist, it is the path for humans to become more authentic.

In Kinsella's work, and particularly in his most recent collections, there is a sense that the progress of mankind, for all the barbarism that still haunts it, is some cause for positivity. That the best of the sciences and the arts leaves a legacy to the next generation upon which they can build is increasingly part of the 'late' Kinsella's outlook. The role of the poet, particularly in contemporary Western societies, may be marginal, but their work can still have importance, almost of an organic nature. 'The significant poetry of the time is, I believe, at the edge, fulfilling virtually a biological function. To speak passively: guarding the basics which, for the time being, count for nothing in the outer world. But, to speak dynamically: fulfilling what might be called an evolutionary function, at the global forefront with other creative efforts – in the physical sciences and in metaphysics, in psychology, archaeology and mathematics – which are making the significant human difference.'[169]

The correlation between poetry and the progressive work of the human sciences is again made in the 2006 poem 'Blood of the Innocent':

> *add our own best and,*
> *advancing in our turn*
>   *outward into the dark,*
> *leave to those behind us,*
> *with Acts of Hope and Encouragement*
> *a growing total of Good (adequately recorded),*
>
> *the Arts and the Sciences,*
> *with their abstractions and techniques*
> *– all of positive human endeavour –*
>
> *in a flexible and elaborating*
> *time-resisting fabric*
> *of practical and moral beauty...*[170]

* * *

Much of Kinsella's poetry embraces the negative response to the question of life's meaning, with all the falls and spinning in space. But at times he answers, warily, in the positive: that there is something infinite, something mysterious, which connects us all, to everything, which we do not know fully. That Kinsella's poetry reads most authentically when it veers towards the negative may be because, despite the reverence for Jung's theories within the poetry, no conclusive meaning of life lies outside in the exterior cosmos, or inside in the personal psyche for that matter. His poetry of the Fall reads more credibly because it reflects the brute fact of our existence.

There is no ultimate balm to be found outside of us, however, the comforts in the poetry, the countermoves of resistance, love, activism against injustice, nature and art, are limited but important. Fundamentally, the greatest act of defiance is to be found in not turning away from life's ordeal. In the final analysis, this is the core of Kinsella's sense of resistance. The final stand in the face of ordeal, injustice and mutability is made on the rugged rock of endurance. It is not endurance merely composed of denial of the negativity; rather, it is an honest form of persistence that does not turn away from difficulties. Adorno described it as the highest form of intellectual and political honesty that one could muster following the catastrophe of the twentieth century, and it has echoes of the major themes in Kinsella's work: 'There is no longer beauty or consolation except in the gaze falling on horror, withstanding it, and in unalleviated consciousness of negativity holding fast to the possibility of what is better.'[171]

The essence of the poetry maintains that many of life's greater difficulties arise from a denial of problems, rather than the problem itself. So whether it is facing the mechanical diggers in Wood Quay in 1979, the elderly trade unionist marching against injustice, an honest appraising of difficult matters in a romantic relationship, or staring at the brute fact of death's finality as the egg falls and cracks on the grate, all must be digested. Endurance does not mean successfully slaying our outer and inner dragons, but we must face these beasts and endure what comes. There is no conclusive, heroic victory to be found here. Rather, it is about enduring the bitterness that is inherent in life, drinking from the cup of ordeal rather than denying its existence, and crucially, learning from that experience, and in so doing we add to the positivity in human endeavour. This is the greatest 'individual joy' according to Kinsella in the introduction of *Wormwood* – the joy found in the 'restored necessity to learn,' because after each ordeal we take what we have learned and 'we begin again in a higher innocence to grow toward the next ordeal.'[172] Any resistance is marginal, and the gains partial, but these marginal gains are ultimately worth the effort. Resistance is found in facing the struggle, enduring it, and transmuting the experience so we can struggle on again.

Neither the bard of hopeful collective victory over injustice and death, nor the poet of indulgent individual despair at humanity's plight, Thomas Kinsella is the realistic poet of resistance as endurance.

Works by Thomas Kinsella

Poetry:

Poems	Dublin, Dolmen, 1956.
Another September	Dublin, 1958.
Moralities	Dublin, Dolmen, 1960.
Downstream	Dublin, Dolmen, 1962.
Wormwood	Dublin, Dolmen, 1966.
Nightwalker and Other Poems	Dublin, Dolmen, 1968.
(Peppercanister Years)	
Butcher's Dozen	1. Dublin, Peppercanister, 1972.
A Selected Life	2. Dublin, Peppercanister, 1972.
Vertical Man	3. Dublin, Peppercanister, 1973.
The Good Fight	4. Dublin, Peppercanister, 1973.

Notes from the Land of the Dead and Other Poems
    New York, Alfred A Knopf, 1973.

New Poems	Dublin, Dolmen 1973.
One	5. Dublin, Peppercanister, 1974.
A Technical Supplement	6. Peppercanister, 1976.
Song of the Night and Other Poems	7. Peppercanister, 1978.
The Messenger	8. Peppercanister 1978.
Fifteen Dead	Oxford, OUP, 1979.
One and Other Poems	Dublin, Dolmen, 1979.
Poems 1956-1973	Dublin, Dolmen, 1980.
Songs of the Psyche	9. Dublin, Peppercanister, 1985.
Her Vertical Smile	10. Dublin, Peppercanister, 1985.
Out of Ireland	11. Dublin, Peppercanister, 1987.
St Catherine's Clock	12. Dublin, Peppercanister, 1987.
Blood and Family	Oxford, OUP, 1988.
One Fond Embrace	13. Dublin, Peppercanister, 1988.
Personal Places	14. Dublin, Peppercanister, 1990.
Poems from Centre City	15. Dublin, Peppercanister, 1990.
Madonna and Other Poems	16. Dublin, Peppercanister, 1991.
Open Court	17. Dublin, Peppercanister, 1991.
From City Centre	Oxford, OUP, 1994.
The Dual Tradition: an Essay on Poetry and Politics in Ireland.	18. Manchester, Carcanet Press, 1995

(Author Note: *The Dual Tradition* is prose, but part of the Peppercanister series.)

The Pen Shop	19. Dublin, Peppercanister, Dedalus Press, 1997.
The Familiar	20. Dublin, Peppercanister, Dedalus Press, 1999.
Godhead	21. Dublin, Peppercanister, Dedalus Press, 1999.
Citizen of the World	22. Dublin, Peppercanister, Dedalus Press, 2000.
Littlebody	23. Dublin, Peppercanister, Dedalus Press, 2000.
Collected Poems 1956–2001	Carcanet Press, Manchester, 2001.
Marginal Economy	24. Dublin, Peppercanister, Dedalus Press, 2006.
Readings in Poetry	25. Dublin, Peppercanister, Dedalus Press, 2006.
Man of War	26. Dublin, Peppercanister, Dedalus Press, 2007.
Belief and Unbelief	27. Dublin, Peppercanister, Dedalus Press, 2007.
Fat Master	28. Dublin, Peppercanister, Dedalus Press, 2011.
Love Joy Peace	29. Dublin, Peppercanister, Dedalus Press, 2011.
Late Poems	Manchester, Carcanet Press, 2013.

Selected Prose

The Dual Tradition: An Essay on Poetry and Politics in Ireland (Manchester, Carcanet Press, 1995.)

A Dublin Documentary (Dublin, O'Brien Press, 2007.)
Prose Occasions: 1956–2006 (Manchester, Carcanet Press, 2009.)

Audio

Fair Eleanor, O Christ Thee Save (Claddagh Records, 1971.)
Thomas Kinsella – Poems 1956–2006 (Claddagh Records, 2007.)

Selected Translation

Ó Tuama, Sean (ed.) (1994) *An Duanaire 1600–1900 Poems of the Dispossessed* (trans. Thomas Kinsella. Portlaoise, Dolmen Press.)
The Táin. (2002) (trans. Thomas Kinsella, Oxford, Oxford University Press.)

Selected Bibliography

Adorno, T., (2001) *The Culture Industry: Selected Essays on Mass Culture* (London: Routledge Classics.)

Adorno, T., (2005) *Minima Moralia: Reflections from Damaged Life* (London: Verso.)

Armstrong, T., (2005) *Modernism: A Cultural History* (Cambridge: Polity Press.)

Berman, M., (1983) *All That Is Solid Melts into Air: The Experience of Modernity* (London: Verso.)

Bloom, H., (2011) *The Anatomy of Influence* (New Haven: Yale University Press.)

Boland, E., (2011) *A Journey With Two Maps: Becoming a Woman Poet* (Manchester: Carcanet.)

Boran, P. and Smith, G., (eds.) (2014) *If Ever you Go: A Map of Dublin Poetry and Song* (Dublin: Dedalus Press.)

Byrne, E., (2012) *Political Corruption in Ireland: 1922–2010: A Crooked Harp?* (Manchester: Manchester University Press.)

Callinicos, A., (1989) *Against Postmodernism: A Marxist Critique* (Polity, 1989.)

Campbell, J., (1993) *The Hero with a Thousand Faces* (London: Fontana.)

Camus, A., (2000) *The Myth of Sisyphus* (UK: Penguin.)

Carey, J., (1992) *The Intellectuals and the Masses: Pride and Prejudice Among the Literary Intelligentsia, 1880–1939* (London: Faber and Faber.)

Childs, P., (2011) *Modernist Literature: A Guide for the Perplexed* (London: Continuum.)

Cleary, J., (2007) *Outrageous Fortune: Capital and Culture in Modern Ireland* (Dublin: Field Day.)

Cleary, J. and Connolly, C., (eds.) *The Cambridge Companion to Modern Irish Culture* (Cambridge: Cambridge University Press.)

Corkery, D., (1996) *Synge and Anglo-Irish Literature* (Mercier: Cork, 1966.)

Coulter, C. and Coleman, S., (eds.) *The End of History? Critical Approaches to the Celtic Tiger* (Manchester: Manchester University Press.)

Donoghue, D., (2008) *On Eloquence* (Yale: Yale University Press.)

Dorgan, T., (1996) *Irish Poetry Since Kavanagh* (Dublin: Four Courts Press.)

Duffy, M., (2013) *The Trade Union Pint: The Unlikely Union of Guinness and the Larkins* (Dublin: Liberties Press.)

Eagleton, T., (2008) *The Meaning of Life: A Very Short Introduction* (Oxford: Oxford University Press.)

Edwards, D. and Ransom, B., (eds.) *James Connolly: Selected Political Writings* (London: Jonathan Cape, 1973.)

Ferriter, D., (2007) *Judging Dev: A Reassessment of the Life and Legacy of Éamon de Valera* (Dublin: Royal Irish Academy.)

Fitzsimons, A., (2008) *The Sea of Disappointment: Thomas Kinsella's Pursuit of the Real* (Dublin: UCD Press.)

Gallop, J., (2011) *The Deaths of the Author: Reading and Writing in Time* (Durham, North Carolina: Duke University Press.)

Garvin, T., (2010) *News from a New Republic – Ireland in the 1950s* (Dublin: Gill & Macmillan.)

Gilsenan, I., (ed.) (2006) *The Body and Desire in Contemporary Irish Poetry* (Dublin: Irish Academic Press.)

Gonzalez, A., (ed.) (1997) *Modern Irish Writers: A Bio-critical Sourcebook* (Westport, Conn: Greenwood Press.)

Goodby, J., (2000) *Irish Poetry Since 1950* (Manchester: Manchester University Press.)

Harmon, M., (2008) *Thomas Kinsella: Designing for the Exact Needs* (Dublin: Irish Academic Press.)

Heaney, S., (1989) *The Place of Writing* (Atlanta, Georgia: Scholars Press.)

Hobsbawm, E., (2000) *The New Century* (London: Abacus.)

Jackson, Thomas H., (1995) *The Whole Matter: The Poetic Evolution of Thomas Kinsella* (Dublin: Lilliput.)

John, B., (1996) *Reading the Ground: The Poetry of Thomas Kinsella* (Washington DC: Catholic University of America Press.)

Jung, C., (1991) *The Archetypes and the Collective Unconscious* (London: Routledge.)

Jung, C., (1998) *The Essential Jung* (London: Fontana Press.)

Jung, C., (2009) *The Red Book, Liber Novus* (New York: W. W. Norton & Co.)

Kenneally, M., (ed.) *Poetry in Contemporary Irish Literature* (Buckinghamshire: TJ Press.)

Kermode, F., (1967) *The Sense of an Ending: Studies in the Theory of Fiction* (Oxford: Oxford University Press.)

Kermode F., (ed). (1975) *Selected Prose of T. S. Eliot* (London: Faber and Faber.)

Kiberd, D., (1955) *Inventing Ireland: The Literature of the Modern Nation* (London: Jonathan Cape.)

Kostick, C., (2009) *Revolution in Ireland: popular militancy, 1917–1923* (Cork: Cork University Press.)

Lee, J. J., (1989) *Ireland 1912–1985: Politics and Society* (UK: Cambridge University Press.)

Liddy, J., (2013) *On Irish Literature and Identities* (Dublin: Arlen House.)

Lynch, D., (2005) *Radical Politics in Modern Ireland: A History of the Irish Socialist Republican Party, 1896–1904* (Dublin: Irish Academic Press.)

McCabe, C., (2011) *Sins of the Father: Tracing the Decisions that Shaped the Irish Economy* (Dublin: The History Press.)

Mc Caffrey, C. and Eaton, L., (2003) *In Search of Ancient Ireland: The Origins of the Irish from Neolithic Times to the Coming of the English* (USA: Ivan R. Dee.)

McLellan, D., (ed.) (1977) *Marx: Selected Writings* (Oxford: Oxford University Press.)

McLynn, F., (2010) *Marcus Aurelius: Warrior, Philosopher, Emperor* (London: Vintage.)

Nevin, D., (2005) *James Connolly: A Full Life* (Dublin, Gill & Macmillan.)

Ní Anluain, C., (ed.) *Reading the Future: Irish Writers in Conversation with Mike Murphy* (Dublin: Lilliput.)

O'Connor, F., (1965) *The Big Fellow* (Dublin: Poolbeg.)

Pierse, M., (2011) *Writing Ireland's Working Class: Dublin After O'Casey* (London: Palgrave Macmillan.)

Puirséil, N., (2007) *The Irish Labour Party, 1922–73* (Dublin: UCD Press.)

Quinn, J., (2008) *The Cambridge Introduction to Modern Irish Poetry: 1800–2000* (Cambridge: Cambridge University Press.)

Regan, J. M., (1999) *The Irish Counter-Revolution, 1921–1936: Treatyite Politics and Settlement in Independent Ireland* (Dublin: Gill & Macmillan.)

Roche, A., (ed). *The UCD Aesthetic: Celebrating 150 Years of UCD Writers* (Dublin: New Island.)

Slavin, M., (2005) *The Ancient Books of Ireland* (Belfast: Mcgill-Queen's University Press.)

Stevens, A., (2001) *Jung: A Very Short Introduction* (Oxford: Oxford University Press.)

Taussig, M., (1980) *The Devil and Commodity Fetishism in South America* (North Carolina: University of North Carolina Press.)

Thomson, A., (2006) *Adorno: A Guide for the Perplexed* (London: Continuum.)

Treacy, M., (2013) *The Communist Party of Ireland, 1921–2011* (Dublin: Brocaire Books.)

Tubrity D., (2001) *Thomas Kinsella, The Peppercanister Poems* (Dublin: UCD.)

Waddell, J., (1998) *The Prehistoric Archaeology of Ireland* (Galway: Galway University Press.)

Yeates, P., (2000) *Lockout: Dublin 1913* (Dublin: Gill & Macmillan.)

Young, J., (2003) *The Death of God and the Meaning of Life* (London: Routledge.)

Suggested Further Reading

This book is not an extensive work of academic literary criticism. However, Thomas Kinsella's poetry has inspired engagement from many leading literary academics over the decades, and so those interested in pursuing the work of the poet in more detail are very much in luck.

Thomas Kinsella: Designing for the Exact Needs (Irish Academic Press, 2008) is by Maurice Harmon, who knows the poet personally and is a leading expert on his work. This is an insightful engagement with the poet's work from one of the country's leading scholars and critics, and is particularly strong on Kinsella's important work in the translation of Gaelic literature. Harmon has consistently engaged with Kinsella over the decades and he wrote the first book-length study of his work in the 1970s, *The Poetry of Thomas Kinsella* (Wolfhound Press, 1974).

Andrew Fitzsimons's *The Sea of Disappointment: Thomas Kinsella's Pursuit of the Real* (UCD Press, 2008) was published around the same time. It is an exhaustive and incredibly impressive scholarly work of detailed primary research that mines Thomas Kinsella's own notebooks for the background to individual poems.

For those interested in tracing the development of the *Peppercanister* series of poems in greater detail, Derval Tubridy's *Thomas Kinsella, The Peppercanister Poems* (UCD, 2001) follows the series chronologically. It also discusses the drawings and designs of the different *Peppercanister* editions.

Now two decades old, both Brian John's *Reading the Ground: The Poetry of Thomas Kinsella* (Catholic University of America Press, 1996) and Thomas H. Jackson's *The Whole Matter: The Poetic Evolution of Thomas Kinsella* (Lilliput Press, 1995) provide interesting insights into the development of Kinsella's early work.

Given Kinsella's importance and the longevity of his career, his work has featured in a vast number of academic journal articles and reviews too extensive to list here.

Obviously, the back catalogue of *Poetry Ireland* is a good place to start. Writers such as Maurice Harmon, Peter Denman and many others have penned reviews of Kinsella collections therein, and it is also an excellent place to discover expert insights into the development of the poet's career. *Irish University Review* had a 'Thomas Kinsella Special Issue' in its Spring/Summer 2001 edition, and so did the *Irish Studies Review* with its 'Kinsella at Eighty' special in August 2008. All are highly recommended.

Acknowledgements

I want to thank my parents, David and Marie, and my talented sister, photographer and designer, Julie Lynch.

Since my last book five years ago, many of my friends have crossed the frontiers of adulthood and have started families — they remain an important source of ideas, friendship and fun: Mark Walsh, Simon Dunne, Anne Marie Quinn, Ruth O'Hara, Clifford Burke, Donal Collins, Dave Parkes, Sandra Cryan, Donal O hAodha, Paul Hartnett, Triona Lynch, Morgan Treacy, Dave Watt and others.

I want to acknowledge everyone at New Island Books, in particular Justin Corfield, Eoin Purcell and Shauna Daly for their huge contribution in deciding to run with this project, and later with the editing process and in helping to clarify ideas.

Finally I want to thank artist Barbara Vasic for entering my life early last year and enhancing it in so many wonderful ways.

Endnotes

1. Entry

1. Kinsella, T. (1956) *Poems*. Dublin: Dolmen Press.
2. Wheatley, D. (1997) 'Going Underground – Review of Thomas Kinsella's Collected Poems 1956–1994'. *Metre 3*. p. 43.
3. Kinsella, T. (1990) Interview by Eileen Battersby for *The Irish Times*, 3 December.
4. Kinsella, T. (2001) *Collected Poems*. Manchester: Carcanet, p.365.
5. O'Siadhail, M. (1989) *Poetry Ireland Review* 26, Summer 1989, p. 20.
6. Gonzalez, A. (ed.) (1997) *Modern Irish Writers: A Bio-Critical Sourcebook*. Westport, Connecticut: Greenwood Press, p. 160 and John, B. (1996) *Reading the Ground: The Poetry of Thomas Kinsella*. Washington DC: Catholic University of America Press, p. 117.
7. Kinsella, T. (2002) Interview by Michael Smith for *Poetry Ireland Review*, Winter 2002, p. 109.
8. Clutterbuck, C. (2005) 'Thomas Kinsella'. In Roche, A. (ed.) *The UCD Aesthetic: Celebrating 150 Years of UCD Writers*. Dublin: New Island, p. 150.
9. See 'Suggested Further Reading, p. 276'.
10. Kinsella, T. quoted in (1997) Interview by Ian Flanagan for *Metre 2*, Spring 1997, p. 114.
11. Kinsella, T. (1987) Interview by John F. Deane for *Tracks* No. 7, 1987, pp. 88–89.
12. *Ibid*.
13. Battersby, Thomas Kinsella Interview.
14. Kinsella, *Collected Poems*, p. 189.

15   Barthes, R. Quoted in Gallop, J. (2011) *The Deaths of the Author: Reading and Writing in Time.* Durham, North Carolina: Duke University Press, p. 29.
16   Stevens, A. (2001) *Jung: A Very Short Introduction.* Oxford: Oxford University Press, p. 137.
17   Kinsella, *Collected Poems,* p. 189.
18   O'Driscoll, D. (1987) 'Reading Patterns: Thomas Kinsella's Poetry', Quoted in *Tracks,* No. 7, p. 9.
19   Kinsella, T. (1989) Interview by Dennis O'Driscoll for *Poetry Ireland Review 25,* Spring 1989, p. 59.
20   *Ibid*, p. 63.
21   Kinsella, T. (2013) Interview by Miles Dungan for RTÉ Radio, *Today with Myles Dungan,* 30 August.
22   Heaney, S. (1989) *The Place of Writing.* Atlanta, Georgia: Scholars Press, p. 57.
23   Kinsella, T. and Kinsella, E. quoted in (2009) 'Thomas Kinsella: Personal Places'. *Arts Lives.* RTÉ One. 24 March 2009.
24   Kinsella, T. (1997) Interview by Ian Flanagan for *Metre 2,* Spring 1997, p. 114.
25   Dawe, G. (1995) 'Poetry as Example: Kinsella's Peppercanister Poems' in Kenneally, M. (ed.) *Poetry in Contemporary Irish Literature.* Buckinghamshire: TJ Press, p. 205.
26   Smith, Thomas Kinsella Interview, p. 117.

2. Working-Class Heroes

1   O'Connor, F. (1965) *The Big Fellow.* Dublin: Poolbeg, 1965, p. 20.
2   Ferriter, D. (2007) *Judging Dev: A Reassessment of the Life and Legacy of Éamon de Valera.* Dublin: Royal Irish Academy.
3   Lee, J. J. (1989) *Ireland 1912-1985: Politics and Society.* Cambridge: Cambridge University Press, p. 334.
4   Nevin, D. (2005) *James Connolly: A Full Life.* Dublin: Gill and MacMillan, p. 97.
5   Lynch, D. (2005) *Radical Politics in Modern Ireland: A History of the Irish Socialist Republican Party, 1896–1904.* Dublin: Irish Academic Press, pp. 112–115.
6   Garvin, T. (2010) *News from a New Republic – Ireland in the 1950s.* Dublin: Gill and Macmillan, p. 104.
7   *Ibid*, p. 116.
8   *Ibid*, p. 117.

9   McCabe, C. (2011) *Sins of the Father: Tracing the Decisions that Shaped the Irish Economy*. Dublin: The History Press, p. 57.
10 Kiberd, D. (1955) *Inventing Ireland: The Literature of the Modern Nation*. London: Jonothan Cape, p. 102.
11 *Ibid*, pp. 1–2.
12 *Ibid*, p. 492.
13 Mc Cormack, W. J. (1987) 'Politics or Community: Crux of Thomas Kinsella's Aesthetic Development' in *Tracks,* No. 7, 1987, p. 74.
14 Kinsella, T. (2001) *Collected Poems*. Manchester: Carcanet, p. 212.
15 Devine, F. (2013). 'Introduction' in Duffy, M. *The Trade Union Pint: The Unlikely Union of Guinness and the Larkins*. Dublin: Liberties Press, p. 10.
16 Kinsella, *Collected Poems,* p. 217.
17 *Ibid.,* p. 214.
18 *Ibid.,* p. 215.
19 *Ibid.*
20 *Ibid.,* p. 217.
21 *Ibid.*
22 Harmon, M. (2008) *Thomas Kinsella: Designing for the Exact Needs*. Dublin: Irish Academic Press, p. xi.
23 Kinsella, *Collected Poems,* p. 218.
24 *Ibid.,* p. 214.
25 *Ibid.*
26 *Ibid.,* p. 210.
27 *Ibid.*
28 *Ibid.,* p. 211.
29 Yeates, P. (2000) *Lockout: Dublin 1913*. Dublin: Gill & Macmillan, p. x.
30 Pierse, M. (2011) *Writing Ireland's Working Class: Dublin After O'Casey*. London: Palgrave Macmillan, p. 15.
31 Liddy, J. (2013) *On Irish Literature and Identities*. Dublin: Arlen House, p. 155.
32 Treacy, M. (2013) *The Communist Party of Ireland, 1921–2011* Dublin: Brocaire Books, p. 171. See also Puirséil, N. (2007) *The Irish Labour Party, 1922–73*. Dublin: UCD Press.
33 Harmon, *Thomas Kinsella: Designing for the Exact Needs,* p. xii.
34 Pierse, *Writing Ireland's Working Class: Dublin After O'Casey,* p. 9.
35 Kinsella, *Collected Poems,* p. 266.
36 *Ibid.*
37 Pierse, *Writing Ireland's Working Class: Dublin After O'Casey,* p. vii.

38 *Ibid.*, p. 13.
39 *Ibid.*, p. 15.
40 *Ibid.*, p. 50.
41 Kinsella, T. (2006) *A Dublin Documentary*. Dublin: O'Brien Press, p. 17.
42 *Ibid.*
43 Kinsella, *Collected Poems*, p. 37.
44 Taussig, M. (1980) *The Devil and Commodity Fetishism in South America*. North Carolina: University of North Carolina Press, p. 3.
45 *Ibid.*
46 Kinsella, *Collected Poems*, p. 36.
47 *Ibid.*
48 Camus, A. (2000) *The Myth of Sisyphus*. London: Penguin.
49 *Ibid.*, p. 32.
50 *Ibid.*, p. 53.
51 *Ibid.*, p. 43.
52 Kinsella, *Collected Poems*, p. 211.
53 Young, J. (2003) *The Death of God and the Meaning of Life*. London: Routledge, p. 165.
54 Camus, *The Myth of Sisyphus*, p. 19.
55 Kinsella, *Collected Poems*, p. 295.
56 Camus, *The Myth of Sisyphus*, p.104.
57 Kinsella, *Collected Poems*, p. 36.
58 *Ibid.*
59 Kinsella, *A Dublin Documentary*, p. 17.
60 Kinsella, *Collected Poems*, p. 36.
61 Young, *The Death of God and the Meaning of Life*, p.138.
62 Camus, *The Myth of Sisyphus*, p. 13.
63 Kinsella, *Collected Poems*, p. 36.
64 Kiberd, *Inventing Ireland: The Literature of the Modern Nation*, p. 492.
65 *Ibid.*
66 Garvin, T. (2010) *News from a New Republic – Ireland in the 1950s*. Dublin, Gill and Macmillan, p. 9.
67 McCarthy, C. (1973) *The Decade of Upheaval: Irish Trade Unions in the Nineteen Sixites*. Dublin: Institute of Public Administration, p. 7.
68 Kinsella, *Collected Poems*, p. 19.
69 *Ibid.*
70 Boland, E. (2011) A Journey With Two Maps: Becoming a Woman Poet. Manchester: Carcanet, pp. 109–110.
71 *Ibid.*

72 *Ibid.*, p. 112.
73 Kinsella, *Collected Poems,* p. 29.

3. Walking Alone

1 Liddy, J. (2013) *On Irish Literature and Identities.* Dublin: Arlen House, p. 154.
2 Kinsella, T. (2001) *Collected Poems.* Manchester: Carcanet, p. 44.
3 *Ibid.*, p. 45.
4 *Ibid.*, p.77.
5 *Ibid.*, p. 261.
6 Theodor A. 'Resignation', in Adorno, T. (ed.) *The Culture Industry: Selected Essays on Mass Culture.* London: Routledge Classics, p. 202.
7 Harmon, M. (2008) *Thomas Kinsella: Designing for the Exact Needs.* Dublin: Irish Academic Press, p. 4.
8 Kinsella, *Collected Poems,* p. 111.
9 Campbell, J. (1993) *The Hero with a Thousand Faces.* London: Fontana, p. 51.
10 Kinsella, *loc.cit.*
11 *Ibid.*, p. 112.
12 *Loc.cit.*
13 Harmon, *Thomas Kinsella: Designing for the Exact Needs,* p. 70.
14 Kinsella, *Collected Poems,* p. 169.
15 *Ibid.*, p. 239.
16 *Ibid.*, p. 303.
17 *Ibid.*, p. 329.
18 *Ibid.*, p. 110.
19 *Ibid.*, p. 90.
20 *Loc.cit.*
21 *Ibid.*
22 Donoghue, D. (2008) *On Eloquence.* Yale: Yale University Press, p. 3.
23 Kinsella, *Collected Poems,* p. 90.
24 *Ibid.*, p. 162.
25 *Ibid.*, p. 159.
26 *Ibid.*, p. 160.
27 *Ibid.*, p. 182.
28 Collins, L. ' "Enough is Enough": Suffering and Desire in the Poetry of Thomas Kinsella' in Gilsenan, I., (ed.) *The Body and Desire in Contemporary Irish Poetry.* Dublin: Irish Academic Press, p. 183.
29 Kinsella, *Collected Poems,* p. 53.

30 *Ibid.*, p. 53.
31 *Ibid.*, p. 98.
32 Kinsella quoted in Jackson, T. (1995) *The Whole Matter: The Poetic Evolution of Thomas Kinsella*. Dublin: Lilliput, p. 3.
33 Kinsella, T. (2002) Interview by Michael Smith for *Poetry Ireland Review,* Winter 2002, p. 115.
34 Kinsella, *Collected Poems,* p. 288.
35 *Ibid.*, p. 289.
36 *Ibid.*, p. 315.
37 *Ibid.*, p. 318.
38 Ibid., p. 316.
39 Denman, P. (1992) 'Review of "Open Court", *Irish University Review*, Vol. 22. No 1. 1992, p. 191.
40 Kinsella, *Collected Poems,* p. 316.
41 Smith, Thomas Kinsella Interview, p. 119.
42 *Ibid.*
43 Kinsella, T. (1989) Interview by Dennis O'Driscoll for *Poetry Ireland Review 25,* Spring 1989, p. 57.
44 Kinsella, *Collected Poems,* p. 310.
45 *Ibid.*, p. 124.
46 *Ibid.*
47 *Ibid.*
48 *Ibid.*, p. 236.
49 Kinsella, T. (1997) Interview by Ian Flanagan for *Metre 2,* Spring, 1997, p. 115.
50 Kinsella, *Collected Poems,* p. 185.
51 Childs, P. (2011) *Modernist Literature: A Guide for the Perplexed*. London: Continuum, p. 1.
52 Armstrong, T. (2005) *Modernism: A Cultural History*. Cambridge: Polity Press, p. 5.
53 Berman, M. (1983) *All That Is Solid Melts into Air: The Experience of Modernity*. London: Verso, p. 15.
54 Cleary, J. (2007) *Outrageous Fortune: Capital and Culture in Modern Ireland*. Dublin: Field Day, p. 117.
55 Carey, J. (1992) *The Intellectuals and the Masses: Pride and Prejudice Among the Literary Intelligentsia, 1880–1939*. London: Faber and Faber.
56 Adorno, *The Culture Industry: Selected Essays on Mass Culture.*
57 Dorgan, T. (1996) *Irish Poetry Since Kavanagh*. Dublin: Four Courts Press, p. 123.

58 *Ibid.*, p. 152.
59 Nolan, E. (2005) 'Modernism and the Irish Revival' in Cleary, J. and Connolly, C. (eds). *The Cambridge Companion to Modern Irish Culture.* Cambridge: Cambridge University Press, pp. 168–169.
60 Quinn, J. (2008) *The Cambridge Introduction to Modern Irish Poetry: 1800–2000.* Cambridge: Cambridge University Press, p. 101.
61 Kinsella, *Collected Poems,* p. 261.
62 *Ibid.*, p. 240.
63 *Ibid.*, p. 175.
64 O'Driscoll, Thomas Kinsella Interview, p. 59.
65 Kinsella, T. (1987) Interview by John F. Deane for *Tracks* No. 7 (1987), p. 87.
66 Wheatley, D. (1997) ' "Going Underground", A Review of Kinsella's Collected Poems 1956–1994', in *Metre 3,* Autumn 1997, p. 43.
67 O'Driscoll, Thomas Kinsella Interview, p. 59.
68 Wheatley, 'Going Underground', p. 44.
69 *Ibid.*, p. 46.
70 Kinsella, T. (1990) Interview by Eileen Battersby for *The Irish Times,* 3 December.
71 Harmon, *Thomas Kinsella: Designing for the Exact Needs,* p. 168.
72 Battersby, Thomas Kinsella Interview.
73 Kinsella, *Collected Poems,* p. 128.
74 *Ibid.*, p. 38.
75 Harmon, M. (2001) quoted in Ní Anluain, C. (ed.) *Reading the Future: Irish Writers in Conversation with Mike Murphy.* Dublin: Lilliput, p. 109.
76 Smith, Thomas Kinsella Interview, p. 115.
77 *Ibid.*, p. 117.
78 Ní Anluain, C. (2001) *Reading the Future: Irish Writers in Conversation with Mike Murphy.* Dublin: Lilliput, p. 100.
79 Kinsella, *Collected Poems,* p. 53.
80 Jackson, Thomas H. (1995) *The Whole Matter: The Poetic Evolution of Thomas Kinsella.* Dublin: Lilliput Press, p. 15.
81 McLynn, F. (2010) *Marcus Aurelius: Warrior, Philosopher, Emperor.* London: Vintage, p. 540.
82 *Ibid.*
83 *Ibid.*, p. 544.
84 Kermode, F. (1967) *The Sense of an Ending: Studies in the Theory of Fiction.* Oxford: Oxford University Press, p. 4.

85 Kearney, R. (2013) Lecture, 'Narrative Imagination and Catharsis', *Big Ideas*. [Podcast] 19 January 2013.
86 Harmon, M. (2012) 'Review of Fat Master' in *Poetry Ireland Review 100,* April 2012, p. 14.
87 *Ibid.*, p. 15.
88 Kinsella, T. (1973) 'The Divided Mind', in Lucy, S. (ed.) *Irish Poets in English*. Cork: Mercier, p. 215.
89 Kinsella, *Collected Poems,* p.118.
90 *Ibid.*, p. 308.
91 Kinsella, T. (2009) *Prose Occasions 1951–2006* Manchester: Carcanet, 2009, p. 67.
92 Campbell, *The Hero with a Thousand Faces.*
93 Eliot, T. S. (1975) 'Ulysses, Order and Myth' in Kermode F. (ed.) *Selected Prose of T. S. Eliot.* London: Faber and Faber, p. 177.
94 Campbell, *The Hero with a Thousand Faces,* p. 3.
95 *Ibid.*, p. 23.
96 *Ibid.*, p. 45.
97 Young, J. (2003) *The Death of God and The Meaning of Life.* London: Routledge, pp. 44–57.
98 Quoted in John, B. (1996) *Reading the Ground: The Poetry of Thomas Kinsella*. Washington DC: Catholic University of America Press, p. 84.

4. The Dreams that Died

1   Young, J. (2003) *The Death of God and The Meaning of Life.* London: Routledge, p. 1.
2   O'Higgins, K. (1989) Quoted in Lee, J. *Ireland, 1912–1985.* Cambridge: Cambridge University Press, p. 105.
3   Garvin, T. (2010) *News from a New Republic – Ireland in the 1950s.* Dublin, Gill and Macmillan, p. 38.
4   *Ibid.*, p. 39.
5   Kinsella, T. (2001) *Collected Poems*. Manchester: Carcanet, p. 57.
6   *Ibid.*
7   *Ibid.*
8   *Ibid.*, p. 37.
9   *Ibid.*
10 *Ibid.*, p. 56.
11 Kinsella, quoted in Fitzsimons, A. (2008) *The Sea of Disappointment: Thomas Kinsella's Pursuit of the Real.* Dublin: UCD Press, p. 90.
12 Kinsella, *Collected Poems,* pp. 273–274.

13 *Ibid.*, pp. 210–211.
14 *Ibid.*, p. 297.
15 John H. (ed.) (1981) *Viewpoints: Poets in Conversation with John Haffenden*. London: Faber and Faber, p. 100.
16 Kinsella papers, quoted in Fitzsimons, A. (2009) *The Sea of Disappointment: Thomas Kinsella's Pursuit of the Real.*
17 Kinsella, T. (2013) Interview by John Kelly for *The Works*, RTÉ One, 23 September 2013.
18 *Ibid.*
19 *Ibid.*
20 *Ibid.*
21 Kinsella, *Collected Poems,* p. 336.
22 *Ibid.*, p. 148.
23 *Ibid.*
24 *Ibid.*, p. 150.
25 *Ibid.*, p. 149.
26 *Loc.cit.*
27 *Ibid.*, p. 151.
28 *Ibid.*, p. 148.
29 Connolly, J. (1973) 'Erin's Hope: The Ends and The Means'. In Edwards, Dudley O. and Ransom, B. (eds.), *James Connolly: Selected Political Writings*. London: Jonathan Cape.
30 Kinsella, *Collected Poems,* p. 150.
31 John, B. (1996) *Reading the Ground: The Poetry of Thomas Kinsella*. Washington DC: Catholic University of America Press, p. 160.
32 Kinsella, *Collected Poems,* p. 151.
33 *Ibid.*
34 *Ibid.*, p. 152.
35 *Ibid.*, p. 147.
36 *Ibid.*, p. 152.
37 *Ibid.*
38 *Ibid.*, p. 153.
39 Kinsella, T. (1973) 'The Divided Mind', in Lucy, S. (ed.) *Irish Poets in English*. Cork: Mercier, p. 215.
40 Kinsella, *Collected Poems,* p. 153.
41 *Ibid.*, p. 154.
42 *Ibid.*, p. 157.
43 *Ibid.*, p. 43.
44 *Ibid.*

45 Kinsella, *Collected Poems*, p. 46.
46 *Ibid.*
47 Harmon, M. (2008) Thomas Kinsella: Designing for the Exact Needs, p. 17.
48 Lynch, D. *Radical Politics in Modern Ireland*. Dublin: Irish Academic Press, p. 10.
49 Regan, J. M. (1999) *The Irish Counter-Revolution, 1921–1936: Treatyite Politics and Settlement in Independent Ireland*. Dublin: Gill & Macmillan.
50 Kinsella, *Collected Poems*, p. 46.
51 *Ibid.*
52 *Ibid.*, p. 274.
53 Byrne, E. (2012) *Political Corruption in Ireland: 1922–2010: A Crooked Harp?* Manchester: Manchester University Press.
54 Kinsella, *Collected Poems*, p. 300.
55 Marx, K. (1997) 'The Fetishisms of Commodities', *Marx: Selected Writings*. McLellan D. (ed.) Oxford: Oxford University Press, p. 436.
56 Kinsella, *Collected Poems*, p. 300.
57 *Ibid.*, p. 280.
58 *Ibid.*
59 Oz, A. (1999) 'When the British Troops Went Home', *Newsweek*, 19 July 1999.
60 Kinsella, T. (2002) Interview by Michael Smith for *Poetry Ireland Review*, Winter 2002, p. 113.
61 Kinsella, *Collected Poems*, p. 351.
62 Kinsella, T. (2006) *A Dublin Documentary*. Dublin: O'Brien Press, p. 69.
63 Kinsella, *Collected Poems*, p. 264.
64 *Ibid.*, p. 17.
65 *Ibid.*, p. 18.
66 *Ibid.*, p. 283.
67 Kinsella, T. Interviewed by Elgy Gillespie for *The Irish Times*, 20 June 1981.
68 Kinsella, *Collected Poems*, p. 133.
69 Goodby, J. (2000) *Irish Poetry Since 1950*. Manchester: Manchester University Press, p. 69.
70 Girvin, B. and Murphy, G. (eds.) 'Review of Politics and Society in the Ireland of Sean Lemass', *Irish Literary Supplement*, Spring 2007.
71 Cleary, J. (2007) *Outrageous Fortune: Capital and Culture in Modern Ireland*. Dublin: Field Day, p. 8.

72. McCabe, C. (2011) *Sins of the Father: Tracing the Decisions that Shaped the Irish Economy.* Dublin: The History Press, p. 115.
73. Donoghue, D. (1982) Quoted in *The Arts Without Mystery.* Reith Lecture for BBC Four.
74. Kinsella, *Collected Poems,* p. 78.
75. *Ibid.*
76. Coulter, C. and Coleman, S. (eds.) *The End of History? Critical Approaches to the Celtic Tiger.* Manchester: Manchester University Press, p. 17.
77. *Ibid.,* p. 18
78. *Ibid.,* p. 123.
79. Kinsella, (2009) *Prose Occasions (1951–2006)* Manchester: Carcanet, p. 1.
80. Kuhling, K. (2003) 'Millenarianism and Utopianism in the New Ireland: The Tragedy (and Comedy) of Accelerated Modernisation' in *The End of Irish History?* Manchester: Manchester University Press, pp. 122–139.
81. Eagleton, T. (2008) *The Meaning of Life: A Very Short Introduction.* Oxford: Oxford University Press, pp. 57–58.
82. Lee, M. J. (1993) *Consumer Culture Reborn: The Cultural Politics of Consumption.* London: Routledge, p. 144.
83. *Ibid.*
84. Thomson, A. (2006) *Adorno: A Guide for the Perplexed.* London: Continuum, 2006, p. 123.
85. Kinsella, *Collected Poems,* p. 116.
86. Callinicos, A. (1989) *Against Postmodernism: A Marxist Critique* London: Polity Press.
87. Donoghue, p. 173.
88. Waters, M. A. (1970) (ed.) *Rosa Luxemburg Speaks.* New York: Pathfinder.

5. The Truth Within

1. Kinsella, T. (2001) *Collected Poems.* Manchester: Carcanet, p. 76.
2. *Ibid.*
3. Kinsella, T. (2002) Interview by Michael Smith for *Poetry Ireland Review,* Winter 2002, p. 117.
4. Kinsella, *Collected Poems,* p. 116.
5. Young-Eisendrath, P. and Dawson, T. (eds.) (2008) *The Cambridge Companion to Jung.* Cambridge University Press, Cambridge, p. 301.
6. Kinsella, *Collected Poems,* p. 96.
7. *Ibid.*
8. *Ibid.,* p. 97.

9   Jung, C. (2009) *The Red Book, Liber Novus*. New York: W. W. Norton & Co., pp. 562–563.
10 Campbell, J. (1993) *The Hero with a Thousand Faces*. London: Fontana, p. 51.
11 Kinsella, *Collected Poems*, p. 98.
12 *Ibid.*, p. 99.
13 *Ibid.*
14 *Ibid.*
15 Kinsella, T. (1997) Interview by Ian Flanagan for *Metre 2*, Spring 1997, p. 111.
16 *Ibid.*, p. 113.
17 Kinsella, *Collected Poems*, p. 76.
18 Kinsella, T. (2013) Interview by John Kelly for *The Works*, RTÉ One, 23 September 2013.
19 Shamdasani, S. (ed.) (2013) *Jung and the Making of Modern Psychology*. Cambridge: Cambridge University Press, p. 1.
20 Jung, C. (1991) *The Archetypes and the Collective Unconscious*. London: Routledge, pp. 3–4.
21 Jung, C. (1998) *The Essential Jung*. London: Fontana Press, pp. 415–416.
22 Kinsella, T. Interviewed by Elgy Gillespie for *The Irish Times*, 20 June 1981.
23 Jung, *The Essential Jung*, p. 418.
24 Jung, *The Red Book*, p. 307.
25 Jackson, Thomas H. (1995) *The Whole Matter: The Poetic Evolution of Thomas Kinsella*. Dublin: Lilliput Press, p. xii.
26 Kinsella, *Collected Poems*, p. 300.
27 Harmon, M. (2012) Thomas Kinsella: Designing for the Exact Needs, p. 35.
28 Fitzsimons, A. (2009) *The Sea of Disappointment: Thomas Kinsella's Pursuit of the Real*, p. 112.
29 Jung, *The Red Book* p. xii.
30 Kinsella, *Collected Poems*, p. 177.
31 Harris, S. (2012) *Free Will*. New York: Free Press.
32 Campbell, p. 23.
33 *Ibid.*, p. 64.
34 *Ibid.*, p 58.
35 Kinsella, *Collected Poems* p. 95.
36 *Ibid.*, p. 11.

37 *Ibid.*, p. 12.
38 *Ibid.*, p. 13.
39 *Ibid.*
40 *Ibid.*
41 Flanagan, Thomas Kinsella Interview, p. 112.
42 Gillespie, Thomas Kinsella Interview.
43 Jung, *The Red Book*, p. xi
44 Shamdasani, S. 'The Introduction', *The Red Book* p. 26.
45 Jung, *The Red Book*, p. 555
46 Bloom, H. (2011) *The Anatomy of Influence*. New Haven: Yale University Press, p. 27.
47 Kinsella, *Collected Poems*, p. 95.
48 *Ibid.*, p. 185.
49 *Ibid.*, p. 184.
50 *Ibid.*, p. 179.
51 *Ibid.*, p. 227.
52 Smith, Thomas Kinsella Interview, p. 109.
53 *Ibid.*
54 Kinsella, *Collected Poems*, p. 229.
55 *Ibid.*, p. 227.
56 Smith, Thomas Kinsella Interview, p. 109.
57 Kinsella, *Collected Poems*, p. 232.
58 *Ibid.*
59 *Ibid.*, p. 237.
60 *Ibid.*
61 *Ibid.*, p. 273.
62 *Ibid.*
63 *Ibid.*
64 *Ibid.*, p. 276.
65 *Ibid.*, p. 196.
66 Flanagan, Thomas Kinsella Interview, pp. 110–111.
67 Kinsella, T. (1987) Interview by John F. Deane for *Tracks* No. 7 (1987), p. 88.
68 Quinn, J. (2008) *The Cambridge Introduction to Modern Irish Poetry: 1800–2000*. Cambridge: Cambridge University Press, p. 103.
69 Kinsella, *Collected Poems*, p. 161.
70 *Loc.cit.*
71 Gillespie, Thomas Kinsella Interview.

6. Resistance

1. Kinsella, T. (2001) *Collected Poems*. Manchester: Carcanet, p. 51
2. *Ibid.*
3. Camus, A. (2000) 'Summer in Algiers', *The Myth of Sisyphus*. London: Penguin.
4. *Ibid.*
5. Kinsella, *Collected Poems*, p. 51.
6. *Ibid.,* p. 223.
7. *Ibid.,* p. 221.
8. *Ibid.,* p. 222.
9. *Ibid.,* p. 200.
10. *Ibid.*
11. Smith, Z. Interview. BBC 4 *Desert Island Discs*, 22 September 2013.
12. Kinsella, *Collected Poems,* pp. 267–268.
13. *Ibid.,* p. 211.
14. *Ibid.,* p. 218.
15. *Ibid.,* p. 219.
16. *Ibid.,* p. 65.
17. *Ibid.,* p. 234.
18. *Ibid.,* p. 12.
19. Fitzsimons, p. 26.
20. Dorgan, T. (1996) *Irish Poetry Since Kavanagh*. Dublin: Four Courts Press, p. 8.
21. Bloom, H. (2011) *The Anatomy of Influence*. New Haven: Yale University Press, p. 6.
22. Martin, A. 'Biographical Note on Kinsella', *Soundings*. Dublin: Gill and MacMillan, 2010.
23. Kinsella, T. (1989) Interview by Dennis O'Driscoll for *Poetry Ireland Review 25,* Spring 1989, p. 58.
24. *Ibid.*
25. Kinsella, *Collected Poems*, p. 12.
26. *Ibid.,* p. 53.
27. Jung, C. (1998) *The Essential Jung*. London: Fontana Press, p. 211.
28. Kinsella, *Collected Poems*, p. 226.
29. *Ibid.*
30. *Ibid.,* p. 107.
31. *Ibid.,* p. 287.
32. *Ibid.,* p. 190.
33. *Ibid.*

34 *Ibid.*, pp. 6–7.
35 Kinsella, E. *Irish Independent*, 22 March 2009.
36 Kinsella, *Collected Poems*, p. 84.
37 *Ibid.*, p. 65.
38 *Ibid.*
39 *Ibid.*, p. 64.
40 *Ibid.*
41 *Ibid.*, p. 66.
42 *Ibid.*
43 *Ibid.*, p. 62.
44 Ellis, C. (1987) 'Above the Salt: The Early Peppercanisters', *Tracks* No. 7, p. 34.
45 Kinsella, *Collected Poems*, p. 88.
46 *Ibid.*, p. 90.
47 Jung, *The Essential Jung*.
48 Forster, J. (2007) *Muses*. London: Oldcastle Books, p. 14.
49 Harmon, M. (2008) Thomas Kinsella: Designing for the Exact Needs, p. 6.
50 Kinsella, *Collected Poems*, p. 91.
51 Jackson, Thomas H. (1995) *The Whole Matter: The Poetic Evolution of Thomas Kinsella*. Dublin: Lilliput Press, p. 138.
52 Kinsella, *Collected Poems*, p. 84.
53 *Ibid.*
54 Clutterbuck, C. Reading of the poetry of Thomas Kinsella. Gate Theatre 17 June 2007.
55 Kinsella, *Collected Poems*, p. 330.
56 *Ibid.*, p. 332.
57 *Ibid.*, p. 188.
58 *Ibid.*
59 Jung, *The Essential Jung*, p. 210.
60 Kinsella, *Collected Poems*, p. 47.
61 *Ibid.*, p. 48.
62 *Ibid.*, p. 49.
63 *Ibid.*, p. 204.
64 *Ibid.*
65 *Ibid.*, p. 205.
66 *Ibid.*
67 Dunne, D. quoted in Denman, P. (2001) 'Significant Elements: Songs of the Psyche and Her Vertical Smile', *Irish University Review* 31, p. 96.

68 Adler, G. and Hull, R. F. C. (eds.) (1980) *The Collected Works of C. G. Jung, Volume 9 (Part 1): Archetypes and the Collective Unconscious*. Princeton: Princeton University Press.
69 Adorno, T. (2005) *Minima Moralia: Reflections from Damaged Life*. London: Verso, p. 28.
70 Fitzsimons, p. 17.
71 Mc Cormack, W. J. (1989) 'Politics or Community: Crux of Thomas Kinsella's Aesthetic Development', in *Tracks* No. 7 (1987), pp. 70–71.
72 Kinsella, *Collected Poems*, p. 324.
73 *Ibid.*, p. 155.
74 *Ibid.*, p. 156.
75 Ellis, P. B. (ed.) (1997) *James Connolly: Selected Writings*. London: Pluto Press, p. 90.
76 Kinsella, *Collected Poems*, p. 291.
77 *Ibid.*
78 Kinsella, T. (1997) Interview by Ian Flanagan for *Metre 2*, Spring 1997, pp. 109–110.
79 *Ibid.*, p. 110.
80 *Ibid.*
81 Cleary, J. (2007) *Outrageous Fortune: Capital and Culture in Modern Ireland*. Dublin: Field Day, p. 176.
82 Adorno, *Minima Moralia*, p. 28.
83 Kinsella, *Collected Poems*, p. 283.
84 *Ibid.*, p. 46.
85 Kinsella, T. (2002) Interview by Michael Smith for *Poetry Ireland Review*, Winter 2002, pp. 110–111 (CP, 279).
86 *Collected Poems*, p. 279.
87 *Ibid.*, p. 280.
88 *Ibid.*, p. 276.
89 Wheatley, D. (2001) "All is Emptiness/and I Must Spin': Thomas Kinsella and the Romance of Decay', *Irish University Review* (2001) p. 329.
90 Kinsella, *Collected Poems*, p. 144.
91 *Ibid.*
92 *Ibid.*, p. 298.
93 Boran, P. and Smith, G. (eds.) (2014) *If Ever You Go: A Map of Dublin Poetry and Song*. Dublin: Dedalus Press, p. 185.
94 Jung, C. (1995) *Memories, Dreams, Reflections*. London: Fontana Press, p. 260.

95 Eliot, T. S. (1975) 'Ulysses, Order and Myth', *Selected Prose of TS Eliot.* Kermode, F. (ed.) London: Faber & Faber, p. 177–178.
96 Campbell, J. (1993) *The Hero with a Thousand Faces.* London: Fontana, p. 4.
97 Waddell, J. (1998) *The Prehistoric Archaeology of Ireland.* Galway: Galway University Press.
98 Slavin, M. (2005) *The Ancient Books of Ireland.* Belfast: Mcgill-Queen's University Press, p. 28.
99 Mc Caffrey, C., and Eaton, L. (2003) *In Search of Ancient Ireland: The Origins of the Irish from Neolithic Times to the Coming of the English.* New York: Ivan R. Dee, p. 56.
100 *Ibid.*, p 7.
101 Litton, H. (1997) *The Celts: An Illustrated History.* London: Wolfhound Press, p. 10.
102 Kinsella, *Collected Poems,* p. 164.
103 *Ibid.,* p. 165.
104 *Ibid.,* pp. 172–173.
105 *Ibid.* p. 173.
106 *Ibid.,* p. 162.
107 *Ibid.,* pp.162–163.
108 *Ibid.*, p. 163.
109 *Ibid.*
110 *Ibid.*
111 *Ibid.,* p. 165.
112 *Ibid.,* p. 166.
113 *Ibid.*
114 Corkery, D. (1996) *Synge and Anglo-Irish Literature.* Mercier: Cork, 1966, p. 14.
115 Kinsella, *Collected Poems,* p. 166.
116 *Ibid.,* p. 167.
117 Jung, *The Red Book,* p. 324.
118 Kinsella, *Collected Poems,* p. 167.
119 *Ibid.,* p. 178.
120 *Ibid.,* p. 175.
121 Campbell, p. 4.
122 Kinsella, *Collected Poems,* p. 172.
123 Ní Bhrolchain, M. (2011) 'Death-Tales of the Early Kings of Tara' in *Landscapes of Cults and Kingships.* Dublin: Four Court Press, p. 45.
124 Kinsella, *Collected Poems,* p. 172.

125 *Ibid.*, p. 269.
126 *Ibid.*, p. 270.
127 Ibid., p. 266.
128 Kinsella, T. (1970) 'The Irish Writer', *Davis, Mangan, Ferguson?: Tradition and the Irish Writer: Writings by W. B. Yeats and by Thomas Kinsella*. Dublin: Dolmen Press, p. 72.
129 Flanagan, Thomas Kinsella Interview, p. 109.
130 *Ibid.*
131 Mount, N. (2010) 'On T. S. Eliot'. *Big Ideas* [Podcast] 23 April 2010.
132 Harmon, M. (2008) Thomas Kinsella: Designing for the Exact Needs, p. 104–163.
133 Pinker, S. (1999) 'In Our Time' BBC Radio 4. 11 February 1999.
134 Kinsella, T. (1995) *The Dual Tradition: An Essay on Poetry and Politics in Ireland.* Manchester: Carcanet.
135 Smith, Thomas Kinsella Interview, p. 110.
136 Kinsella, *Collected Poems*, p. 82.
137 *Ibid.*
138 Kinsella, *The Dual Tradition.*
139 Kinsella, *Collected Poems*, p. 12.
140 *Ibid.*, p. 13.
141 *Ibid.*, p. 254.
142 Young, J. (2003) *The Death of God and The Meaning of Life* London: Routledge, p. 210.
143 Kinsella, *Collected Poems*, p. 355.
144 *Ibid.*, p. 352.
145 *Ibid.*
146 *Ibid.* p. 353.
147 *Ibid.*, p. 205.
148 *Ibid.*, p. 208.
149 *Ibid.*, p. 92.
150 *Ibid.*, p. 45.
151 *Ibid.*, p. 275.
152 *Ibid.*
153 *Ibid.*, p. 193.
154 Hobsbawm, E. (2000) *The New Century.* London: Abacus, pp. 149–150.
155 Kinsella, *Collected Poems*, p. 30.
156 *Ibid.*, p. 62.
157 *Ibid.*, p. 191.

158 *Ibid.*, p. 83.
159 Clutterbuck, C. (2005) 'Thomas Kinsella', Roche, A. (ed.) *The UCD Aesthetic*. Dublin: New Island, p. 151.
160 Flanagan, Thomas Kinsella Interview, p. 108.
161 *Ibid.*
162 Kinsella, *Collected Poems*, p. 99.
163 *Ibid.*, p. 116.
164 *Ibid.*
165 Stevens, A. (1994) *Jung – A Very Short Introduction*. Oxford: Oxford University Press, p. 42.
166 Marino, G. (ed.) (2004) *Basic Writings of Existentialism*. New York: Modern Library. p. 470.
167 'Hebrews 11:1' The King James Bible.
168 McLellan, D. (2005) *The Thought of Karl Marx*. London: Papermac, p. 151.
169 Smith, Thomas Kinsella Interview, p. 108.
170 Kinsella, T. (2013) *Late Poems*. Manchester: Carcanet, p.21.
171 Adorno, *Minima Moralia*, p. 25.
172 Kinsella, *Collected Poems*, p. 62.

Praise for David Lynch's *A Divided Paradise* (New Island Books, 2009)

'Captures the tension and beauty of a partitioned paradise. Lynch is studiously fair in mapping out the tragedy of the Israeli/Palestinian conflict.'
— *The Irish Times*

'An excellent collection of memories intertwined with political analyses and history. With a fresh and very accessible narrative, Lynch has enriched the literature available on the Arab–Israeli conflict.'
— *Digest of Middle East Studies*

'A heartrending account of the suffering of Palestinians under occupation … [Lynch] impressively and seamlessly combines story-telling with reportage and fact-finding.'
— (Starred Review) *Publishers Weekly*

'An endlessly entertaining delve into a serious issue.'
— *Midwest Book Review*